The Dalton Gang Story

23 July 1992

NOLA   Vernal, Utah

To: Ed Davis

Nancy B Samuelson

SOUTHERN PACIFIC COMPANY.

(PACIFIC SYSTEM.)

$3,000 REWARD.

Supplementing circular letter of W. E. Hickey, Special Officer S. P. Co., dated San Francisco, Feb. 26, 1891, wherein is offered a reward of $5,000 for the arrest and conviction of all parties concerned in the attempted robbery of train No. 17, on the night of Feb. 6th, 1891.

The Grand Jury of Tulare County have indicted **Bob and Emmett Dalton** as principals in said crime, and William Marion Dalton and Gratton (or Grafton) Dalton, as accessories; the two latter named being now in jail in Tulare County awaiting trial.

The Southern Pacific Company hereby withdraw said general reward in regard to Bob and Emmett Dalton, and in lieu thereof offer to pay $1,500 each for the *arrest* of said Bob and Emmet Dalton, described below, *upon their delivery to a duly authorized Agent or representative of the State of California, at any jail in any of the States or Territories of the United States.*

In addition to the foregoing, the State and Wells, Fargo & Co. have each a *standing reward of $300* for the arrest and conviction of each such offender.

About 8 o'clock in the evening of Feb. 6th, 1891, two armed men attempted, unsuccessfully, to rob the south-bound train, No. 17, near Alila, Tulare Co., California. The Express Messenger offered a gallant resistance, and during the interchange of shots the fireman, G. W. Radliff, received a wound, from the effects of which he died the following day.

It is now known that the attack was made by two brothers, viz: Bob and Emmet Dalton, described as follows:

BOB DALTON: About twenty-three years of age (but might be taken for 25); height, 6 ft. 1½ inches; well built and straight; light complexion, but florid and healthy looking; boyish beard and mustache; light hair and eyes; weight, 180 to 190 lbs.; large, bony, long fingered hands, showing no acquaintance with work; large nose and ears; white teeth; long, sunburned neck, square features. Was wearing square, box-toed, custom made, new, calfskin boots with morocco legs, size 8½. Is a good poker and card player; drinks whisky in moderation, but does not chew tobacco; smokes brown paper cigarettes occasionally.

EMMETT DALTON: Between 20 and 21 years of age; nearly 6 feet in height; weight, about 180 lbs.; well built; hair lighter than Bob's; no mustache nor whiskers; looks the counterpart of Bob; has scar on forehead, over eye; also plays cards and drinks in moderation, but does not use tobacco.

On the 2d inst. they left San Luis Obispo County, on horseback, and on the 8th disposed of their horses at Ludlow, a station on the A. & P. Railway, about 100 miles east of Mojave, and there took passage on an East-bound train, since which time no trace of them has been obtained.

The Daltons are brothers, and it is believed that Bob and Emmett came to California from Indian Territory in the latter part of 1890, and Grat. in January, 1891, and that they now have relations and friends in that region.

Any communications regarding them, addressed to E. W. Kay, Sheriff Tulare County, Visalia, Cal.; Jas. B. Hume, Special Officer, Wells, Fargo & Co., San Francisco, Cal., or the undersigned, will receive prompt attention, and if so desired, will be treated confidentially.

Railroad and Express Agents receiving a number of these circulars, are respectfully requested to place them in the hands of local officers, or citizens who will take an interest in the matter.

W. E. HICKEY,
Special Officer, S. P. Co., S. F.

San Francisco, March 26th, 1891.

Courtesy Wells Fargo

The Dalton Gang Story
Lawmen To Outlaws

by
Nancy B. Samuelson

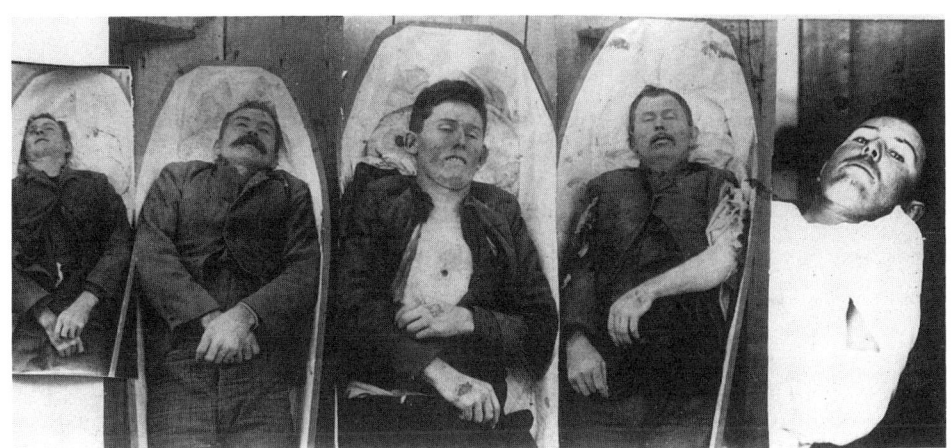

The end of the Dalton Gang Coffeyville, KS 5 Oct. 1892.
Courtesy of The Kansas State Historical Society

Design & Layout By:
Girard Paperworks Co.
(203) 928-9540

Printing By:
Thomson-Shore, Inc.
7300 West Joy Road
P.O. Box 305
Dexter, MI 48130-0305

© 1992 by Nancy B. Samuelson
All Rights Reserved

ISBN No. 0-9633362-0-7

Printed in the United States of America

First Published July 1992

SHOOTING STAR PRESS

P.O. Box 359
Eastford, CT 06242

Table of Contents

Preface 1

Chapter I: Separating Fact From "Faction" and "False Teeth" 3

Chapter II: Forefathers & Mothers 6
    The Daltons
    The Youngers
    The Rabourns

Chapter III: The Dalton Gang Family 27

Chapter IV: When The Dalton Brothers Wore Badges 78

Chapter V: The Daltons Versus The Southern Pacific Railroad 87

Chapter VI: The Dalton Gang 100

Chapter VII: The Coffeyville Affair 114

Chapter VIII: Bill Dalton: Most Notorious Outlaw of All 131

Chapter IX: Emmett and Julia 149

Chapter X: Dubious, Doubtful and Deceptive Daltons 163

Sources & Author's Notes 173

The Dalton Gang Story - Lawmen to Outlaws

Preface

This book actually began the summer of 1984 at a reunion of my Dalton family in St. Louis. I had retired from the Air Force in February 1984 so when the reunion conversation turned to the question, "Are we related to the Dalton Gang?" I opened my mouth and said, "Now that I have retired I think I will research the family history and find out." (Fools rush in.) Now in 1992 I know my Dalton family and the Dalton Gang family all share a common ancestor, Timothy Dalton, who claimed his first land in Albemarle County, Virginia in 1732.

I now also know that most of the books and magazine and newspaper articles that have been written about the Dalton Gang are mostly fiction. (I won't even comment on the movies.) In fact, I now know that most of the literature about the Old West is filled with inaccuracies and a lot of outright lies. I cannot help but wonder how much else that passes for history is just as biased and inaccurate as is the material about the Old West.

My state of nativity is Missouri but I think that I have a genetic "Show Me" attitude as well. In addition to this, I have developed some specific techniques during my Air Force career to insure that staff, co-workers, or students gave me facts, instead of heresay or opinion. One of the techniques was to ask, "Have you counted teeth?" or to give instructions to "Go count teeth". The "Count teeth" comments never failed to get attention. I stole the idea from Bertrand Russell's ESSAYS IN SKEPTICISM. "To avoid the various foolish opinions to which mankind is prone, no superhuman genuis is required. A few simple rules will keep you, not from ALL error, but from silly error. If the matter is one that can be settled by observation, make the observation yourself. Aristotle could have avoided the mistake of thinking that women have fewer teeth than men by the simple device of asking Mrs. Aristotle to keep her mouth open while he counted. He did not do so because he thought he knew. *THINKING THAT YOU KNOW, WHEN IN FACT YOU DON'T IS A FATAL MISTAKE, TO WHICH WE ARE ALL PRONE*".

As I began my search for my ancestors and for the truth about the Dalton Gang it quickly became clear that all too few of the so-called western historians had bothered to count teeth.

I began by consulting a few basic "How To" books about genealogy. The next step was checking many public and official records such as census records, birth, death, marriage, and other such vital records. Later I investigated many other sources such as church records, local histories, old newspapers, court records, and a variety of other types of orginal source documents. I joined a number of state and local historical and genealogical societies and later became a member of a number of organizations that are dedicated to the study of the outlaws and lawmen of the Old West. I made a number of trips to all of the areas where the Dalton Gang lived and where they operated, first as lawmen, then later as outlaws. I have written hundreds of letters, made hundreds of phone calls and have visited any number of libraries and archives while counting the Dalton teeth.

I read the books and magazines about the Daltons, then returned time and time again to the search for official records, newspapers of the time and area, and any other source I could think of that would give me a more complete inventory of the teeth. I eventually discovered that not a single book existed that told the complete and true story of the Dalton Gang. I decided it was time for someone to tell the REAL story of the Daltons. Thus I decided to write this book.

I previously (1989) wrote and published a small booklet THE DALTON GANG FAMILY. This put me into contact with Daltons and others interested in Daltons all over the United States and in at least four other countries. I have had dozens of letters and phone calls about Daltons. A generation or two ago people wanted to deny any connection with outlaws. Now it seems everyone wants to claim kin to outlaws, or at least to the Dalton outlaws. I have had to tell a lot of folks that grandpa's story of riding with the Daltons or holding the horses in Coffeyville just ain't so. I have adopted much the same attitude as Andy Devine, the well known movie comedian. When he visited Coffeyville in 1940 Andy said he doubted the accuracy of the 1890 census figures which showed Coffeyville's population at 5,000 because at least 50,000 persons now claim to have been living in Coffeyville at the time of the Dalton Raid. He further stated, "If everybody who claims really to have seen the Daltons shot really did—I don't see how they ever got the bleachers built in such a little alley, and if the Daltons really had as many friends as now claim that distinction, I don't see how the boys ever got killed."

While counting the teeth, I had a lot of assistance from many different people. Space will not permit a mention of all, but here are some of the key people who provided a lot of help. William Dalton "Bill" Phillips, grandson of Bea Elizabeth Dalton, and his entire family have shared documents, photos, and family stories. Lora Miller of Oklahoma has helped in so many different ways it would take pages to list her contributions. She has dug through tons of dusty records in various Oklahoma courthouses and many other places for me. Writers Carl Breihan, Harrell Mc Cullough, and Marley Brant have all encouraged me to write this book and have shared material on the Daltons and Youngers with me. Hazel Chapman, step granddaughter of Emmett Dalton, shared documents, photos and family stories. Pat Waddle provided genealogical and other material on the Power family. Christopher Brewer kindly allowed me to consult all of Frank Latta's files and papers. Linda Brown Allie tackled the Fort Worth branch of the National Archives and various other Texas libraries for me. Janet Baker Burks dug through Texas court house records and located what few source documents remain of the trials of Jim Nite for the Longview bank robbery. Lois Copley mined the files of the Oklahoma Historical Society. Rowena Horr provided like service at the Kansas State Historical Society. Verna Gail Johnson located all of the records on the "Introducing" charges against Bob and Emmett Dalton in the Kansas City branch of the National Archives. Several agencies and individuals provided photographs. They all get credit lines with the photos. Librarians everywhere were wonderful but special thanks goes to Mary Anne Terstegge at the Tulare County Library in California for the newspaper accounts of Grat and Bill Dalton's trials for the Alila train robbery. She also dug out biographical material on many of the key players involved in the California episode. Special thanks also to Barbara Packenham and Selene Bennett at my home library in Eastford, Connecticut. If the book I needed was in a library anywhere, Barb and Selene got it on interlibrary loan.

Two outstanding researchers have provided marvelous assistance with the genealogical material in this book. Mark Dalton (a member of the tribe) and Steve "Mr. Pittsylvania County" Harris. They have dug through records, walked the creeks, checked the property boundaries, and provided all kinds of help on tracking down the early Virginia Daltons. The three of us have spent hours on the phone going over and over the records on the early Daltons. In addition to counting teeth, Mark frequently cautioned, "You have to do the arithmetic!". There is still more research to be done on the Dalton genealogy. We may have some people assigned to the wrong generation and thus to the wrong set of parents (many records before 1850 for this area of Virginia are often sketchy or missing entirely); however, we know without a doubt that all of the Daltons in the genealogical section of this book are from one Dalton family. This is the family that produced not only the Dalton Gang, but also the late Governor of Virginia, John Dalton and John's father, the grand old man of the Virginia Republican Party, Judge Theodore Roosevelt "Ted" Dalton and many other very respectable Daltons as well.

Two more very special people also deserve a great deal of credit for making this book happen. One is my cousin Kay Dalton Henneberger who accompanied me on several of the Dalton research trips, and assisted with some of the research. The other is my husband, Reid Samuelson, who tolerates my Dalton mania with good humor, provides moral support at all times, and tames THE BEAST a/k/a the personal computer when it does not do what I want it to or does not work.

The credit for any mistakes goes only to the author; it is a dead certainty that I missed a tooth or two somewhere along the way.

Nancy B. Samuelson
Eastford, Connecticut
Feburary 1992

I. Separating Fact From "Faction" and "False Teeth"

Everyone knows they were the Desperate Daltons; they formed a formidable gang in old Twin Territories. They rustled cattle, stole horses and robbed stages, trains, and banks. They were a band of cold blooded murderers that roamed the midwest without challenge, robbing and killing at will. Or so the "historians" have said. In fact, the Daltons were first lawmen, and their outlaw activities were less than spectactular (until Coffeyville anyway) in an era when violence was common. The career of the Dalton Gang was of less that two years' duration. There is no evidence of cattle rustling, very slim evidence of any horse stealing, and they never robbed a stage. The Dalton Gang did rob four trains and did "go for the gold" while trying to establish a new record in the outlaw olympics when they attempted to rob two banks at once in Coffeyville, Kansas. They were not cold blooded murderers. They were, in fact, rather gentlemanly train robbers, for they never molested nor stole from a passenger, unlike many other practioners of this profession.

After the Coffeyville fiasco, brother Bill then supposedly turned outlaw too. Bill allegedly became part of the Doolin Gang, and latter branched out on his own with three other men to rob the bank at Longview, Texas. Not long after this robbery Bill Dalton was shot and killed by a posse of nine U. S. deputy marshals. Bill Dalton has been accused of almost everything under the sun, but there is very little real evidence to support most of the accusations. Furthermore, two years after Bill Dalton's death all nine of the deputies in the posse that killed him were arrested for the murder of Bill Dalton. Why the deputies were charged with murder and what the outcome of their trial was, if in fact there ever was a trial, remains one of the greatest unsolved mysteries of the Old West. The files of the National Archives, and all county and district files that relate to the supposed outlaw activities of Bill Dalton, the Longview bank robbery, and the death of Bill Dalton appear to have been stripped. Just about all the documents that remain in the official archives that mention Bill Dalton relate to the "flap" that ensued when someone spread the false story that Bill had been appointed a U. S. deputy after the Coffeyville raid. This dearth of records concerning one of the supposedly most wanted men of the Old West simply cannot be accidental.

One of the earliest books about the Daltons is THE DALTON BROTHERS written by "An Eyewitness". This book has been reprinted at least twice and many other writers have relied heavily on this material. In the introduction to one edition of this book, a well known and respected western writer said ,"An Eye Witness was one of those rarities among writers of the period who chose to write about outlaws, namely, in that he is one who has sought out the facts conscientiously, checked them, and presented them without fictional elaboration, colorful inventions, surmises or sermonizing." Nothing could be further from the truth! This book was written by, or at least the material for the book was furnished by, then U. S. deputy marshal Ransome Payne. Payne was fired as a deputy because of the outrageous untruths he told in the book. Any facts in this book are there purely by accident.

Several writers relied a great deal on interviews with or the written accounts of Chris Madsen. Madsen was another U. S. deputy marshal who became very well known as one of the "Three Guardsmen" of law and order in the Indian and Oklahoma Territories. Six different accounts of the history of the Daltons by Madsen have been found. Madsen's accounts do not agree with each other; all are full of misstatement of fact and many fine examples of creative fiction.

Emmett Dalton wrote two books about his outlaw experiences. His books do not agree with each other and both are filled with fiction. All the material he added to WHEN THE DALTONS RODE about Bob's girlfriend and about his own youthful romance with Julia Johnson is pure moonshine, probably added to enhance book sales.

Frank Latta interviewed an older brother of the Gang, Littleton, several times when he was writing DALTON GANG DAYS. But Littleton had not been near any of the family for over forty years when Latta interviewed him, and information in Latta's files indicate that Littleton was somewhat senile at the time of these interviews. The records of Grat's and Bill's trials for the California train robbery disprove much of what Littleton told Latta. Latta also relied heavily on interviews with and letters from Chris Madsen.

Throughout the literature many "well known facts" that simply are not true are repeated over and over again. Other statements appear that are clearly absurd; many of these could have been avoided by "counting teeth" or by "doing the arithmetic". Here is a sampling of some most common of the many "false teeth".

Bob Dalton shot Charley Montgomery in the back and killed him, because Charley had taken up with Bob's girl (also his first cousin), Minnie Johnson. Bob shot and killed Charley all right, but he did it the line of duty and Bob never had a cousin named Minnie Johnson. All other stories about Bob Dalton and other women, Flo Quick, a/k/a Tom King, Daisy Bryant, Eugenia Moore,etc. are also fiction. (Sorry folks, the Daltons did not practice equal opportunity for women; there were no female gang members.)

There is no evidence that Bob was ever the Chief of Police for the Osage Indian Nation. Emmett made the claim that Bob even organized the Osage Police. Bob did serve as a detective in the Osage Nation, but that is all the records show.

The Daltons did not start their career in outlaw activities by shooting up a crooked card game in a mining camp near Silver City, New Mexico. This is another tale invented by Emmett. Repeated queries to numerous libraries, historical societies, and individuals that have made a lifelong study of the history of the Silver City area have not turned up one iota of evidence to support this yarn.

Bill Dalton never served in the state legistature in the state of California. Neither did Bill father a child by a woman named Mary Hughes in Hugo, Oklahoma. The Mary Hughes story has been repeated numerous times both in published and in unpublished sources. Here the simple matter of doing the arithmetic for birth and conception dates of the William Dalton Jr. in question show this story to be ludicrous.

One of the wilder tales about Grat has been repeated by writers far and wide. This is the story of how Grat jumped from a speeding train while he was enroute to the California State Prison, after he had been sentenced to 20 years for the Alila train robbery. Grat was never sentenced for that robbery; he broke out of jail while awaiting sentencing. And anyone with a lick of common sense knows it takes a professional stunt man to leap out of a speeding train without killing one's self.

Horse stealing stories abound but there is just the slimmest bit of evidence to support only one of these stories. Most of the writers appear to have received most of their inspiration for the horse stealing tales from a single newspaper story that appeared in the FORT SMITH ELEVATOR of 8 May 1891; even brother Littleton repeated the ELEVATOR account almost verbatim.

Another yarn that combines horse stealing and murder, has been widely repeated in the literature and is as follows: After one of their train robberies the Daltons stole several head of horses from a group of farmers on Beaver Creek, near Orlando, Oklahoma. The farmers formed a posse and followed. W. T. Starmer was killed and another farmer, William Thompson, was badly wounded. Later versions of the tale usually add that Starmer has three bullet holes in his chest, so close together than any one of the shots could have killed him, or that all three bullet wounds could be covered by one hand. Then some famous deputy arrived on the scene and observed, "The only man in territory that can shoot like that is Bob Dalton.". Not one shred of evidence has been unearthed to support this tale. This story appears to be an invention of an early writer; then later writers picked up the story and added to it in each telling. One well known and highly respected western historian repeats this yarn in two or three of his books. In one book he footnotes the story, then in the footnote takes issue with FOUR other authors for getting the dates and place of the killing of Starmer all wrong; however, he neglects to provides any source documentation for the story in the first place. (He does not answer letters about the Daltons either.)

Charley Bryant is one of the least known and written about members of the Dalton Gang, but even he gets the works. Early in the career of the gang Charley became ill and was captured by Ed Short. Then Short and Bryant manage to shoot and kill each other on the train enroute to prison. Poor old Charley has been said to have been suffering from any and everything ranging from gunshot wounds to an advanced case of syphilis. On the other hand, Ed Short was a hired gun in some of the infamous county seat wars in Kansas, and he may have committed more criminal acts than all of the Dalton Gang combined. But the "historians" have gradually made Ed Short into a bright and shining hero who stood ten feet tall.

Then there are the stories of Emmett and Julia Johnson as childhood sweethearts, married in prison, etc., etc. Also the one about Grat (or was it Bob?) that played William Tell with the six-shooter and shot an apple off a Negro boy's head. Then Charley Bryant did not only the unlikely but the impossible when he killed a station agent during the robbery at Red Rock in June 1892, almost a year after Ed Short shot him dead. There never was a station agent killed during any of the Dalton train robberies. There is also the Sixth Man at Coffeyville, Madsen's story that he warned Coffeyville before the raid (he conveniently forgot to explain why the City Marshal was walking around unarmed when the Daltons struck), and dozens more tall tales about the Daltons.

Some of the above stories are understandable to a degree. As the stories about outlaws are told and retold, the stories grow. We are a nation of story-tellers; the knack for telling a good story has always been highly regarded, especially on the frontier. It is almost an unwritten law, that if you can't improve the story, you should not tell it in the first place. The Daltons have become the stuff of legends and have entered into the folk tales of the nation. However, the legends and the folk tales should not be confused with history and far too many writers do not seem to be able to make the distinction between legend and historical fact.

Another aspect of the Dalton story is even more puzzling. Most writers, with the exception of a few California historians, and a few who claim the Daltons were never in California at all, accept without question that the Daltons were guilty of the Alila, California, train robbery. The large, gleaming, and greedy teeth of the Southern Pacific Railroad [hereafter the SP] in this matter has been almost completely ignored. Not one writer (until yours truly) has bothered to look at the court records, or the newspaper accounts of the trials of the Daltons for the Alila robbery. Even the most casual researcher should have have able to locate volumes of data that attest to the conspicous criminal behavior of the founders and managers of the SP. Stanford, Huntington, the rest of "The Big Four" and their minions bought and sold congressmen before breakfast, openly bought votes on the streets of San Francisco, ran the state house in Sacramento, bombed and murdered their competitors, and arranged stock-watering deals and other financial shenanigans that Ivan Boesky and Mike Milken could only dream about. The SP wanted to nail somebody (did not matter who) for robbing their trains. When the SP detectives found out the Daltons were in the area, and that the Daltons were related to the infamous Youngers, of James and Younger outlaw fame, the SP went after the Daltons lock, stock, and barrel. The Daltons were simply no match for the SP "Octopus" and its tentacles.

Note: In the next two chapters standard abbreviations for states, counties, etc. have been used. Standard genealogical abbreviations have also been used.

Examples: b. - born, d. - died, m. - married, ca. - circa, etc. The term tithable is synonymous with taxable. There has been no attempt to place any of the early Daltons in chronological birth order within family groups. Dates of birth are seldom known, and can only be estimated from tax and marriage records.

II. FOREFATHERS & MOTHERS
The Daltons

The Dalton name is very old and may be Viking in origin. There are stories that a D'Alton accompanied William the Conqueror into England during the Conquest. William was the leader of a former Scandinavian speaking province of France and these people were descendants of Viking adventures who settled in the Seine Valley around 911. Another story claims that a Le Sieur de Dalton arrived in England from France with King Henry II about 1153. In any event, by the thirteenth century the name was well established in the British Isles.

The first record of a Dalton in America is that of Philemon Dalton who came to New England with his wife and son, Samuel, in 1635. By 1637 Philemon's brother, Rev. Timothy Dalton, was also in New England. Some researchers believe that this New England family and the early Virginia ancestors of the Dalton Gang were related.

Tristram Dalton, a descendant of Philemon, served as one of the first Senators from Massachusetts after the American Revolution. Tristram was a known associate of George Washington and other prominent Virginia families. So were some of the early Virginia Daltons.

By the time of the American Revolution there were numerous Daltons found in Virginia and several served in the Revolution.

Five early Daltons in Fairfax, Louisa, and Albemarle Counties appear to be connected and are probably related. These men are John and Robert of Fairfax and Timothy, Samuel, and David of Louisa/Albemarle. These men had business dealings with the same people and witnessed wills, deeds, and other legal documents for some of the same families. In addition the same given names appear over and over in these families.

There is a common story passed down that says a whole ship load or a group of Dalton brothers came to America from Yorkshire, England. This group reportedly first landed in New Jersey then moved on to Virginia.

ROBERT DALTON: Little is known about this man. He died in Fairfax County ca. 1792. He and John are believed to be brothers. There are surviving legal documents that Robert and John witnessed together and John named one of his sons Robert.

JOHN DALTON married Jemima Shaw and had seven children. Only two daughters survived to adulthood and married. John was a personal friend of George Washington and a business partner of John Carlyle in Alexandria, VA. John was a Vestryman in the church (Church of England-Episcopalian) and was very active in the civic and military affairs of the county. He was a member of the Committees of Safety and Correspondence for the county and an officer in the militia. However, he died about the time the Revolution started, in either 1776 or early 1777.

DAVID DALTON lived in Albemarle Co. and later moved to North Carolina. His wife is unknown. David is believed to have been born ca. 1730 possibly in England. He died in 1804 in Rutherford Co., NC. He had eleven children and three of his sons, John, William, and Thomas, served in the Revolution. Most of this family went to NC and some later went to TN and other areas. David's family do not seem to have been as well off as most of the other Daltons. This branch of the family appear to have remained poor and uneducated. David's son John became a Primitive Baptist minister and many others of this family were also of this religion.

SAMUEL DALTON is often refered to as Samuel of Mayo because in his later years he lived along the Mayo river on the Virginia/North Carolina line. Sam is believed to have been born ca. 1699 and he died ca. 1806 in Rockingham Co., NC. His wife was Anne Redd and there were probably twelve children in this family; ten children are fully documented. Samuel obtained early land grants in Albermarle Co. in 1746 and 1756. He and various members of his family lived in Louisa, Albermarle, and Pittsylvania (the portions that were later Patrick Co. and Henry Co.) County,

VA. Some of the family went to Georgia for a short time but most settled in the northern counties of NC. This family is the best documented family of all the early VA Daltons. Samuel's family remained in the Church of England and therefore almost all of the early marriages for this family have been recorded. Known children are: 1. William m. Rachel Harris 2. Samuel Jr. m. 1767 Charlotte Gallihue 3. David m. 1st Susannah Davis, m. 2nd Eleanor Good 4. Letitia m. 1757 Col. Matthew Moore 5. Rachel m. William Martin 6. Mary (Molly) m. Archelaus Hughes 7. Nancy (Anne) m. 1769 Adonijah Harbour 8. Sarah (Matilda) m. Jonathan Hanby 9. Virginia (Jenny) m. David Hanby 10. Jane m. Joseph Winston and possibly 11. Robert 12. Charles.

TIMOTHY DALTON appears to be the earliest American Dalton ancestor of the Dalton Gang. Timothy may have been born in England but the date is unknown. He names his wife, Elizabeth, in his will but nothing further is known about her. Timothy was probably a very old man when he died in 1767. He made his will in 1755 and stated that he was weak in body at that time. The first record of a land grant for Timothy is in Albemarle Co. in 1732. He later owned land in Halifax Co. (the area that was previously Lunenburg Co. and later Pittsylvania Co. - hereafter Pitts. Co.). Other records are found for Timothy that indicate he may have owned land in Brunswick, Spottslvania, and other counties. In 1738 Timothy Dalton Jr., almost certainly the son of the older Tim, also received land by grant in Albemarle Co. Timothy Sr. may have had some falling out with most of his family, because he left his entire estate to his son William and nothing to his wife or to any other children. His son William may be the William Dalton that died in 1783 in Albemarle. Other possible children are Richard and John who died in Albemarle in 1774 and 1787.

No early marriage records have been found for the Timothy Dalton family. Early tax records show that few of this Dalton family owned slaves. These two facts raises the possibility that some of this family may have been Quakers in the early days. Further research is needed to check the validity of this theory.

Note: Ages are not known for certain for the Timothy Dalton family members. In the following group it is possible that some of these men are either brothers or grandsons of Timothy Jr. instead of his sons.

TIMOTHY DALTON JR. AND ELIZABETH DALTON

Timothy Dalton Jr. d. 1775 Bedford Co., VA; wife, Elizabeth, may have been a Talbot. He too left a will but names only wife Elizabeth and oldest son James. Other children are mentioned but not named.

Children:

1. James, named as the oldest son in his father's will. Probably d. 1811 in Franklin Co., VA. Wife Elizabeth. Children: Randolph, Anna, Judah, Elizabeth (probably), and likely others.

2. Elizabeth m. 1st _____ Bennet, one child, Richard; m. 2nd James Bobbitt, children: John, William, James Jr., Randolph, Dinah, Ann, Mary, Livisia.

3. DAVID, wife Hannah. The record for his family follows.

4. Robert died ca. 1779 Pitts. Co. VA, wife Mary Key. Children: John, Robert Jr., Soloman, Agatha, Nancy, and probably others.

5. William, wife Elizabeth (Sturman?). William d. ca. 1811 in what is now Carroll Co. VA. Children: James, Timothy, Lewis, William, Patience, Rachel, Nancy, John, Reuben, Susannah.

6. Timothy. Very little is known about him. He appeared on the tax list in Montgomery Co., VA (the area that is now Carroll Co.) in 1782 along with William, Reuben, and Samuel Dalton, all believed to be his brothers. Wife was probably named Sarah. It is believed that he went to Hawkins Co., TN and died there. Timothy Dalton b. 1803 d. 1870 m. Susan Kelly in Hawkins Co. is thought to be his son, other children not identified.

7. John F. b. ca. 1750 d. 1833 Sumner Co. TN, wife Mary Ann Flannagan. Children: Winston, Booker, Shelton, John R., Martin, and probably others. There are several John Daltons in Pitts. Co. and trying to sort them out is a real chore. However, there is positive proof that Winston Dalton was the son of John F. and Mary Ann Flannagan Dalton. Winston was a school teacher and kept a "register" that names many of his relatives and friends. Winston's register has been kept and handed down with the original land grant of Tim Dalton Jr. for several generations. Therefore, it seems logical that John F. is the son of Tim Jr.

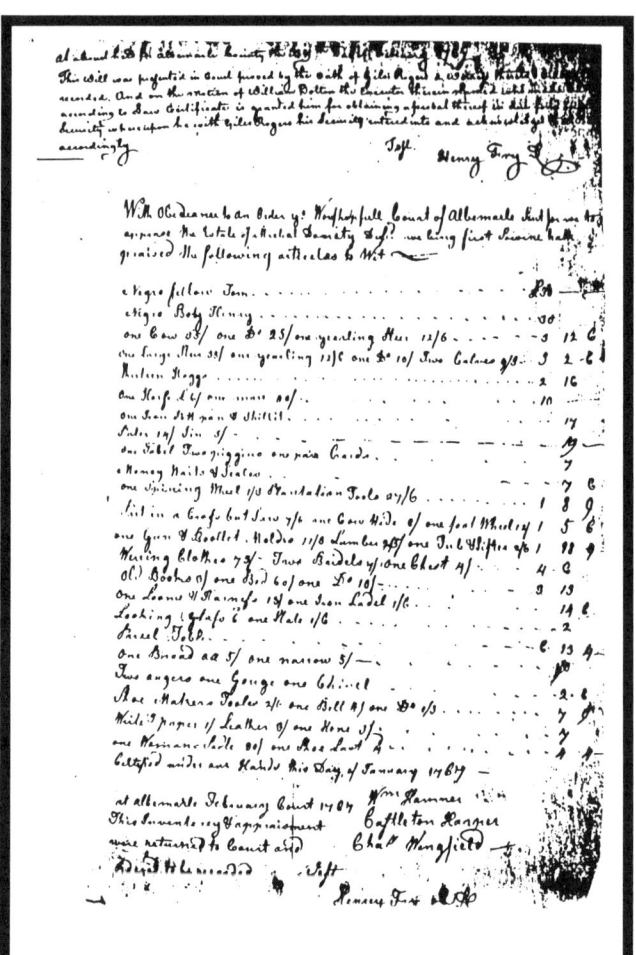

The will of Timothy Dalton Sr.

8. Reuben d. 1822 Grainger Co., TN, wife Elizabeth Shockly. Children: Enos, Timothy, Meredith, Carter, Reuben, Polly Dodson, Elizabeth Rucker, Ann Harrell, and dau. m. _____ Shockley (grandson William Shockley named in Reuben's will).

9. Samuel, little is known about him for sure. He is probably the Samuel who died ca. 1798 in Pitts. Co. His wife was probably Milly. He likely went to Montgomery Co. in 1782 with his brothers William, Reuben, and Timothy. He only appeared on the Montgomery Co. tax lists for a year or two, so he probably returned to Pitts. Co. and died there. Possible children: Isham, Samuel, Lewis (ordered bound out after Samuel's death), and Phoebe. After Samuel died his wife, Milly married Daniel Slayton.

DAVID DALTON SR. AND HANNAH DALTON

David Dalton appeared on the tax or tithe lists of Lunenburg Co., VA from 1748-1751. Part of Lunenburg became Halifax Co. and later a portion of Halifax became Pitts. Co., VA. Early tax records for Halifax have not been located but a number of early Pitts. Co. records are available. Records for both David and David Jr. appear on various census records for Pitts. Co. from 1782-1790. In 1797 David and Hannah Dalton appeared on the Camden Parish register and their support was to be deposited in the hands of Thomas Smith. In 1802 Hannah was listed alone and after 1804 she too was gone from the register. It is believed that David d. 1802 and Hannah d. 1804. Hannah may have been a Goad.

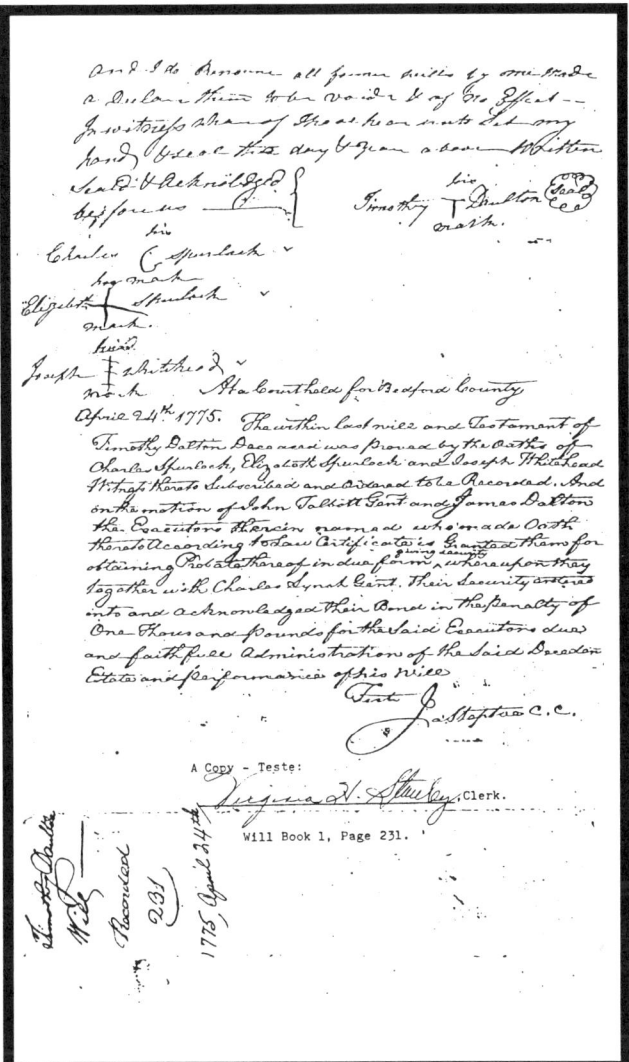

The will of Timothy Dalton Jr.

Children:
1. ? dau. m. John Hill or Hall. John appeared on the 1748 tax list with David Dalton.

2. ? dau. m. James Henley. James appeared on the 1752 tax list with David Dalton.
Note: There is no proof that these two men are sons-in-law of David. They could be hired men. The name Hanley in Gratton Hanley Dalton may be a variation of the Henley name.

3. Benjamin was listed on the 1767 tax list with his father, David. No other record has been found for this Benjamin. He probably either died young or left the area.

4. DAVID JR. appeared on the Pitts. Co. tax list for the first time in 1773. Other records identify his wife only as Judith. Records for this family follow.

5. James was on the tax list with his father, David from 1773-1775 and again in 1779 and 1780. He is probably the James that m. Agness Dyer 18 April 1782.

Other likely children are:
6. Rachel Dalton m. George Dyer and had children named James, Benjamin, Francis, Phoebe, David Dalton, Elizabeth, Louisa, Rachel, and Martha Dyer.

7. Nancy Dalton m. 1788 Nathan Dyer. She probably died young as Nathan m. 15 Feb. 1793 Mary Payne.

DAVID DALTON JR. AND JUDITH DALTON

Judith Dalton appears on the roll of Camden Parish in 1821 for the first time. She must be a widow by this time. In 1822 her support is in the hands of Walter Pickerall. After that her support is in the hands of various individuals and she is last found on the rolls in 1831. She probably died about this time. Children:

1. Thomas Dalton, first appeared on the 1787 tax list and was not tithable; probably not yet 21 years of age. In 1788 he married Elizabeth Patterson. (See James Dalton and Agatha Patterson for more information on the Patterson family). Thomas and Elizabeth appear on the Camden Parish roll in 1848; by 1850 Elizabeth is listed alone and her support was in the hands of a James P. Lewis. Thomas probably d. ca. 1849. Death records of Pitts. Co. show Elizabeth d. 1860. Thomas and Elizabeth had a number of children.

2. JAMES m. 19 Jan. 1791 Agatha Patterson. Records for this family follow.

3. Benjamin Dalton m. Caty Mayhue 11 Nov. 1803 and m. 2nd Elizabeth Pickerall 11 Sept. 1819.

4. Isham Dalton m. 19 Jan. 1795 Mary Goad. Surety was Samuel Dalton.

5. Lewis Dalton m. 12 Nov. 1797 Mary (Polly) Keeze. Lewis d. ca. 1847. His eight children are named in the records of the estate settlement.

6. Judith Dalton m. 21 Dec. 1801 Watte (Walter) Pickerell (Pickerall). Surety was Lewis Dalton.

7. Sally Dalton m. 24 Dec. 1805 Thomas Pickerall. Surety was Benjamin Dalton.

There are possibly other children.

JAMES DALTON AND AGATHA PATTERSON DALTON

James Dalton m. Agatha Patterson 19 Jan. 1791 in Pitts. Co., VA. She was the dau. of Littleberry and Nanney Thomas Patterson. Littleberry Patterson d. ca. 1796 in Pitts. Co. and his wife Nanney d. sometime after that. Patterson children: Elizabeth b. 1772 m. 1788 Thomas Dalton (brother of James), John b. 1774 m. 30 July 1794 Polly Mustain, Agatha b. 1776, William b. 1778 m. 1799 Nancy Farris, Edward b. 1780, Robert b. 1782, Thomas b. 1784 m. 18 June 1804 Mary "Polly" Jane Harvey in Madison, Co., KY, Milley b. 1786, and Fanney b. 1788. Note: Most of this information was furnished by a member of the Patterson family. The dates given here do not always agree with census and other records.

On the 1850 census of Hawkins Co., TN there is a James Dalton age 80 and his wife Aggy age 79. Birthplace of both is listed as TN but this is probably in error as both were most likely born in Pitts. Co., VA. Aggy is gone by 1860 but James is listed on the 1860 census as age 110 (clearly a mistake in this age), by 1870 James is also gone. Aggy must have died between 1850-60 and James sometime in the 1860s.

Children:

1. Littleberry. James and son Berry appeared on the 1810 tax list for Pitts. Co., VA. Berry m. Fanny Dove 6 Jan. 1812 and 2nd m. Nancy C. Camp 21 Jan. 1819 in Pitts. Co., VA. He divorced Fanny and both remarried; there were children of both of his marriages. Berry probably d. in Benton Co., TN before 1850 as wife Nancy, son Littleberry, and other family members are on the 1850 census of Benton Co.

2. BENJAMIN m. Nancy Rabourn 16 April 1815 in Montgomery Co., KY. Records of this family follow:

NOTES: The Benjamin Daltons get confusing. The first Benjamin, son of David and Hannah appears on the tax records of Pitts. Co. in 1767. The next appearance of Benjamin Dalton is on the 1810 tax list/census. In 1810 there are two of them, Ben Sr. and Ben Jr. Ben Sr. is also a grandson of David and Hannah Dalton but he is not the father of Ben Jr. Ben Sr. married twice, 1st m. Caty Mayhue 11 Nov. 1803 and 2nd m. Elizabeth Pickerall 11 Sept. 1819. On the 1820 census of Pitts. Co. there is only one Ben Dalton and he is over 45, his wife between 26-45, 1 son and 4 daus. under age 10, and 2 daus. 10-16. Children of Ben Sr's. 1st. marriage: Rebecca, Booker, Cyrena, Anna; 2nd marriage: Nella, Caleb, Sally, John, Elizabeth, Doctor Lynch (Doctor is a name not a title and this son was generally known as Lynch), and Benjamin. In 1848 Camden Parish records show that Joseph East was paid for making a coffin for Benjamin Dalton.

The terms Sr. and Jr. were often used in times past to distinguish between two or more men of the same name living in the same vicinity. The current custom of using these abbreviations to denote only father and son is of fairly recent origin.

3. James Lewis m.20 Feb. 1821 Matilda Rabourn, sister of Nancy, in Montgomery Co., KY. Records on this family also follow in order to establish proof that this man is not the father of James Lewis Dalton, the father of the Dalton Gang.

4. Agatha or Aggy Dalton. She was probably unmarried when she gave birth to a son, Willis, 14 March 1811 and to a second child, name unknown, 28 April 1816. She is probably the Aggy on the census index for Pitt. Co. in 1830. Her son Willis was later living in Lawrence Co., Ohio. A Thomas Dalton (probably a son of Thomas and Elizabeth Patterson Dalton) m. Nancy Taylor 23 Jan. 1823 in Pitts. Co., VA and by 1850 the Willis, Thomas, and at least two other Dalton families from Pitts. Co. are all in Lawrence Co., Ohio.

5. Coleman Dalton b. ca. 1800 m. Dolly Shelton 26 Oct. 1820 in Pitts. Co., VA. He later moved to Patrick Co., VA and died there in 1882. Known children were Jane, Fredrick, Aggy, Andrew J., James W., Coleman J., Willis, and Nancy.

There were probably other children not yet identified. Some of the Hawkins Co., TN Daltons also may be children of James and Agatha.

BENJAMIN DALTON AND NANCY RABOURN DALTON

Benjamin Dalton m. Nancy Rabourn, dau. of Henry Rabourn 16 April 1815 in Montgomery Co., KY. Ben died 15 Jan. 1835 in Decatur Co., IN. Nancy Dalton filed for a War of 1812 Widow's Pension on 3 May 1879. She was 86 years old when she filed the application in Belton, MO. Appearing with her and signing her application were Lewis Dalton age 79 and Henry M. Dalton age 57, her brother-in-law and nephew.

Children:

1. JAMES LEWIS b. 16 Feb. 1826 in Montgomery Co., KY. Wife Adeline Lee Younger. This couple are the parents of the Dalton Gang. Records of this family follow in Chapter III.

2. Henry. Nothing known except his name, he reportedly died in KY.

3. Tillie (Matilda) married ____ Louis. Believed to have been living in MO when the Dalton Gang family lived there.

4. Nancy Emaline m. Robert Noel in KY and later moved to California. They are on the 1850 census in Clark Co., KY and Robert Callaway or Robert C. Noel (Noell) appears on the 1867 and 1886 voting records of Sutter Co., CA.

5. Agnes m. William Chism 16 May 1856 in Jackson Co., MO. She was born in KY.

There were probably other children. The following may also be the dau. of Ben and Nancy.

6. Adeline m. Joshua Corn 16 April 1854 in Jackson Co., MO. Adeline Dalton age 21 also appears on the 1850 census for Montgomery Co. KY in the household of William Baldwin. She is the only Dalton in that county that year.

NOTES: Most of the available information on Ben and Nancy comes from Ben's War of 1812 military records and Nancy's pension application. They were m. in 1815 in Montgomery Co., KY by Rev. David Barr. In 1785 Rev. David Barr was granted a license to perform marriages by the Pitts. Co., VA court. He was the resident minister of the Presbyterian Church on Wet Sleeve Creek in Pitts. Co. In 1796 Barr sold property in Pitts Co. and supposedly moved to North Carolina. He was replaced at the Wet Sleeve church by Revs. James Mitchell and James Turner of Bedford Co. A James Mitchell married Agatha Dalton, dau. of Robert and Mary Key Dalton 25 Nov. 1768 in Pitts. Co., VA.

Benjamin Dalton served in the War of 1812 Co. D, 2 Reg't KY Vol. Militia. Dates of service were 1 Sept. 1812 to 26 March 1813. There is also a War of 1812 record for a Benjamin Dalton in Co. D, 6 Reg't VA Militia service dates 28 Aug. 1814-22 Dec. 1814. This is probably the same Benjamin Dalton with two enlistments as the dates of service do not over lap. There is also a Berryman Dalton who served in the 6th Reg't VA Militia. Berryman is almost certainly a close cousin of Benjamin.

The following two entries are found in the Court Records from Estill Co. KY (Estill joins Montgomery Co.) in 1815:

"2 Feb. 1815, Garland Jones VS Benjamine Dalton was to recover of Dalton $55 for trespass."

"22 March 1815, Garland Jones VS Benjamine Dalton, trespass, exchanging horses, Jones doubts the soundness of the eyes of Dalton's horse. If horse was to go blind before a certain date, he was to take horse back and give him a stear valued at $16. Sues for $100."

JAMES LEWIS DALTON AND MATILDA RABOURN DALTON

NOTE: Numerous supposed family histories of the Dalton Gang are floating around and some have even been published that claim that James Lewis and Matilda Rabourn Dalton are the grandparents of the Dalton Gang. THIS IS NOT TRUE; this couple are the great uncle and aunt of the Gang. The records of this family are included here in order to establish, beyond any doubt, the proper relationship of this family to the Dalton Gang.

James Lewis Dalton m. Matilda Rabourn, sister to Nancy who married Ben Dalton, 20 Feb. 1821 in Montgomery Co., KY. The family remained in Montgomery Co., KY until about 1841 when they went to TN for a short time and then moved on to Jackson Co., MO. Matilda d. 19 Feb. 1879 age 76 and James Lewis d. 22 June 1879 age 80. They are both buried in the Dalton or Luttrell Cemetery in Jackson Co., MO.

Children:

1. Henry Milton b. 29 Nov. 1821 Mt. Sterling, Montgomery Co., KY, m. Nancy Martha Johnson 13 Feb. 1853 in Jackson Co., MO, d. 16 Feb 1896. Henry names his parents, siblings, and all of his children in his family bible.

2. Nancy b. ca. 1828 in KY, m. 1st James Helms 28 March 1844 and 2nd Isaac Andrews and lived in Jackson Co., MO.

3. Armilda (Ormilda) b. ca 1833 in KY, m. Samuel H. Luttrell, d. 12 Feb. 1914 at age 82. She, her husband and some of their children are buried in the Dalton/Luttrell Cemetery in Jackson Co., MO.

4. James Lewis b. 14 Mar. 1835 in KY, m. Margaret Elizabeth Smith 10 Feb. 1858 in Jackson Co., MO. James, his wife, and one son are buried in the Westport Cemetery, Bates Co., MO.

5. David Gillam (Gillom) b. ca 1837 in KY, m. Georgia C. Hannen 28 Nov. 1867 in Jackson Co., MO.

NOTES: The Warranty Deed filed in Jackson Co., MO 2 Oct. 1880 to settle the estate of James Lewis Dalton names all five of his children and spouses that were still living. Jackson Co., MO census records of 1850 show the younger James as age 15 still in the household of his parents Lewis and Matilda Dalton. In 1870 the following are all living in one household. Lewis 71, Matilda 67, David G. 32, Georgia C. 20, Lewis 35, Elizabeth 27, Anna E. 8, William N. 7, Charles 5, Robert L. 2.

The 1850 census records give the birthplace of Lewis Dalton age 52 as KY; however, both the 1860 and 1870 census give his birth place as VA.

988 Sheila Court,
Mt. Sterling, Ky. 40353
August 1, 1986

Dear Nancy,

Thank you so much for all the Dalton information.

You are quite correct with your suspicion that Lewis Dalton and Ben Dalton were brothers and married to sisters, however, all records indicate that the father of the Dalton Gang was Ben and not Lewis.

One Henry Raybourn settled in Montgomery County by 1803 and purchased land on Lulbegrud Creek some three miles nearly due south of Mt. Sterling. As the years passed by, he made additional land purchases.

On October 25, 1823, Benjamin Dalton bought land in this same area adjoining the lands of Henry Rabourn; the deed is recorded in Deed Book 11, Page 147. Ben kept the land until February 1, 1825 when he and Nancy sold it. This deed is recorded in Deed Book 12, Page 90. On August 29, 1827, Benjamin mortgaged to Lewis Dalton a horse and colt, 5 head of cattle, 16 head of sheep, 30 geese and 3 fields of corn to purchase a horse from Lewis; this mortgage is recorded in Deed Book 13, at Page 265.

As yet I have not researched the Ky. tax lists but I would suspect that soon after this date of August, 1827, Ben and Nancy migrated to Indiana where according to her pension application Ben died August 25, 1835.

The will of Henry Rabourn was probated at the May term of court, 1838, and recorded in Will Book "E", Page 32. He devised the home place to his son, John Westley, and gave instructions for John Westly to build homes for his two single daughters, Margaret and Sally. He further devised furniture to his grandson, Henry Milton Dalton. He then gave $100 to his daughter, Nancy Dalton. He instructed that his remaining farm land was to be sold, the proceeds to be equally distributed among his other children, William, James, Henry, Hiram and Matilda Dalton. A William Baldwin and a James McKee witnessed the will.

An apprasal of the estate of Henry Rabourn was made May 31, 1838 and recorded in Record Book A1, Page 249. On the next day, June 1, 1838, the sale of his estate was held and by this date, Nancy Dalton was back in Montgomery County for she made two purchases of sewing materials at the sale; this sale is recorded in Record Book A1, Page 250. On October 20, 1840, the estate was settled after 60 plus acres of land was sold; the settlement was recorded in Record Book A1, Page 382.

The recollections of Littleton Dalton appear very true; the naming of the eldest Dalton son, Charles Benjamin, indicates that his grandfathers were Charles Younger and Benjamin Dalton; so far there are no contradictions in our story.

We're rolling; I'll keep you informed of our progress.

Sincerely,

Stanley

988 Sheila Court,
Mt. Sterling, Ky. 40353
Sept. 12, 1986

Dear Nancy,

Thank you for your last two letters with the enclosed transmittals.

I made one trip to the Ky. Historical Society Library in Frankfort in late August and found Ben Dalton appeared on the Estill County tax lists for the first time on May 3, 1812; he also appeared on this same county list for the years of 1813 and 1814. Today I researched the Montgomery County tax lists and found Ben was shown on the 1816 list and continued on this list thru 1829. The tax lists for 1823 and 1824 showed his ownership of his farm for these two years confirming the past deed references I gave you in my last letter. It appears that Ben and Nancy migrated to Indiana around 1830 so he might possibly be on the 1830 Decatur County, Indiana census.

Lewis Dalton first appeared on a Montgomery County tax list in 1821 and as you know continued to reside in this county for another 20 years.

While in Frankfort I copied the following Pittsylania County, Va. marriages:

```
22 Sept. 1767 - Sameul Dalton, Jr. and Charlotte Gollilee -
17 Dec.  1778 - Winston Dalton and Sarah Pullin
         1778 - Thomas Dalton and Elizabeth Patterson
15 July  1788 - John Dalton and Luvenia Pickrall - Surety, John Dalton
18 Apr.  1782 - James Dalton and Agnes Dyer
19 Jan.  1791 - James Dalton and Agatha Patterson - Surety, Ambrose Dalton
19 Jan.  1795 - Isham Dalton and Mary Goad - Surety, Samuel Dalton
12 Nov.  1797 - Lewis Dalton and Mary Keezee
11 June  1801 - Lewis Dalton and Betsy Chambers - Surety, Benjamin Dalton
20 June  1803 - Martin Dalton and Caty Crider
11 Nov.  1803 - Benjamin Dalton and Caty Mayhue
10 Mch.  1804 - Eligy Dalton and Nancy Brogen - Surety, Lewis Dalton
 5 Sept. 1804 - James Dalton and Molly Dalton
17 Nov.  1804 - William Dalton and Winifred Foster - Father of Wm. is George
26 Dec.  1804 - Jesse Dalton and Catharine Clark
19 Dec.  1805 - Berryman Dalton and Sarah Cook
```

Will look for more Pittsylvania County, Va. information on my next trip to Frankfort.

Sincerely,

Stanley

The Youngers

In his book, THE STORY OF COLE YOUNGER by Himself, Cole described his family as follows:

"My people had always been prominent, politically. It was born in the blood. My great grandmother on my father's side was a daughter of "Lighthorse Harry" Lee whose proud memory we all cherish. The Youngers came from Strasburg, and helped to rule there when it was a free city. Henry Washington Younger, my father, represented Jackson county three times in the legislature, and was also judge of the county court. My mother, who was Bursheba Fristoe of Independence, was the daughter of Richard Fristoe who fought under General Andrew Jackson at New Orleans, Jackson county having been so named at my grandfather Fristoe's instance. Mother was descended from the Sullivans, Ladens and Percivals of South Carolina, the Taylors of Virginia and the Fristoes of Tennessee, and my grandfather Fristoe was a grand nephew of Chief Justice John Marshall of Virginia."

Adeline Younger was the daughter of Charles Lee Younger, and therefore she is the aunt of Cole Younger and the other Younger brothers who were part of the James-Younger band of outlaws. It has often been reported that the Youngers and the Daltons were all related to the James Family. There is no evidence of any blood ties of either the Youngers or the Daltons to the James family. The third wife of Thomas Coleman (half brother of Adeline) Younger, Augusta Peters Inskeep, was related to Benjamin Simms, second husband of Zerelda James (mother of Jesse and Frank James). Augusta was also a sister to the mother of outlaw Johnny Ringo.

It is entirely possible that there was some distant relationship between Adeline Younger and James Lewis Dalton. Both the early Dalton and Younger families were in the same sections of Virginia and Kentucky. Both families also seemed to have ties of some kind to the Coleman family of Virginia. The name

Cole Younger in his later years. Photo Author's collection.

Coleman is found as a given name in both the Dalton and Younger families several times.

Which woman is really the mother of Adeline? This question has been a subject of some debate. Most researchers agree that Parmelia Dorcus Wilson is the mother but Sarah Sullivan Purcell is listed on Adeline's death certificate. The 1850 census lists Adeline Younger in both the Charles Younger household and Parmelia Wilson household. On these records Adeline is shown as age 14 and Sarah Younger as age 62. Sarah would have been 48 or 49 when Adeline was born. It is not impossible that Sarah is the mother but it is unlikely at that age. In the Wilson household Adeline is listed as age 15 and Parmelia as 35. The date of the census for the Younger household is Aug. 23, for the Wilson household Sept. 11. Adeline's death certificate gives her birth date as 15 Sept. 1835, she was four days away from her 15th birthday when the Wilson household was counted. It seems more logical that Parmelia is the mother of Adeline.

JOSHUA LOGAN YOUNGER b. 11 May 1752 VA, d. 2 Aug. 1834 Lawrence Co., IN, m. Elizabeth Lee b. 1755, VA d. before 15 Sept. 1787.

Children:

1. Peter Younger, d. before 1841 Grant Co., KY, m. 18 Mar. 1798, Abigail Dennis, dau. of Elisha and Elizabeth Dennis. Children:
    1. Elizabeth m. Jan. 1823, Harrison Co., KY John Coulson.
    2. Catherine, d. before 1833, Grant Co., KY, m. 7 Feb 1825 Jediah Ashcraft, Harrison Co., KY, son of Jediah and Sarah Ashcraft.
    3. Charles, d. 1833 (cholera) Grant Co., KY m. 14 Feb.1828 Maria Burnley.
    4. Sally m. 3 Apr. 1833 Cyrus Williams
    5. Nelly (Milly) m. 13 Aug. 1834 Willis Marksberry.
    6. Polly m. 1st 3 April 1833 David Rains.
    7. John B. m. 14 Nov. 1858 Lucinda Heflin.

2. CHARLES LEE, b. 28 Dec. 1779, Hampshire, VA d. 12 Nov. 1854, Osceola, St. Clair Co., MO, m. 1st 13 April 1798 Nancy Toomey, Garrard Co., KY, m. 2nd 1800-1808 Sarah Purcell.

Note: This is the grandfather of Cole Younger and father of Adeline Younger Dalton.

3. Elizabeth Lee b. 27 Feb. 1772 d. when? Orleans, Orange Co., IN.

JOSHUA m. 2nd 15 Sept. 1787 Catherine Yoter,

Cole Younger just after his capture for the Northfield, MI bank robbery, Sept. 1876. The three Younger brothers were sentenced to life in Stillwater Prison. Photo Tacket Collection. Courtesy of Herb Osborne.

Forefathers & Mothers - The Youngers

Hampshire, VA.

4. Stephen d. 23 Dec. 1893 m. 8 April 1819 Sarah Kern.

5. Rachel m. 29 Oct. 1806 William Ward, Garrard Co., KY.

6. Garrett m. Polly Parrott.

7. Lewis b. 3 Dec. 1802 KY d. 17 Feb. 1890 Lawrence Co., IN m. 28 Aug. 1823 Nancy Crosse.

8. Polly (Mary) b. 30 March 1793 Lawrence Co., IN d. 4 July 1880 m. Thomas Welborn.

9. Sallie b. KY m. 7 Sept. 1823 Horatio Morris.

10. Mary.

11. John m. Elizabeth Kern 17 March 1818. One child Catherine; both parents died young and Steven Younger was appointed guardian.

SOURCES: KENTUCKY ANCESTORS V 16-3 1981 and Stanley Kern.

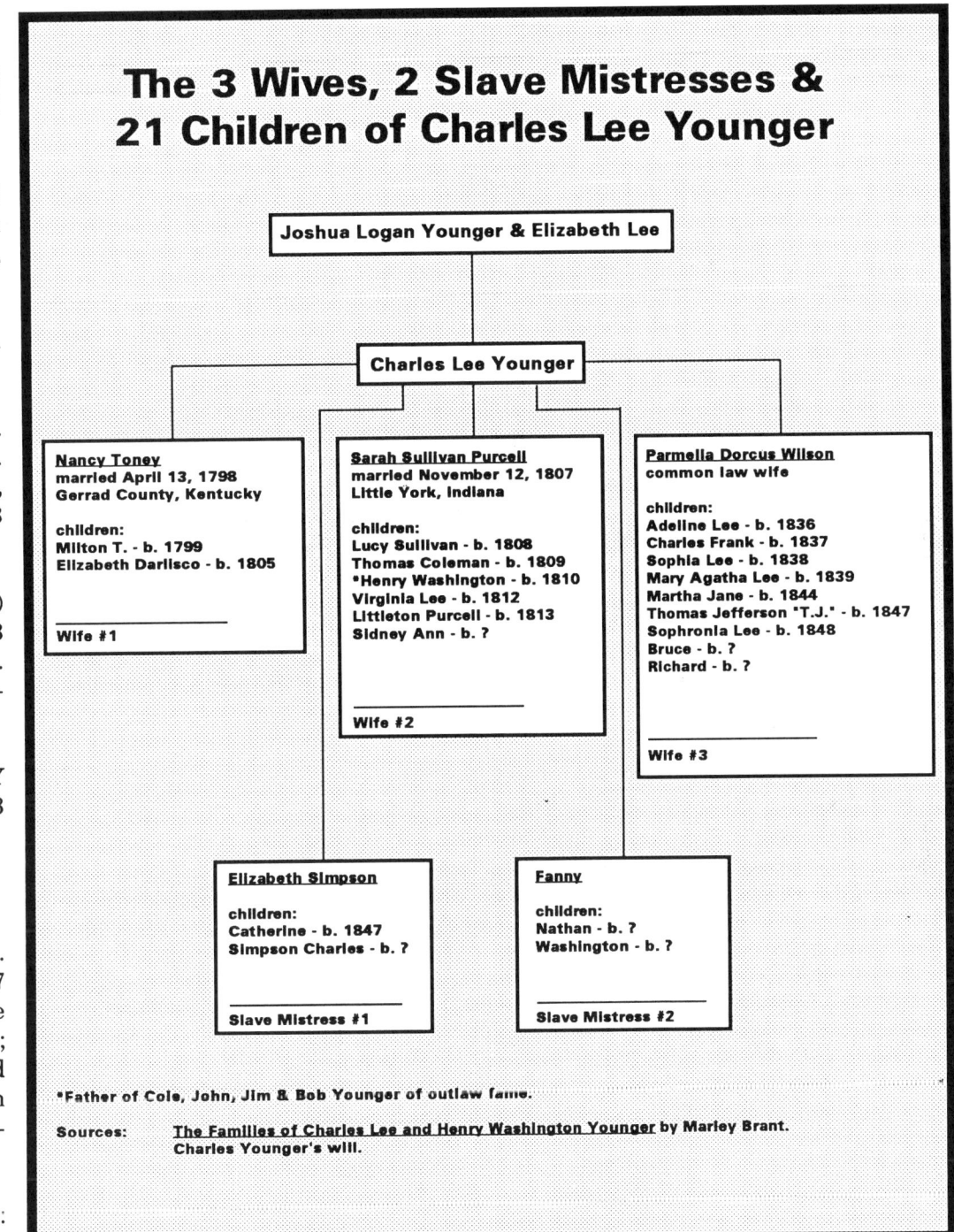

WILL AND CODICIL OF CHARLES YOUNGER

IN THE NAME OF GOD, AMEN:

I, Charles Younger of the County of Jackson in the State of Missouri, being of sound mind and memory, in view of the uncertainty of life and wishing to dispose of my property differently from the laws of decents as in all good conscience I feel that I ought to do, do make and publish the following, my last will and testament, hereby revoking all other wills or parts of wills, which I may have heretofore made.

ITEM 1st. In view of the fact that I have heretofore by deed of gift, conveyed to the six next named persons upwards of Thirty Thousand Dollars worth of Real Estate in common, which is an equal share of my Estate with others hereinafter named whom I am bound by every tie of honor to provide for. I will and bequeath to my beloved wife Sarah S. Younger the sum of one dollar, which with the property given her in said deed of gift is in lieu of dower in my Estate. I give and bequeath to Harry W. Younger the sum of one dollar. I give and bequeath to Littleton Younger the sum of one dollar. I give and bequeath to Virginia L. Creek, wife of Jacob Creek the sum of one dollar. I give and bequeath to Elizabeth D. Woods, wife of Thomas Woods the sum of one dollar, and to Lucy S. Burten the like sum of one dollar.

ITEM 2nd. I give and bequeath to Parmelia Wilson of Jackson County, the eighty acre tract of land situated in said County which I bought of Hampton, reference being had to Hampton's deed to me. To Have and To Hold the same to her and her heirs forever.

ITEM 3rd. I give and bequeath to Adeline L. Dalton,

Louis Dalton, father of the Dalton boys.

Mrs. Louis Dalton, mother of the Dalton boys.

These photos have been widely published and are usually identified as Louis (proper spelling is Lewis) and Adeline Dalton. However, these are photos of Henry Washington and Bursheba Fristoe Younger, the parents of the outlaw Younger brothers. Photos courtesy of Western Historical Collections University of Oklahoma. Identification by Marley Brant and Carl Breihan.

wife of Lewis Dalton, Jr., the tract of land containing two hundred and ten acres on which said Dalton and wife now live in Cass County near Harrisonville, and one negro girl, slave named Minerva, about twenty-seven years of age, which girl slave was hired to Todds at the Noland House. To Have and To Hold the above land and negro girl unto her the said Adeline and to her heirs after her in tail and not to the said Lewis Dalton, Jr., nor his heirs nor assigns.

ITEM 4th. I will and bequeath that after my death the following slaves belonging to me be maumitted and forever set free from slavery or service or bondage to any man, to wit: Elizabeth, aged 22 years, of mulatto color and her two children named Catherine and Simpson. Also Fanny, aged between 35 and 40 years, and her two children named Nathan and Washington, and that their freedom commence at my death.

ITEM 5th. I give and bequeath to said Elizabeth, Fanny, Catherine, Simpson, Nathan and Washington, named in the 4th Item, jointly, the 300 acre tract of land situated on Little Blue in Jackson County, which I bought in part from John Ross and from Hawkins Estate and in part from the U. S. Land Office, all which land is easily ascertained by reference to the deeds from the last named parties to me and from the Land Office Certificate. To Have and To Hold the same to said last mentioned legatees after their freedom, Forever.

ITEM 6th. I give and bequeath to the children of Milton Younger, deceased to wit: Rebecca, Charles and Catherine Younger, the sum of one dollar each and this I do because I have already given them as much as I intended to do besides this legacy.

ITEM 7th. After the payment of my just debts and the special legacies herein mentioned, I give and bequeath to Sophia S. Wilson, Charles F. Wilson, Mary S. Wilson, Martha L. Wilson, Jefferson Wilson, Bruce Wilson and Sophronia Wilson, who are sometimes called by the name of "Younger" instead of "Wilson" (and whom I acknowledge as my children by the said Parmelia Wilson their mother), all the remainder of my Estate both real and personal to be divided equally between said seven children. In this testimony I hereunto set my hand and affix my seal this 26th day of February A. D. 1852.

CHARLES YOUNGER (SEAL)

At the request of said Charles Younger we hereunto subscribe our names as witnesses to the forgoing Will and Signature.

J. BROWN HOVEY

JOHN R. SWEARINGER

At the request of Charles Younger we hereunto subscribe our names as witnesses to the foregoing Will and Signature in the presence of the said Younger in St. Clair County, MO this 28th day of October 1854.

THEODRICK SNUFFER

JOHN BEDELL

IN THE NAME OF GOD, AMEN:

I, Charles Younger, of the County of St. Clair and State of Missouri, being of sound mind and memory, in view of the uncertainty of life, and wishing to make some farther provisions in regard to my temporal affairs after my death, I hereby confirm each and every provision in my will made in Jackson County, Mo., on the 26th day of February 1852 and reattested by Theodrick Snuffer and John Bedell as witnesses at my request on the 28th day of October 1854, ratifying said will in every particular not altered in this codicil No. 1, and revoking all other wills and codicils heretofore made by me, save and except the will above described and this codicil No. 1 to said will. It is my will and desire that the slaves Catherine and Simpson, mentioned in my will, shall, after my death, be known by the names of Catherine Younger and Simpson Younger, and in addition to their freedom absolutely at my death it is my will and desire that my Executor hereinafter named, shall, as soon as convenient after my death, take said Catherine and Simpson to a free state and place them in a respectable school where they shall be well clothed and cared for in every respect and their morals particularly guarded until they arrive at the age of twelve years each, and when they respectively arrive at the age of twelve years each it is my will and desire that my executor hereinafter named shall place each of said children, Catherine and Simpson, at an academy or college of a high grade where each may receive a thorough classical education, and each be kept at said accademy or college or some other institution of similar character until each of them shall have graduated according to the rules of such institution or institutions of learning, and if necessary, to be kept at school until they are each twenty-one years of age, all the expences of educating said Catherine and Simpson, including board, tution and incidental expences and cost of traveling, to be paid out of my estate. It is my will and desire and I hereby give and bequeath to the above named Catherine and Simpson the sum of three thousand dollars to be paid to them in equal parts when they shall respectively arrive at the ages of twenty-one years, and in case either of them shall die before he or she shall arrive at the age of twenty-one years, then, in that event the whole of the said three thousand dollars to be paid to the survivor, and in case both the said Simpson and Catherine should die before either arrive at the age of twenty-one years, then said sum of three thousand dollars to be considered part of my Estate and to be included and disposed of according to Item 7th of my will above described and I hereby direct my executor to pay it over accordingly and said persons mentioned in Item 7th of the aforesaid will are hereby confirmed as residuary legatees. In order that there may be no mistake as to the identity of said Catherine and Simpson for whom I have made and wish to make by this codicil, the most liberal provisions, I here state that Catherine is about 8 years of age and Simpson about 6 years of age, both of bright mulatto colour, both the children of my mulatto woman Elizabeth, and that said Catherine and Simpson and their mother are now living with me in St. Clair County, Mo., and it is my wish and desire that the provisions of my above described will as well as this codicil be liberally construed to promote the Freedom, Happiness, Education and Respectability of said Catherine and Simpson. It is my wish and desire that my son Coleman Younger have and I hereby give and bequeath to him one half of the farm in Jackson County, MO., upon which I formerly resided for a few days but upon this express condition, that he pay to my executor twenty-five dollars per acre for the other half of said farm or pays to me during my life the said sum of twenty-five dollars per acre for one half of said farm, in either event I give and bequeath to said Coleman Younger the other half. The land included in this bequest to Coleman Younger is the Hamilton tract of land and all the Ross Wilkerson tract of land both lying east of the state road running from Independence south, except a little of the Hamilton tract and lying east of the Moultry tract of land and said tracts of land above mentioned bequeathed on the above condition contain between three and four hundred acres. I hereby revoke the bequest made in Item 5th of the above mentioned will which shall hereafter be set aside, revoked and held for nought, and the said land is hereby included in the bequest made in Item 7th of my above described will and I hereby give and bequeath to said persons mentioned in Item 7th the land mentioned in Item 5th and who are confirmed as my residuary legatees. I hereby confirm unto all the slaves mentioned in my above described will, their absolute freedom at my death. I hereby give and bequeath to Fanny and Elizabeth, who are made free by my will, and whose freedom is confirmed to them by this codicil No. 1 the tract of land I own in St. Clair County, Mo., which I purchased of Comstock, containing 40 acres, and also the tract of land upon which I now reside known as the Gilliam Farm, it is hereby given and bequeathed to them jointly, and their heirs and assigns forever. I hereby constitute and appoint Waldo P. Johnson Executor of my Will above mentioned as well as of the codicil No. 1 and enjoined on him the duty of strictly carrying out all the provisions of said will and codicil.

In Testimony Whereof I have hereunto set my hand and seal this 11th day of November, 1854.

CHARLES YOUNGER (SEAL)
At the request and in the presence of Charles Younger we have hereunto set our hands as witnesses to this codicil No. 1 and to his signature.

L. LEWIS

S. A. BRUCE

SAM'L. P. HEDGES

Filed November 15th 1854

JAMES W. BECK, Clerk.
State of Missouri)
County of St Clair) SS (for State Seal) I James W. Beck Clerk of the County Court of St. Clair County Missouri Do hereby Certify that the foregoing Eight Pages contains a full and true Copy of the Last Will and testament and Codicil No. 1 thereto of Charles Younger, Deceased which hath in due form of law been Exhibited proved and recorded in the office of the Clerk of the county Court of St. Clair County Missouri by the order of the County Court of said County all of which Manifestly appears of record in my office.

In Testimony whereof I hereunto subscribe my name and affix the Seal of Said Court at office in Oseola this 11th day of January AD 1855.

(SEAL)

James W. Beck Clerk.

Recorded in Book "E" Page 106

WILL OF SARAH S. YOUNGER OF THE STATE OF MISSOURI AND COUNTY OF CLAY

Liberty Courthouse 5 Nov. 1858. Will Book D. page 240-244, Probated 11 Jan. 1859

I Sarah S. Younger do make this my last Will & Testament as regards the wordly goods with which God has been pleased to intrust me with, I wish to make the following disposition of viz.:

(1) I leave after my funeral expenses were paid, I will

(2) At my death a young negro woman named Lydda to my daughter, Virginia Creek, & also 3 cows & one calf, to be hers absolutely.

(3) I wish my negro man named George to be set free at my death, by paying four hundred dollars ($400.00) at my death, & I will that the four hundred dollars ($400.00) coming from said negro George be divided equally between my two daughters, to woll [(?)] Lucy S. Buster & Virginia Creek, & also my household and kitchen furniture to be divided equally between my two above mentioned daughters. At my death, I will that my daughter, Virginia L. Creek, at my death be intitled to my mare. I appoint my soninlaw, Jacob Creek, will executor. I also will my son, Henry W. Younger, at my death one dollar ($1.00)

This fifth day of Nov. A. D. 1858 (Nov. 5, 1858)

Given under my name & seal,

SARAH S. YOUNGER, [(her mark X)]
Attest: Jno. Walker, (word illegible)

SOURCE: Copies of both wills are from Mid-Continent Public Library, North Independence Branch, Independence, MO.

COPY OF A LETTER WRITTEN BY COLE YOUNGER IN PRISON

Stillwater, Minn. Jan. 28, 1894

St. Paul, Minn.

Hon. W. R. Marshall

My dear Governor:

I received a letter not long since from The Hon. S. C. Ragan informing me of the death of an uncle Steve Younger, a halfbrother of my Grandfather. He also sent me a paper containing a short scetch of Uncle's life. As the paper was a daily, the usher cut out the piece and sent it in so I will inclose the same to you thinking you would like to read it as your line in some respects are the same.

Natives of Ky. emigrated North and Republicans from the start. Though he told me the last time I ever saw him there was never a time he would have accepted (of) an office of any kin. My grandfather was the same, except he was Capt. of a Volunteer Company to fight the Indians in an early day in Missouri. I think, in fact, I know the writer is in error as to the birth of my Great Grandfather, he puts it 1775 while my grandfather Charles Younger was born 1783-4 and he was the third and youngest child by my great grandfather's first wife who was a Miss Lee of Va. where my grandfather was born and was a baby when his father and mother moved to Ky. where she died. My Great Grandfather married Uncle Steven's mother, a lady of German decent.

The eldest of the first three children was Peter Younger who married in 1802, was with (Gen. Andrew) Jackson at the Battle of New Orleans. So was my mother's father, Judge Richard Fristoe of Nashville, Tenn. afterward of Jackson City, Mo. In fact, he organized and named the County and was the first Representitive of that County in the State Legislature. I speak of that here because my grandmother so often spoke of my grandfather and Uncle Pete Younger being at the great Battle of New Orleans and I go into the details of Uncle Peter to show he could not have been born later than 1780. That would leave him but about five years younger than his father according to details in the sketch I sent you.

My own father was born in 1810, my grandfather had the family tree, it got burned with the house, going back over 200 years when the first of the family from Strausburg on the Rhine entered on the Eastern shore of Maryland.

When the Hon. W. W. Erwin was over here I had a talk with him. He wore a button of the Sons of the Revolution I told him Jim and I were entitled to the same. He asked me to write him and offered to get it, said it would help us but I have so many friends that I cannot write to one tenth of them. I have not written him, but if it is convenient sometimes, will you please let him see the article concerning Steven's death, it will say more than merely talking for buncum.

Cole Younger

Jim and I both had LaGrippe but we are well at present only I have rheumatism in my right shoulder and arm that hurts me while I write.

With our best wishes from your true and grateful friend,

Cole Younger.

SOURCE: KENTUCKY ANCESTOR V 17-1, 1981.

Left to right: Bob, Henrietta, Jim, and Cole Younger. Photo taken at Stillwater Prison, 1889. Bob died in prison of consumption the same year this photo was taken. Cole and Jim were paroled in July 1901. Jim killed himself in Oct. 1902 and two years later Cole received a full pardon. Author's collection. The April 1989 issue of WILD WEST magazine identified this photo as James and Adeline Dalton and two of their progeny.

2519 Etna St.,
Berkeley 4,
California.

Missouri Historical Society,
Jefferson Memorial,
St. Louis, Mo.

Dear Mrs. Gieseker:

Thank you for your letter of May 18 regarding the Younger family. I question whether the local libraries would have the books you suggested but would like to buy a couple anyway if they are still in print. I thought the two books, Bronaugh, Warren Carter -"The Youngers' Fight for Freedom", and Younger, Cole, "The Story of Cole Younger, by Himself" seemed the most pertinent. Do you happen to have the name of the publishing house and date of publication or do you know of any copies that are for sale? If neither of these are obtainable I would try to get one or two of the others listed, if you could give me this additional information.

My great grandfather, Coleman Younger, was not the famous bandit but I believe was his uncle and namesake. He was known as Colonel Younger and came to San Jose, California from Missouri in the fifties.

All of my paternal ancestors seem to have lived in Kentucky and moved westward to Missouri and thence to California in the days of the gold rush. My grandmother's parents, William White Waddell and Elizabeth Bailey Hudson were both born in Ky., but married in Lexington, Mo where their children were born. My great grandmother is presumably buried in Lexington, i.e. Elizabeth Bailey Hudson Waddell. My grandmother, Jeannie Hudson Waddell came to California after she had finished her schooling and met and married Charles Bruce Younger in Santa Cruz, Calif.

Dr. Malloy is the historian for the Army Supply Depot at Ogden, Utah. We hear from him frequently and I shall write him to tell him of your letter.

I appreciate your courtesy in replying to my request.

Very truly yours,

Jane Younger McKenzie.
(Mrs. Gordon McKenzie)

The Rabourns

WILLIAM RABOURN SR.

William Rabourn Sr. b. ca. 1725 m. ca. 1754, wife unknown, d. ca. 1795, still living in 1792 when he made a deed of gift to his son Henry in KY. William reportedly came from the "settlements" of VA to KY with Daniel Boone ca. 1782.

Children:

1. Robert b. ca 1756 m. 1st Sarah Mc Guire 2 March 1778 m. 2nd Milly Savage 17 Sept. 1799 d. ca. 1831 Montgomery Co., KY.

2. William b. ca. 1758 m. Amelia Skaggs 1780 d. ca. 1834 Fair Co., OH.

3. Ralph "Rafe" b. ca. 1760 m. Nancy Ann White ca. 1783 d. 25 Nov. 1832 Ripley Co., IN.

4. George b. ca. 1761 m. ca. 1782 wife unknown, d. ca. 1828 Pulaski Co., KY.

5. HENRY b. ca. 1763 m. ca. 1784 wife unknown, d. ca. 1838 Montgomery Co. KY., Records follow.

6. David b. ca 1765 m. ca. 1790 Stacy Fitzgerald Hambrick (previously married to William Hambrick) d. ca. 1817 Fleming Co., KY.

7. John b. ca. 1772 m. Jane McDowell 1796.

At least two other children, both sons.

Note: William, son of Rafe Rabourn m. Mary (Polly) Younger 17 Jan. 1811 Montgomery Co., KY.

Note: William Rabourn Sr. is believed to be the son of Richard Rabourne who d. 1732 Henrico Co., VA leaving six sons: John, Charles, Richard, Thomas, George, and William.

HENRY RABOURN

Henry Rabourn served under Benjamin Logan on an expedition against the Shawnee Indians up the Big Miami. An old account book in the Kentucky State Historical Society archives reflects that Henry was paid $4.41 for this service on 6 Nov. 1800. One expedition headed by Benjamin Logan up the Big Miami occurred in 1782 and a similar one in 1786. It is not clear which one Henry took part in. Henry married ca. 1784 but the name of his wife is unknown.

Children:

1. Margaret b. ca. 1786 never married d. after 1860.

2. William b. 30 Jan. 1789 m. Esther Phillips d. 1858.

3. James b. ca. 1789 m. Margaret Anderson after 1820.

4. David b. ca. 1793 m. Suca Henson (?) 28 Mar. 1811 d. ca. 1825.

5. NANCY b. ca. 1793 m. Benjamin Dalton d. after 1879. Records on this family are found with the Dalton family.

6. Henry b. ca. 1795 m. Lucy Garrett 20 Dec. 1820 d. 1 Sept. 1878.

children 7 & 8 names unknown

9. Hiram b. ca. 1801 m. Mary Daniel d. 1838.

10. Matilda b. 6 April 1802 m. James Lewis Dalton d. 10 Feb. 1879.
Records for this family are found with the Dalton family.

11. John Westley b. 24 April 1805 m. Nancy Moore 2 Aug. 1829 d. 15 Jan. 1849.

12. Sally (Sarah) b. ca. 1809 m. Samuel Moore 11 Oct. 1853, Jackson Co., MO d. 16 Feb. 1862.

SOURCES: Manuscript "The Early Raburns of Montgomery County, KY and clippings from the MT. STERLING ADVOCATE, Mt. Sterling, KY

WILL OF HENRY RABOURN

The last will and testament of Henry Rabourn of Montgomery County, and State of Kentucky who being of sound mind and of disposing memory make ordain and appoint this as my last will and testament after paying my just debts. My Will is that the balance of my estate real and personal be disposed of in the following manner towit:

First, I give to my son John Westley Rabourn the following boundary of land towit: Beginning at a beech corner in the hollow, corner to James McKee and Nicholas Madden and to run west so as to include all the water to his westly side of the stream and the orchard until it intersects the line at Jas. Kitchens fence and thence with the line between said Kitchens and myself until it shall strike the line of James McKee to a Linn corner and with him line to be beginning the same more or less for him and his heirs forever, that is on the following condition that Westley is to build a comfortable house for my two daughters Margaret and Sally Rabourn to live in near his own dwelling and to see that they are kept free from want during their lives or remaining single.

2nd. I give my two daughters as aforesaid a feather bed each now, by their choice, with a sufficient quantity of clothing to be judged by my executors and all their wearing apparel my cupboard and furniture my bureau, my fire irons and the teakettle and pot tramel and as much of the pot vessels as they think proper, to take my cherry table, and a set of windsor chairs, a cow a peace known by the name of Rose and the heifer and my largest Gray mare and also the dressing glass and my Rockhill plow, and one chain pair of gears.

3rd. I also give my son John Westley Rabourn my duke filly & her colt.

4th. I give to my grandson Henry Milton Dalton a Bed and furniture known by the name of Jimmy's bed.

5th. and when the above items are taken, my will is that all the balance of my estate of all and every kind be sold on a credit of 12 months to the highest bidder, and the proceeds divided between my children towit: Nancy Dalton is to have one hundred dollars and the balance after that to be equally divided between the following named children towit: William, James, Henry and Hiram Rabourn & Matilda Dalton. GIVEN under my hand this 25th of April, 1838; signed in the presence, having thought after disposing of my effects that my two daughters Margaret and Sally are not sufficiently provided for I think proper to annex this as an addition to my will that, I give to them during their life the spot of ground by my orchard containing about six or seven acres of land more or less for them to use as they may think proper during their life and at their death to Westley or his heirs, and my will is that Andrew Wills and Wm. Barrow be my Executors. In Testimony Whereof I have unto set my hand and fixed my seal this day and date first above written.

his
HENRY X RABOURN (SEAL)
mark

Attest:
WILLIAM BALDWIN
JAMES MCKEE

Source: DALTON DATA Vol. I published by Mary Ann Van Zant Bell. Spokane, WA 1985.

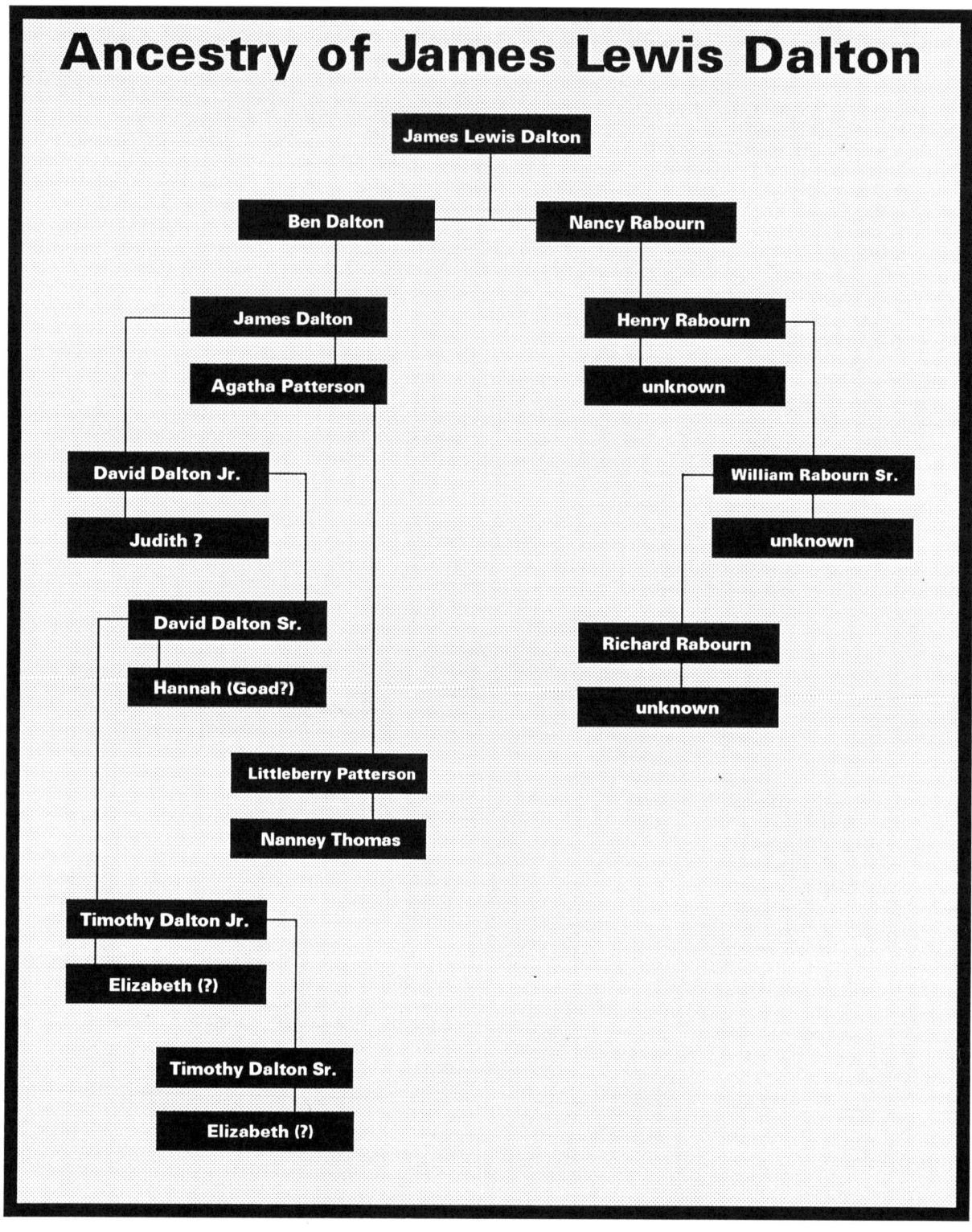

III. THE DALTON GANG FAMILY

LEWIS AND ADELINE DALTON

James Lewis Dalton was born 16 Feb. 1826 in Montgomery Co., KY according to his pension record for the Mexican War. He supposedly attended McGee college (no record of this school has been found in KY and it may have been in a neighboring state) before he enlisted in McKerson Turpin's Co. of the 2nd Regiment of the Kentucky Infantry on 9 June 1846. He was a musician (fifer) and served for a year in Mexico. He was discharged in New Orleans 9 June 1847. He married Adeline Lee Younger 12 March 1851 in Jackson Co., MO.

Lewis did not stay in one place for very long. He repeatedly moved his family and in later years he followed his horses from race track to race track and was rarely home. In 1860 the family lived for a short time near Denver, CO., then they went to the Lawrence, KS area where Grat was born. They lived in both Cass and Bates Counties, MO and probably in Clay Co., MO for a time also. Later they lived near Coffeyville, KS, and in the Indian Territory near what is now Vinita, OK. In 1890 the Dalton's were in the process of moving back to OK from KS when Lewis died near Dearing, KS. Adeline went on to OK and lived in or near Kingfisher, OK for the remainder of her life.

Lewis was six feet one inch tall, weighed about 220 pounds, and had a clear, rosy complexion. He was described as jovial and easy going and the more lenient of the parents. He ran a saloon before he married but gave this up, probably to please his wife. Many of the books and movies about the Daltons protray Lewis as a heavy drinker or even a drunk. His sons insisted this was not true; they described their father as a teetaler or a very temperate drinker. Littleton said he only saw his father take three drinks of whiskey in his life, all three to treat a cold. He did not use tobacco either and his sons never heard him swear. Littleton said gambling was his father's one fault and that was plenty.

Lewis was a farmer, horse breeder and trader, and was probably an expert saddler and a skilled carpenter as well. He had musical talent and may have been a fiddler and barker with a circus at one time. Missouri neighbors reported that he was a religious man. Every morning after chores he would read his Bible and then kneel and pray.

Adeline was described as comparatively small in stature and as a heavy, strong woman. She had dark red hair and blue eyes. She was the disciplinarian of the family and was described as agressive, determined, and ambitious for her children. She was a good manager, as well she had to be with fifteen children and a husband who gambled on horses constantly. She was said to express her tenderness in deeds instead of words. She played the piano and hymns were her usual choice of music. For twenty years she did the cooking for her family in a fireplace and acquired her first cookstove in 1871. Her life had to have been mostly episodes of birth and death with long periods of hard work and worry in between. She lived to bury nine of her fifteen children and four of them died violent deaths; yet she remained a fond and caring mother and never lost her faith in the Almighty.

There are several stories that Adeline divorced Lewis before his death. This story appears to be a complete fabrication and first appeared in print in an early newspaper story about the Dalton Gang train robberies. Lewis clearly stated that Adeline was his wife in his pension application and she promptly applied for and received a widow's pension after his death. She would not have been eligible for the pension if they had divorced. Further, divorce records of both Montgomery and Labette, Co. KS have been checked and there is no record of a divorce for the Daltons in either county.

Lewis and Adeline just possibly picked the worst place in the world to try and raise a family in the 1850s and 1860s. Independence, MO was the jumping off place for "The West" and the town was full of fur traders, freighters, bull whackers, mule skinners, and settlers heading West. Independence was the beginning of the Santa Fe, Oregon, and California trails and here in Jackson County was brawling, sprawling America straining at the seams to make "Manifest Destiny" a reality.

shooting, and killing all of the time. In addition to the war there were booze and bottleggers, whiskey runners and prostitutes by the hundreds. The old Whiskey

Mexican War Pension, widow's application of Adeline Lee Dalton filed 28 Aug. 1890.

In 1850 there had been the Missouri Compromise that made an attempt to settle the slavery question, then in 1854 the Kansas-Nebraska Act was passed and in effect repealed the Compromise. Then all hell broke loose on the Kansas-Missouri border. An era of mayhem began as theft, murder, torture, and arson became almost daily occurrences along the border. This state of affairs was to continue to some extent until long after the Civil War.

Littleton said he could remember nothing but fight, fight, fight during his early years. He reported fighting,

Trail, also called the old Border Ruffian Trail ran close to the Dalton home near Belton, MO. This trail was strung with graves and Littleton reported an average of a murder a night between Kansas City and the Red River.

Emmett described the area as the dark and bloody ground where the very soil was fertilized with atrocity. Red Legs, Jay Hawkers, Quantrill's Raiders, Missouri "Border Ruffians", as well as more formally organized Union and Confederate forces fought all over this territory, and left little but chimneys standings in many areas.

During the war, the area where the Daltons lived became known as the "Burnt District" as a result of General Thomas Ewing's infamous "Order No. 11" issued on 25 Aug. 1863. This order read in part as follows: "All persons living in Jackson, Cass, and Bates counties, Missouri, and in that part of Vernon ... are hereby ordered to remove herewith. Those who, within that time, establish their loyalty to the satisfaction of the commanding officer of the military station nearest their present place of residence will receive from him certificates stating the fact of their loyalty, and the names of the witnesses by whom it can be shown. All who receive such certificates will be permitted to remove to any part of the State of Kansas, except the counties on the eastern border of the State. All others shall remove out of this district. Officers commanding companies and detachments serving in the counties named will see that this paragraph is promptly obeyed." This area was almost entirely leveled, even the crops were burned. The Dalton home remained standing throughout the war but it was shot full of holes. For a time the Daltons hid out in the bush and probably moved into Kansas again for a time during this period.

Letter of Adeline Dalton to the Pension Board in 1916 asking for an increase in her pension.

After the war came the railroad and cowboy era. The cattle followed the railheads and as the railroads were built another class of characters, far more unsavory than the cowboy, moved into the area. The Indian Territory was the American Frontier at its worst. The area was refered to as "Robbers' Roost" and "The Land of the Six Shooter". Crime was rampant and the phrase: "There is no Sunday west of St. Louis—and no God west of Fort Smith" was often heard.

It was here, amid war and the aftermath of war, on the wild frontier that the Daltons were born and raised. Is it any wonder that eventually some of them became involved in some criminal activities?

JOURNAL OF SOPHIA LEE YOUNGER BRADEN

"...Bruce [Younger] was doing so well in his business but started to take a lot of time in the company of Lewis Dalton and the horse racing. Bruce traveled with Mr. Dalton over several states and it was common for Bruce to find trouble with companions who he had not known before Mr. Dalton introduced them."
(Courtesy of Marley Brant)

(Retyped Newspaper Article)
MRS. ADALINE LEE DALTON

Adaline L. Younger was born in Jackson County, Missouri, September 15, 1835; died at Kingfisher, Oklahoma, January 24, 1925, at 7:15 p. m. age 89 years, 4 months and 9 days.

She was married to James L. Dalton March 12, 1851, at Independence, Mo. in 1890 the family started to Oklahoma in a covered wagon to make their home. Mr. Dalton died July 16, 1890, from a sudden attack of cholera morbis, about a week out on their trip and was buried at Deering, Kansas. Mrs. Dalton and the family came on to Oklahoma and located on a school quarter in Cimarron township. She made the race in the "C and A" county opening and secured a claim in Cooper Township, now owned by Thomas Saunders.

Mrs. Dalton joined the Presbyterian church at Belton, MO., when a young woman and remained true to her faith to the last.

She leaves to mourn their loss, six living children; Ben of Kingfisher, Littleton and Emmett, living in California,; Mrs. E. D. Whipple of Siloam Springs, Ark,; Simon of Okeemah, Okla., and Miss Leona of Kingfisher. Ben and Leona have always made their home with their mother. Ben, Simon, Mrs. Whipple and Leona and a grandson, Roy Clute, were present at the funeral.

Funeral services were held at the Presbyterian church Monday morning, January 26, at 10 a. m., conducted by Rev. A. M. McInnis and all that remained mortal of Mrs. Dalton was laid to rest in Kingfisher Cemetery to await the resurrection morn.

Pall bearers were C. P. Wickmiller, Josiah Gooden, J. B. Cockrill, M. E. Pennington, Geo. Foster, A. H. Schowalter.

CARD OF THANKS

We wish to thank our many friends and neighbors for their many acts of kindness and assistance during the illness and death of our mother, and to express our appreciation to those who so kindly remembered us with flowers and other tokens.
THE DALTON FAMILY
THE KINGFISHER FREE PRESS 29 Jan. 1925

(Retyped Newspaper Article)
MOTHER DALTON DEAD

**Mother of Famous Dalton Gang
Passed Away at Kingfisher Saturday
at Home of Her Daughter**

Reports reached Bartlesville Sunday of the death of Mrs. Adeline Dalton, 94, mother of the Dalton brothers, who gained nation wide notoriety in the early nineties through their raids on banks in Oklahoma and southern Kansas. Mrs. Dalton died Saturday at the home of her daugher, Miss Leona Dalton, in Kingfisher, Okla.

There were nine boys in the Dalton family. Those who became notorious as desperadoes were Bill, Bob, Grat, and Emmett. Their first big crime was the robbery of a Santa Fe train at Red Rock in 1891. Then followed a series of robberies along the Kansas-Oklahoma border. The gang was practically wiped out in a raid on two banks in Coffeyville a year or so later when Emmett was captured and Bob and Grat were said to have been killed. Bill Dalton who later joined the "Bill Doolan" gang, was killed in a raid on a farmhouse near Ardmore in 1894. Emmett is reported to be the proprietor of a motion picture business in Missouri.

Ben Dalton 70, the eldest of the brothers, was not identified with the gang and is a farmer near Kingfisher. The father died about 30 years ago.
Unidentified [BARTLESVILLE?] newspaper

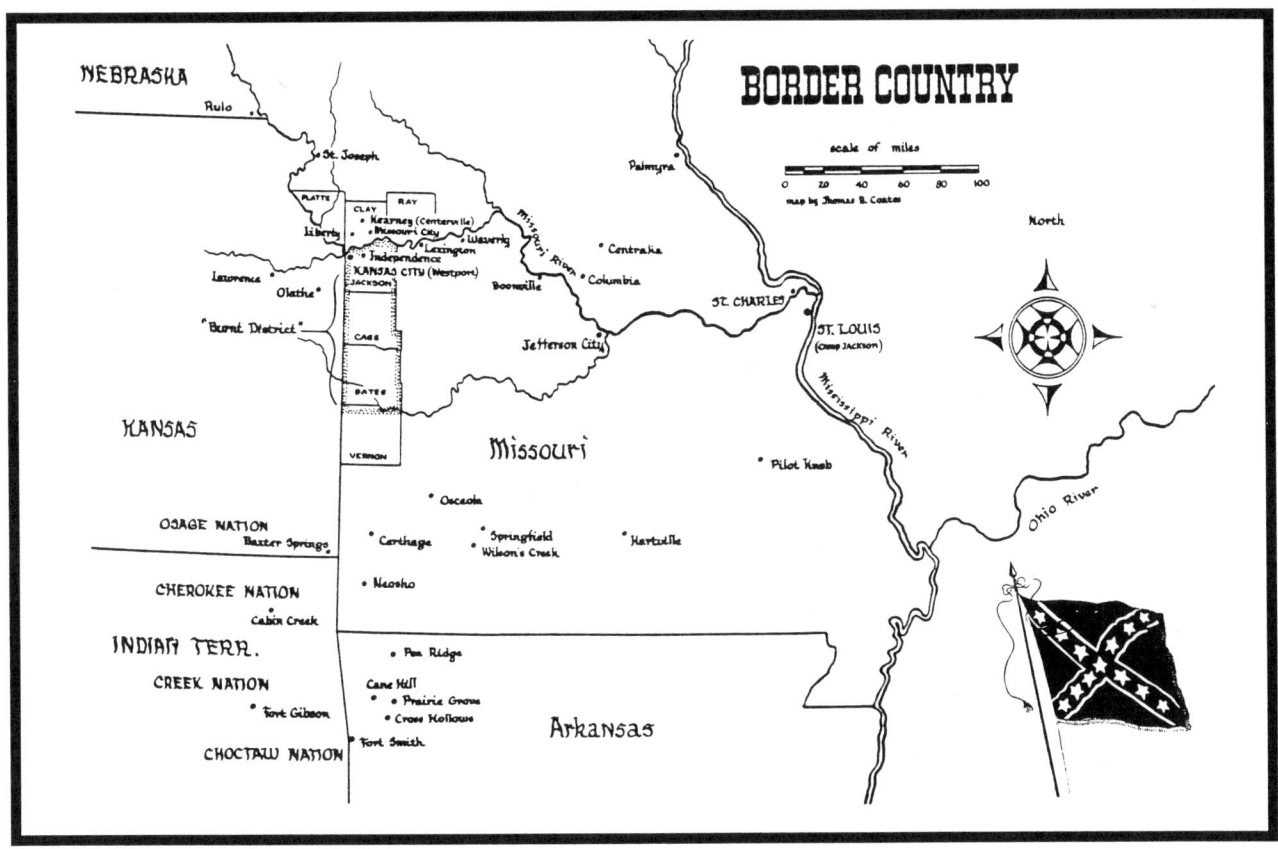

Lee Boecher from SHORTGRASS COUNTRY

"My first contact with the Daltons was in the spring of 1902, when Mrs. Dalton hired me to cut the weeds in her apple orchard, which occupied a two-or three-acre tract to the east of her house. The space between the tree rows had been cultivated both east and west and north and south. However, an area about eight or ten feet square under each tree had not been touched and was overgrown by lambsquarter, rosin weeds and some other varieties. I was given a light hoe, and a file so rusty it no longer had any "bite" with which to sharpen it, and told to cut the weeds that surrounded each tree. It had been a dry spring and the weeds were as tough as sassafras sprouts. I was only 11 and though I worked valiantly I made little progress. I had no coffee breaks, but I made frequent trips to the oaken-bucket well. Each afternoon, Leona brought a tall glass of lemonade made with the well water. There were more than a hundred trees and I calculated that if I worked all summer there would still be weeds to cut. At the end of the second day, Mrs. Dalton gave me a silver dollar and told me that she would need me no longer. I was grateful both for the dollar and the termination of my employment. A very tired boy, I walked the mile and a half home.

...The house was almost bare of furniture. The kitchen contained a small cook stove, a cabinet, a cupboard, a table, two or three chairs and a couple of wooden benches. Upstairs there were only three or four pallets on the floor, on one of which I slept the one night I stayed there. I could hear Leona's sewing machine whirring in the bedroom every time I approached the house.

The Daltons' cooking was southern frontier—biscuits or cornbread, beans, potatoes, bacon and white gravy. The Daltons, like most of the settlers, were poor, though it was rumored tht Adaline received a small pension, the result of her husband's service in the Mexican war.

Adaline kept six or eight cows, which she and Leona milked. The cattle ranged in a pasture along the bend of the creek and crossed to the opposite side at a point where the water was hardly more than three feet deep. Leona had a boat which she used in crossing the stream to retrieve them each evening. At night they were kept in a small corral. The two women churned butter for their own table and a bit to be traded at the grocers.

There were no men on the farm, except at the planting and harvesting seasons when a hired man was employed. Ben Dalton spent all his time on the Cooper creek claim. Adaline's workstock was small and ill-kept and her farm implements in a sad state of repair. Her farming operations were truly those of a widow woman. After all, she was now more that 65 years old. However, she kept a fairly good driving horse and an open buggy and could be seen passing along the highway at a fast clip, always dressed in black with a black slatted sunbonnet.

Adaline depended upon her neighbors to perform the many little "thank you" farm tasks that women usually are unable to do. Old Charlie, a German farmer, rented the Jake Admire farm that joined the school quarter on the east. Since he lived nearest, he got most of these little jobs. He never refused to help, though he always worked with his hackles up. Once when the horses broke down the corral fence and escaped, Adeline called upon him to repair the damage. It took old Charlie several hours to dig holes, set posts and rebuild the gate. All the while, quite angry, he swore in German under his breath. When he had finished, Adaline said, "Ten thousand thanks, Charlie." "Aw, hell," said the old man, "one thousand is enough."

Lee Boecher (pronounced Baker), "The Daltons I Knew", SHORTGRASS COUNTRY

Both photos this page - the old Dalton home near Belton, MO. The house survived the Civil War but was shot full of holes. Identity of the people in the photos is unknown. From the Latta collection. Courtesy of Christopher D. Brewer.

CHARLES BENJAMIN "BEN" DALTON

Ben was probably named for both of his grandfathers. Records do not agree as to the date of his birth. His death certificate gives his birth date as Feb. 1853 but the 1870 census taken on 26 Aug. of that year gives his age as 18 which would mean he was born in 1852. At about age 16 Ben went to McGee College, the same school his father attended. Ben traveled with his father from time to time and by the fall of 1879 Ben was living and working in California. The Dalton boys were mostly engaged in heavy farm work in California. They often worked as mule skinners (drove large strings of mules to plow ground, pull harvesters, etc.) Ben remained in California until after Grat was jailed for the Alila train robbery; he then returned to Kingfisher to raise money for Grat's trial. He stayed on in Oklahoma and farmed for many years. He had a farm on Cooper Creek near Kingfisher and worked and lived there for a number of years. In 1919 Adeline bought a small house in Kingfisher and Ben moved in with

Both photos this page - Dalton Cabin at the Chisholm Trail Museum, Kingfisher, OK. Photos by Nancy B. Samuelson

her. In 1931 Ben was committed to the state hospital at Fort Supply because he was senile (Alzheimers?). Ben died in the state hospital on 16 March 1936 and according to the hospital records he was buried in the hospital cemetery, grave #590. Other records indicate that he is buried in the family cemetery plot in Kingfisher. Ben was generally described as well built with dark hair and dark eyes. Lee Boecher described Ben as a slow fellow and said that in 1909 Ben had the appearance of being older than his mother.

(Retyped Newspaper Article)
OLDEST OF DALTON BROTHERS DIES AT 83

Charles Ben Dalton, 83, brother of Miss Leona Dalton of Kingfisher, died in the State hospital for the insane at Supply, Okla., Monday following a stroke of paralysis. Dalton, who was committed to the institution from Kingfisher county in 1931, had been in poor health the last few months.

The deceased man was not associated with the Dalton Brothers gang of bank robbers which virtually was wiped out in a raid on two Coffeyville, Kansas, banks in 1892. Two of the brothers, Grat and Bob, were slain along with two other members of the gang and a third brother, Emmett, who lives now in Los Angeles, was critically wounded. Mrs. E. D. Whipple, Siloam Springs, Ark., is a sister.

Burial is reported to have been made near Supply.
THE KINGFISHER TIMES 19 March 1936

Death certificate of Ben Dalton

Charles Benjamin Dalton, oldest child of James Lewis and Adeline Dalton. Courtesy Wells Fargo

HENRY COLEMAN "COLE" DALTON

Littleton said this brother was named for brothers of both his mother and father. Records do not agree on his birth date and age but he was probably 67 when he died as that age is in agreement with the Aug. 1870 census record. Cole lived and worked in California for a number of years. He moved to New Mexico about ten years before his death because of his health problems. He also reportedly attended McGee college but Littleton said he only got a whiskey and poker education. Littleton claimed he took Cole back to Kingfisher from California in 1908 and that Cole was suffering from stomach ulcers and was drinking heavily at the time. There is no indication that Littleton was back in Oklahoma at this time in other records, so this story should be questioned. Cole did return to Oklahoma in 1908 and was on the 1810 census record in Union County, New Mexico.

(Retyped Newspaper Article)
THE DALTON OUTLAWS

COLE DALTON, A BROTHER OF THE
NOTORIOUS BANDITS, TALKS

Round Pond, OK., April 25—Cole Dalton, brother of the notorious Bill and Emmett and Bob and Grat Dalton, deceased was in the city yesterday. To a reporter he said that many of the newspaper reports concerning himself and others were totally false and misleading. He positively asserts that none of the Dalton gang were concerned in the attempted train robbery which took place one mile south of this city on April 9, in which one of the gang was killed. He said: "Their method shows that they were new at the business, or they would never have allowed a man to get out of the express car."

"What was your opinion of the report that Bill Dalton and Bill Doolin were killed near

Stillwater?" was asked.

"I knew it was false." he replied. "Bill is not in the United States. If he was to get killed I would know it before twenty-four hours. I would hear of it immediately."

Cole Dalton is an excellent specimen of manhood, about five feet ten inches high and is about 35 years old. He says that he has never been concerned in any robbery, and has no desire to live other than as a peaceful and law abiiding citizen. He said that it was generally believed that desperadoes were intellectual men and asserts that this is a mistake, as he has been associated with that class for twenty years in Arizona, California and Mexico. "While they often are men of nerve and courage," he asserted, "they are mentally deficient. Courage and nerve are born with a man and are not acquired by cultivation."

GUTHRIE DAILY LEADER [Guthrie, OK] 26 Apr. 1894

(Retyped Newspaper Article)

Cole Dalton comes into Enid frequently. He neither drinks nor swears and has very little use for his brothers.

STATE HERALD [Ardmore, OK] 31 May 1894

(Retyped Newspaper Article)

COLE DALTON IS COMING HOME TO DIE

Kingfisher, Okla., Aug 28. Cole Dalton, brother of the famous Dalton band of outlaws who terrorized Oklahoma 15 years ago, is on his way to this place where he will visit his mother, who resides on a farm four miles northeast of here.

Cole is one of the older boys, and has been a successful ranchman in San Luis, Obispo county, California, for a number of years. He is now dying with consumption, and a telegram received here yesterday by Mrs. Dalton stated that it was hardly probable that he

WESTERN STATE HOSPITAL

FORT SUPPLY, OKLAHOMA 73841

TELEPHONE 405-766-2311

March 11, 1987

Mr. Bill Phillips
402 West Seminole
Wynnewood, Oklahoma 73098

Re: Charles Ben Dalton
Hosp. Reg. #4153

Dear Mr. Phillips:

Our records contain almost the same information that you sent concerning Mr. Dalton. He was admitted here on 23, September, 1931, from Kingfisher County Oklahoma. According to court papers dated 22, Sept., 1931, he was the son of John Lewis Dalton (b. Mt. Sterling, KY) and Adeline Lee Younger (b. Lee Summit, MO). He was of the protestant faith, a farmer, and had 1 yr. college education.

Quoting from the Clinical Record dated 31, Oct., 1931, he was the oldest of his parent's children, was born 24, February, 1858, in Cass County MO. He lived there until he was 28, then for a few years he was unsettled and moved back and forth between Missouri and California. About 35 years ago he came to Kingfisher County Oklahoma and has lived on a farm about four miles from the town of Kingfisher since. He and his brothers and sisters own the farm and some property in the town of Kingfisher. He went to school about three years, can read and write, and has been a member of lodges but no longer attends.

The only correspondent listed was his sister, Leona Dalton of Kingfisher.

Mr. Dalton died here at 6:05 p.m., on 16, March, 1936, and was buried here in our hospital cemetery grave #590 on 18, March, 1936. He was 86 years and 22 days old.

Since we do not send copies of information to family members I hope this information will be of help to you.

Sincerely,

Rita M. Boyle

(Mrs.) Rita M. Boyle
Medical Record Department

This Agency conforms to provisions of Title VI of the Civil Rights Act of 1964.
HOSPITAL VISITING HOURS 1:00 P.M. to 4:00 P.M. Saturday, Sunday & Wednesday
In writing concerning patients, address letters to Superintendent. Give full name of patient. Telephone calls regarding patients should be placed person to person to the patients personal physician.

Letter from Western State Hospital, OK concerning Ben Dalton.

could live till he reached Kingfisher.

Emmett Dalton, one of the members of the famous Coffeyville raid, lives in Tulsa; Ben, the older brother, is in Kansas; Simon, the younger, lives with his mother here; Lytton is in California; one daughter lives here; one in El Reno, one in Chicago. Frank was killed near Ft. Smith while serving as a deputy United States marshal; Bob and Grat were killed in Coffeyville, and Bill was killed near Ardmore, by Bud Ledbetter.
OKLAHOMA CITY TIMES, 28 Aug. 1908

(Retyped Newspaper Article)
COLE DALTON DEAD

Cole Dalton, son of Mrs. A. Dalton of this city, died Saturday, in Des Moines, New Mexico, where he had gone a few weeks ago for his health. The remains will be shipped here for burial. Funeral Announcements will be made later.

(Retyped Newspaper Article)
OBITUARY OF COLEMAN DALTON

Henry Coleman Dalton was born in the state of Missouri, November 26th, 1853 and died in Des Moines, New Mexico last Friday, February 27, 1920, aged 66 years, 3 months and 1 day.

Mr. Dalton went from Missouri to Colorado and later to California and then came to Kingfisher County, Oklahoma, where he resided until about ten years ago, when he went to New Mexico for his health. He visited his mother and sister here this winter, returning to his home three weeks ago. He was taken ill with influenza and lived only a few days. He was at one time a member of the Presbyterian Church of this city.

The deceased is survived by an aged mother, two sisters, Miss Leona Dalton of this city and Mrs. Whipple of Purcell, Okla., and four brothers, C. B. of this city, Littleton and Emmet of California and Simon of Blackwell.

Funeral services were held this morning at the Bracken Undertaking Parlors, conducted by Rev. Job Ingram, assisted by Rev. R. B. Norton, pastor of the Presbyterian Church. Music was furnished by a quartette, consisting of Mr. and Mrs. R. A. Frakes and Mr. and Mrs. Russell Dunlap. Interment was made in Kingfisher cemetery.
KINGFISHER FREE PRESS. The obituary from the 2 March 1920 issue; the other undated but likely a few days earlier.

This is a typical California harvest crew. The Daltons worked on many such crews. This photo was taken ca. 1900 on the Merced River, Merced Co., CA. Bill Dalton's son "Chub" is a member of this crew. Chub is the sack server, the man in the center of the rig holding the grain sack. Courtesy of the California State Library.

(Retyped Newspaper Article)
COLE DALTON DEAD

Cole Dalton, a highly respected citizen, who lived in Trabasellia Park section, died at the "El Capulin" hotel in Des Moines on Saturday last at 2 a. m., the cause of death being tuberculosis.

Dalton came to this section about ten years ago hunting for a climate to recover from tuberculosis which he had contracted. After staying around Des Moines a short time he lived with George Thomas and later filed on some land. He prospered and we understand leaves quite a lot of property.

He is a brother of Emmett Dalton, the only surviving member of the Dalton gang, famous in the annuals of Coffeyville, Kansas. Cole was teaching school in California at the time his brothers pulled off the spetacular bank raid at Coffeyville.

He was a quiet, unassuming man who made many friends. He might be counted one of the old settlers of this section. [two words illegible] He was aged about 65 years at the time of his death.
UNIDENTIFIED NEWSPAPER CLIPPING
Des Moines, NM 5 Mar. 1920

Note: There is no record elsewhere of Cole Dalton teaching school. Probate records show that his estate consisted of only six horses valued at $400.00.

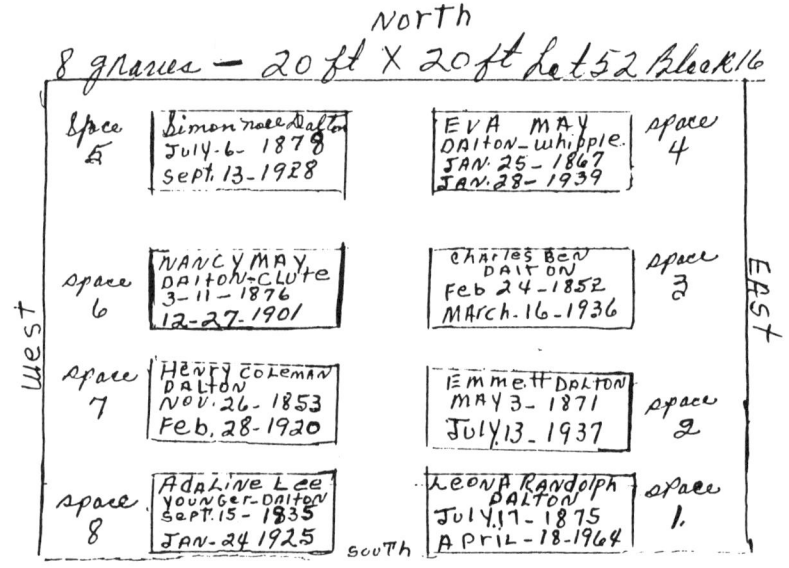

Records supplied by Sanders Funeral Home of Kingfisher, OK. Note this does not agree with hospital records concerning Ben's burial place.

LOUIS KOSSUTH DALTON

Louis was probably born in 1855 and died around 1862. No records have been found for him but Littleton said he died at about age six or seven when Littleton himself was about four. He was named for a famous Hungarian patriot who was popular in this country at the time. (Lajos Kossuth was a Hungarian patriot who fought, unsuccessfully, for Hungary's independence from Austria.) "Louis" may have been from the surname Louis of the man who married Lewis Dalton's sister Tillie or it is possibly that his name should be spelled Lewis.

BEA ELIZABETH "LELIA" DALTON

There have been few records found for Bea Elizabeth. Emmett names her as sister "Lelia" in one of his books. Her descendants have had a "delayed filing" death certificate created from Family Bible records. According to her Phillips family she was born 14 March 1856 and died 28 Dec 1894. She first married a man named Harrison and had a little girl during this marriage. The child was killed in a grassfire when she was very young. The child's braid was kept with the Phillips Family Bible for many years. Her first husband died or they divorced and she married a second time. She was reportedly working in a hotel in Brownsville, Texas when she met and married Tom Phillips, a Texas Ranger. The family later settled near Tussey, Oklahoma. Tom Phillips died in May 1930. There were five children born to this couple: John William b. 1882, d. 1963, Alford Lee b. 1884, d. 1931, Robert Louis b. 1888, d. 1953, and twins Jack Jesse b. 1891, d. 1974 and Pearl Katie b. 1891, d. 1920. Several grandchildren and great-grandchildren still live in Oklahoma.

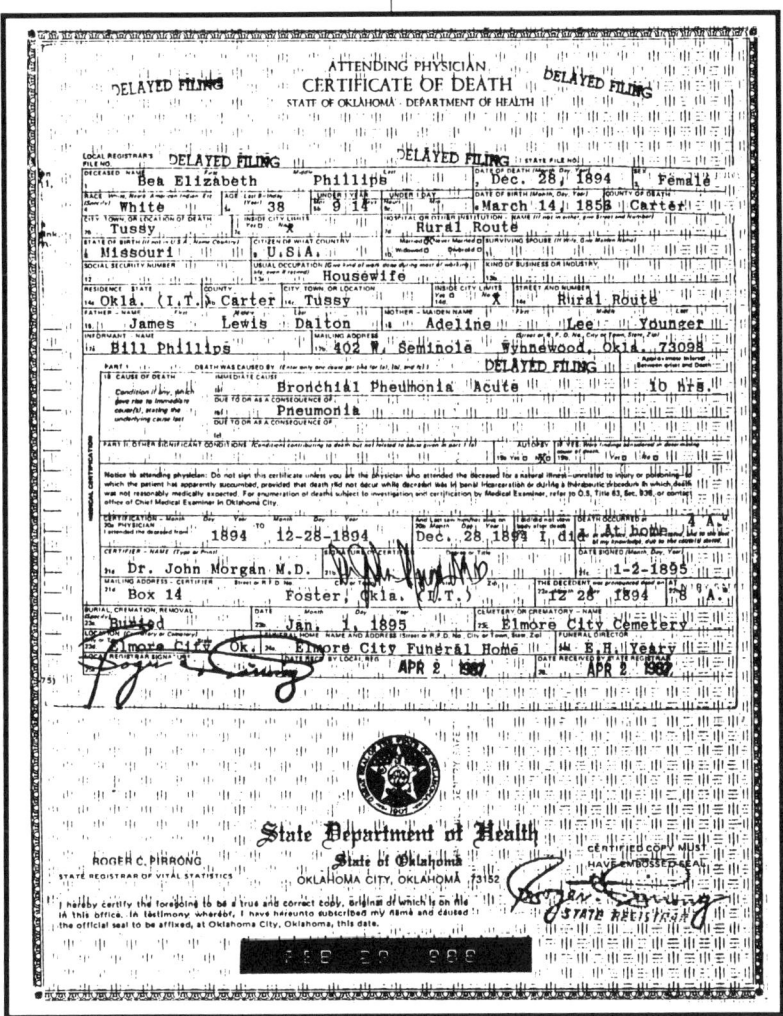

Death certificate of Bea Elizabeth Dalton Phillips

Death certificate of Jack J. Phillips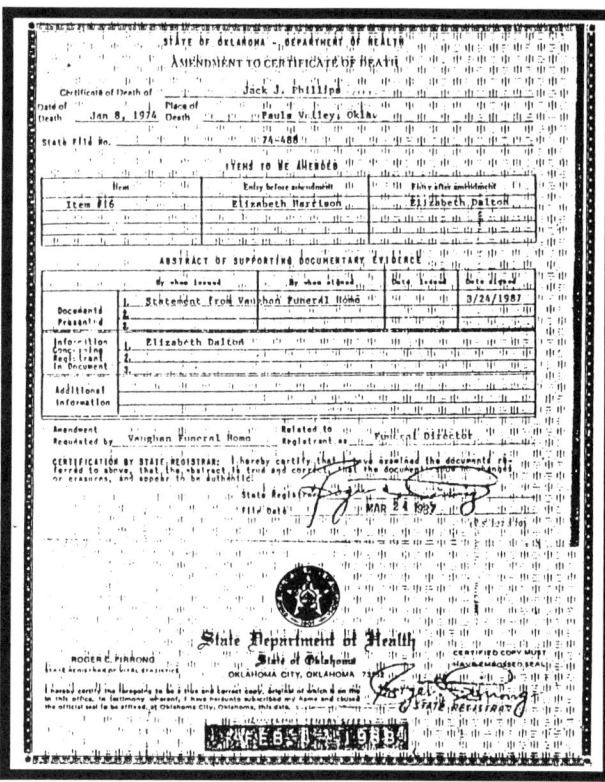

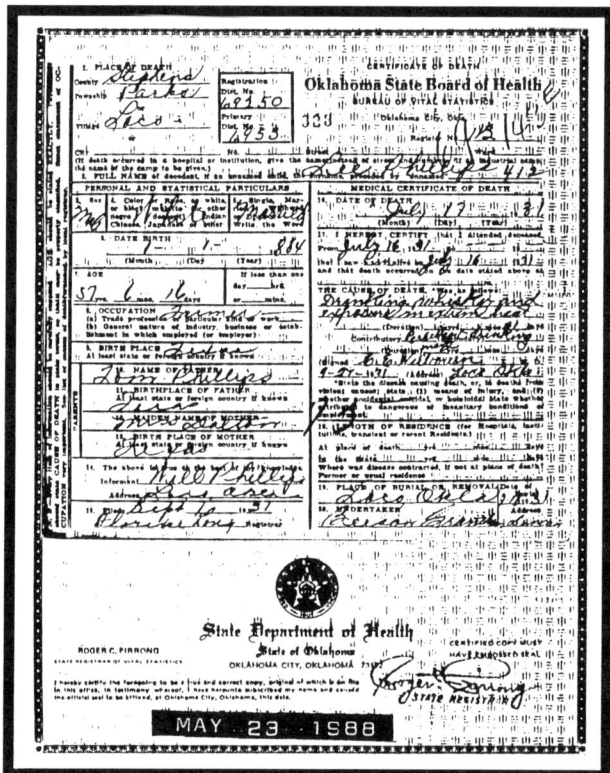
Death certificate of Alford Lee Phillips

The Dalton Gang Family

Three photos this page are George Phillips' Bible records. Courtesy of Bill Phillips.

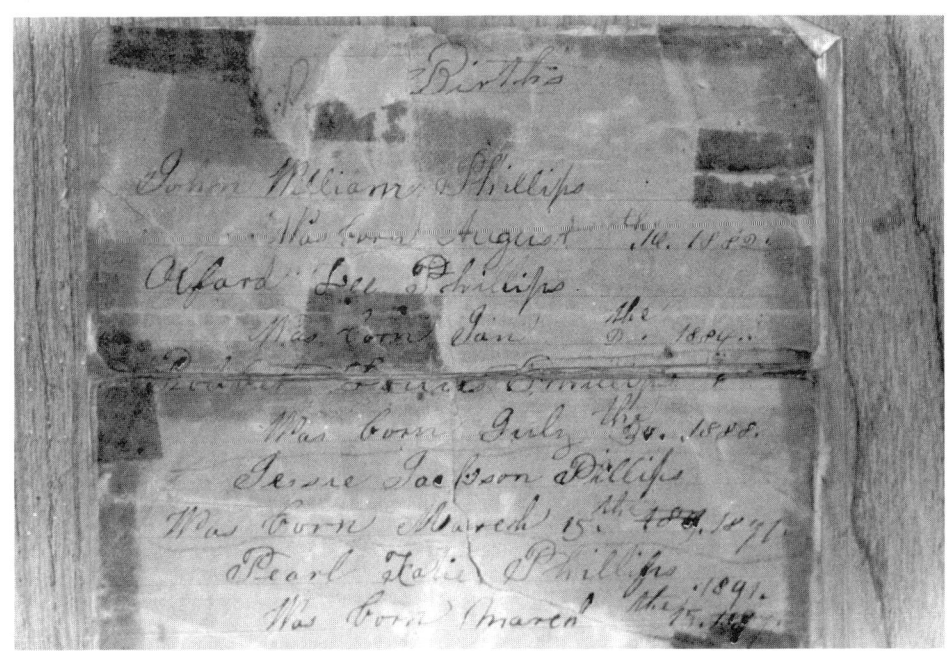

State of Texas.

Crosby Co Feby 28th 1881

I Hereby Certify, That _T. Phillips_ a _3d sergeant_ of Captain _Arrington's_ Company (_"C"_), of the Frontier Battalion, was mustered into the State Service on the _1st_ day of _September_ 1880 and is this day honorably discharged.*

The said _T. Phillips_ has pay due him from _1st December_ to the present date.

There is due said _T. Phillips_ the sum of _One Hundred Twenty_ dollars. He is indebted to the State of Texas, _____ dollars, on account of _____

Approved, $ _120.00_

G. W. Arrington.
Capt Commanding Company

Adjutant-General.

Received, of _____, this _____ day of _____ 188__, dollars in full of the above account.

Signed in duplicate.

*Note.—When this Certificate is given without discharge, the line, "and is this day honorably discharged," will be stricken out.

One of the records for Tom Phillips' service as a Texas Ranger. Courtesy of Texas State Library

The Dalton Gang Family

Jack Phillips, son of Lelia Dalton & Tom Phillips, and his wife Annie. Also pictured here are three of their children.

William Dalton "Bill" Phillips

Dorothy Phillips Lynn

Jay Phillips

All photos on this page courtesy of Bill Phillips

LITTLETON LEE "LIT" DALTON

Lit was born 2 Oct. 1857 at Blue Cut, near Independence, MO. He said he was named for his uncle, Littleton Younger. Lit was five foot seven inches tall and in later years weighed about 160 pounds. He had blue eyes, a florid complexion, and sandy hair. He said that he and his brother Bob most resembled their mother. Lit never married and he spent most of his life in California working as a mule skinner, sheepherder, or cattleman. He also ran a saloon for about eight years. He rarely drank and rarely used tobacco. He told Frank Latta, author of DALTON GANG DAYS, "I used to smoke occasionally and take a chew when I felt I wanted one and I still do—occasionally. The last occasion was, I believe, about forty years ago." Latta interviewed Littleton extensively for his book on the Dalton Gang. However, Lit had not seen any of the family for over forty years when Latta interviewed him. There was also evidence in Latta's papers that Littleton was already becoming somewhat senile.

Lit was very bitter toward his family and the disgrace of the Dalton Gang weighed heavily on him in later years. He had moved to Northern California from the Fresno area after his brothers got into trouble. He claimed that he was back in Oklahoma during or right after the Coffeyville raid, but there is no evidence at all to support this statement. He is never mentioned in any of the newspaper articles about the Coffeyville disaster; both Ben and Bill were there and they are both mentioned in various newspapers. Lit also said he was in Oklahoma when Bill was killed and claimed he had Bill's body embalmed and shipped to Kingfisher and then to Livingston, CA. This story has a bit more validity as he is mentioned in one newspaper article about Bill's death and was supposedly interviewed by a reporter from the same paper a day later. However, Bill's body was never sent to Kingfisher; it was shipped directly from Ardmore to California. It is also doubtful that Lit paid any of the bills for Mrs. Bill Dalton as she clearly had a considerable sum of money in her possession at the time.

Frank Latta also contacted Leona Dalton when he was working on DALTON GANG DAYS. Here is what Leona's letter to Mr. Latta had to say about Lit: "We believe any information that Littleton gives out could hardly be considered authentic as he has not been in touch with the family for over 42 years and for only a short time at that having gone west at 16 years of age and only back home twice."

Littleton Dalton as a young man. Latta Collection Courtesy of Christopher D. Brewer.

Littleton undoubtedly knew who family members were, where and about when they were born, etc; but his information about the criminal activities of his brothers and other facts must be considered questionably at best. Much of what he told Frank Latta does not agree with other sources of information about his brothers; and much of what Lit said is demonstrably false.

(Retyped Newspaper Article)
THE DEAD BANDIT
PARTIES OFFERING REWARDS ARE SATISFIED WITH THE IDENTIFICATION

Ardmore I. T. June 11—Littleton Dalton an elder brother of the dead outlaw arrived this evening from Kingfisher. He was on his way from his claim near Hennesey to Kingfisher to superintend his mother's harvesting when he learned of his brothers death, but did not believe it until shown the telegram signed, Jeanie Dalton, informing him of the fact.

Mrs. Bill Dalton accompanied by C. B. Dalton, a brother of the deceased, left this morning for the Wallace place where her husband was killed to bring her two children and remaining effects. At a late hour tonight they had not yet returned. The body of the dead bandit will not be taken to Guthrie or Longview as was talked of. Marshal Williams informs The News correspondent that the authorities in both Longview and Guthrie are fully satisfied as to the identity of the deceased as is Superintendent [illegible] of the Wells-Fargo express and the Santa Fe officals.

Immediately upon Mrs. Dalton's return to the city the body of her husband will be turned over to her to dispose of as she desires. In conversation with The News reporter tonight Littleton Dalton expressed it as his desire that the remains of his brother Bill be interred in the family lot at Coffeyville alongside of his father and brothers Robert, Grat and Frank who are buried there and where he has errected a handsome monument to their memory. However he will respect the wishes of his brother's widow in the matter and if she still wishes the remains taken to California he will be buried at Livingston in Merced county. Mrs. Dalton had stated her husband has expressed a desire to be buried in California.

Early yesterday morning Mrs. Dalton sent a message to the Wallace place where her husband was killed for some money she had left concealed in the place, which by some means the marshals had missed in the search of the premises. The messenger returned about noon

Littleton Dalton ca. 1938. Courtesy of the California State Library.

bringing [$800 or $850—copy very dim] in currency which he found done up in gingham rags in an old valise.

A Dodge City, Kan, bank to-day telegraphed the authorities here asking if any of their bank bills were found on the dead bandit's person or were secured in the prize captured. They replied that none were.

The south-bound passenger train both yesterday and to-day waited at the station here for their passengers to visit the undertaker's establishment and view the remains.
THE DALLAS MORNING NEWS 12 June 1894

(Retyped Newspaper Article)
NOT A LAWMAKER

Longview, Tex. June 11—The News correspondent met B. C. Weir, who is familiar with California state politics, and when shown the article going the rounds of some papers to the effect that Bill Dalton was once worth $100,000 and had twice represented his county in the state legislature he said that Bill Dalton's depredations had most all been confined to the rich valley in which Fresno county is located and in this county lived a very prominent gentleman, in no way related to Bill Dalton, named H. C. Dalton, who was worth $250,000 and who had twice represented Fresno county in the state legislature.

Mr. Weir had often visited the fine estate of H. C. Dalton. The old gentleman who was nearly 60 years old was killed at his home last August by being thrown from a horse and dragged to death.

Mr. Weir does not say positively that Bill Dalton never represented his county in the legislature, but he says his, Mr. Weir's, business has been in and about the state legislature for twenty years and he never heard of Bill Dalton being in the legislature and thinks the story of his wealth and prominence is drawn from H. C. Dalton.
DALLAS MORNING NEWS 12 June 1894

(Retyped Newspaper Article)
**STORY OF DALTON'S LIFE
AS TOLD BY HIS BROTHER—HE SERVED
TWO TERMS IN THE CALIFORNIA LEGISLATURE**

Ardmore I. T., June 12—Littleton Dalton who came here to identify his brother Bill the dead bandit, has been eagerly sought since his arrival for some of the history and

Littleton Dalton ca. 1938. Courtesy of the California State Library.

personal characteristics of his noted brother. Mr. Dalton is averse to talking of the matter, but to-day in the presence of a few friends and The News correspondent he recounted a few brief chapters in the life of Bill Dalton.

Mr. Dalton said he saw Bill last in the road near Enid shortly after the opening of the Cherokee Strip. Mr. Dalton, continuing, said he didn't know Bill's alias at that time nor did he know where he was destined when he met him. "It would have been useless to ask him" continued Mr. Dalton, "for he would have told no one, not even his wife. His intentions were known only to himself, he had no confidants. We never even heard from him and all we know of his movements were what we learned from the press reports which we seldom believed.

Mother last saw Bill in September. Late one night the night after his wife arrived at mother's from California, Bill rode up to the house and remained until a short time before daybreak. That was the last time he was at mothers. He never wrote, but occasionally we would hear from him through friends."

One of the party asked: "Did any of your brothers ever die a natural death, Mr. Dalton?"

"No," he replied.

"Where was Bill born?"

"He was born in Colorado, near Denver. The family moved from there during the sixties, going to Clay county, Missouri, about twenty miles from Kansas City. There Bill lived until he was 16 years of age, when he went to Butte, Mont. He drove mules at the mines for awhile, then went to Oregon, and later drifted down to California, where he married Jane Bilvens in the early part of 1884."

Speaking of his other brothers, Mr. Dalton said, "I helped to nurse all of them and I know Grat's was the strongest character of the outfit. What he set his head to was as good as accomplished. Bob was not the leader of the brothers as he has been given credit for being, nor did he lead the raid at Coffeyville."

"Emmett," continued Mr. Dalton, "was the coolest headed and smartest one in the family; Frank was killed at Fort Smith, Ark. He was working on the marshal's force and he was intending to quit when he was shot down by a gang of horse thieves and whisky peddlers whom he was pursuing.

Bill was much grieved by the death of his brothers in the Coffeyville affair. He was of a lively disposition, always cheerful and good-natured, and trouble bore more heavily on him than on any of the family."

"Was Bill prosperous in California?"

"Very. From working as a common farm laborer he amassed a fortune and had a magnificent home, and finally served two terms in the legislature of that state."

"Where was Bill at the time of the Coffeyville robbery?"

"Bill was in Kingfisher at that time. Whether he knew that the attempt to rob the Coffeyville bank was to be made I don't know; nor do I know that he tried to stop the boys, but he was known to have secured a horse and do some mighty hard riding some place."

THE DALLAS MORNING NEWS 13 June 1894

Note: If Littleton actually gave this interview as reported, he was sure stretching the truth a long way even then.

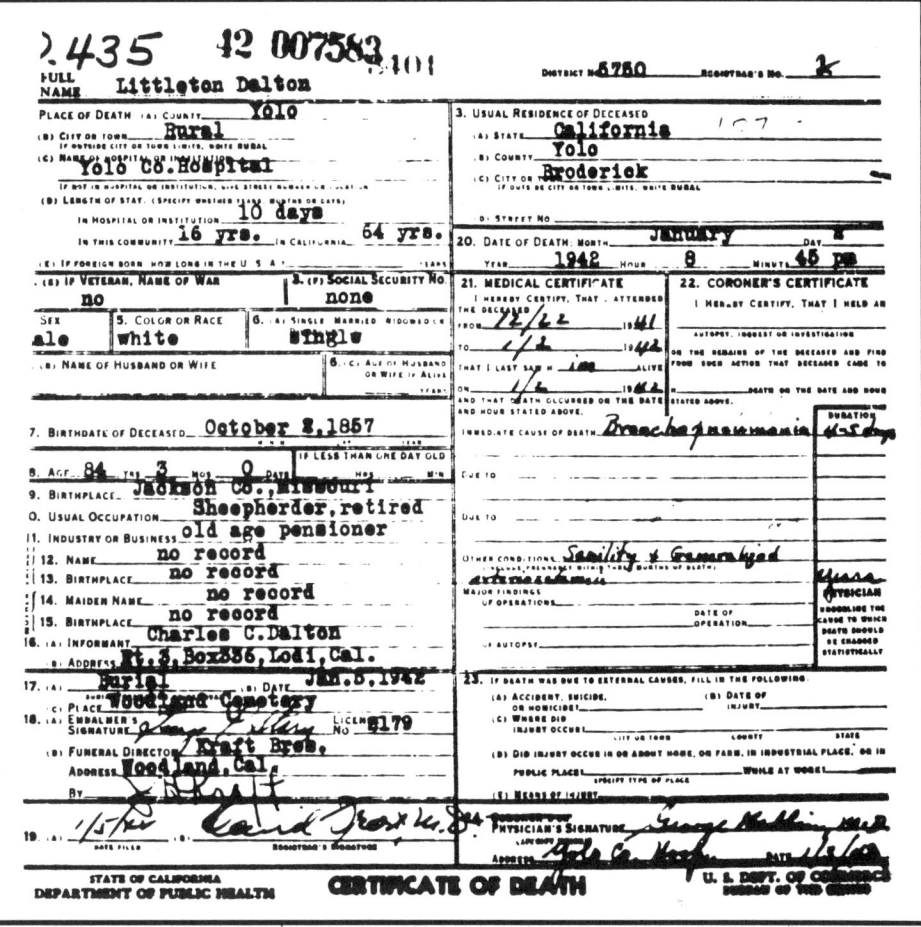

(Retyped Newspaper Article)
YOLOAN DIES; CLAIMED KIN WAS OUTLAW

Littleton Dalton, 84, resident of Broderick for 19 years and formerly of Willows, died at 8:45 p. m. Friday at the county hospital after being gravely ill for 10 days. He often had told his many friends in the river district that his late brother, Jack, was a member of the notorous Dalton Gang.

Kraft Brothers are making funeral plans.

Mr. Dalton was born in Jackson County, Missouri. He came to California in 1878 and worked throughout the state before going to Glenn county where he worked as a sheepherder for 20 years before moving to this county.

He is survived by a nephew, Charles C. Dalton of Lodi. Two sisters, Miss Leona Dalton and Mrs. Eva J. Whipple reside in Arkansas. A brother, Simon, died recently in Arkansas.
WOODLAND DAILY DEMOCRAT 28 Jan 1942

FRANKLIN "FRANK" DALTON

Frank Dalton was born in 1859 and was commissioned a U. S. deputy marshal at Fort Smith, Arkansas in 1884. He was killed near Fort Smith on 27 November 1887 while trying to arrest whiskey runners. (His tombstone in Coffeyville gives 1888 as the year of his death, this is incorrect). It is not known for certain if Frank was married. Some of the dime novels about the Daltons have him married to women named either Naomi or Julia. The newspaper articles about Frank's death do not agree on his marital status. No marriage record has been found for Frank. However, if he married while living in the Indian Territory there probably would not be a record of the marriage. There was no official authority to issue marriage license in the Indian Territory until March 1889 when the first federal court was established at Muskogee. There were 1324 marriage licenses issued during the first thirty

Frank Dalton, age 28, -- Deputy U. S. Marshall. Killed Nov. 27, 1887, while making an arrest.

Frank Dalton. This photo was in the N.H. Rose Collection and has been significantly retouched. Courtesy of Western Historical Collections, University of Oklahoma.

days of the Muskogee court's operation. Many of these for marriages that had taken place some years before. Frank was a widely respected law enforcement officer and his death was a real blow to his family and friends.

The Dalton Gang Family

This photo has not been retouched. This was reproduced from a tintype and is believed to have been taken at Fort Smith, AR in the 1880's. Left to right are Frank Dalton, Ben Dalton, George Maledon, the Fort Smith hangman, and Judge Isaac C. Parker. Courtesy of Armand De Gregoris.

(Retyped Newspaper Article)

MORE BLOODSHED IN THE INDIAN TERRITORY

A dispatch from Ft. Smith to the St. Louis Globe Democrat, under date of November 27, 1887, says: A bloody tragedy took place this morning in the Cherokee Nation, about two miles from this city, in which Deputy United States Marshal Frank Dalton, Dave Smith and Mrs. Lee Dixon were killed, while the husband of Mrs. Dixon and Deputy Marshal J. R. Cole were badly wounded. Deputy Dalton came in with six prisoners on Friday last, and late yesterday evening started with his outfit on another trip: Dalton had a writ for Dave Smith on a charge of larceny, and Cole had one for the same party on a charge of violating the intercourse law. They knew Smith was in the bottom and Cole accompanied Dalton for the purpose of arresting him and coming back today. The marshals camped last night just across the river from here and this morning Dalton and Cole went to a tent where Smith was supposed to be. Several men and women were at breakfast in the tent when the officers rode up and dismounted, not thinking of having trouble. Dalton stepped up to the door and was immediately confronted by Smith, who shot the officer in the breast, mortally wounding him. As Smith turned after shooting

Dalton, Deputy Cole shot him in the body and he fell forward into the tent. Will Towerly then rushed out and shot at Cole, who retreated backwards and tripping on a tent rope, fell, when he was shot in the right breast the ball ranging out at the right side. He sprang to his feet and used his Winchester as best he could, but the women rushing out of the tent checked his fire to some extent and he took refuge behind a tree, several shots hitting the tree after he reached it, the men all having by this time taken refuge in the tent. Cole left on foot, under the impression that Dalton was dead. He was not dead, however, and after Cole got out of range Will Towerly came out and shot him in the head twice with a Winchester, not-withstanding the officer begged him piteously not to, as he was mortally wounded. Cole made his way here and a posse of officers at once repaired to the scene, where they found Smith, Dalton and Mrs. Dixon dead and Mr. Dixon badly wounded. Towerly had escaped unhurt, and a large and determined posse went in pursuit of him. Dixon was brought in and is now in the jail hospital. Dalton resided at Tulsa, I. T., with his mother, and his body will be forwarded to that place on tonight's train in charge of his brother and a posse under Bud Heady. He was one of the most brave and efficient officers on the force, and an upright, honest man. He is the same party who was with Deputy Marshal Jack Richardson when that brave officer was murdered by the notorious Cherokee outlaw Bill Pigeon. Mrs. Dixon was killed by a stray bullet from either Cole or the parties who were shooting at him. Her husband was shot by Cole.

Notes of Frank Dalton's interview with a witness in January 1887. From: Forth Worth Branch, National Archives.

The Dalton Gang Family

THE WESTERN UNION TELEGRAPH COMPANY.

Nov 30, 1887

Dated Fort Smith Ark 30

To The Attorney General Wash'n DC

Sir, On last Sunday morning deputy Marshalls Frank Dalton & James R. Cole rode up to a tent near Fort Smith in the Cherokee Nation where they were informed that one David Smith for whom they had writs could be found. Dalton and Cole dismounted & as Dalton walked to the front of the tent Smith appeared and presented his

THE WESTERN UNION TELEGRAPH COMPANY.

Nov 30, 1887

pistol at Daltons breast & fired, Dalton dropped mortally wounded, instantly deputy Cole killed Smith, some woman & two or three armed men ran out of the tent & the men opened fire on Cole. He was shot through the clothing some six or seven times and through the breast once. He returned the fire mortally wounding one Dixon slightly wounding another man and killing one woman accidentally of course Coles ammunition

Western Union telegraph-Frank's death

THE WESTERN UNION TELEGRAPH COMPANY.

Received at Corcoran Building, S. E. Cor. 15th & "F" Sts., Washington, D. C.   Nov 30 1887

Strength gave out & he escaped, after he departed one (Wm Towerly, a party engaged in the shooting walked out to where Dalton lay and presented his gun at him, Dalton begged him not to shoot saying he was mortally wounded and wanted to prepare for death, Towerly replied "Oh! You Son of a bitch" and fired his winchester into Daltons Mouth. He reloaded and blew out Daltons brains.

THE WESTERN UNION TELEGRAPH COMPANY.

Received at Corcoran Building, S. E. Cor. 15th & "F" Sts., Washington, D. C.   Nov 30 1887

He got a horse & although pursued has thus far eluded arrest. In view of the foregoing we respectfully ask that a reward for the capture and delivery to the Marshal at Ft Smith of the Murderer of Frank Dalton supposed to be William Towerly be offered and in view of the atrocity of the crime we recommend that the reward be one thousand dollars. Respectfully

John Carroll
U.S. Marshal M P Sanders

Received at Corcoran Building, S. E. Cor. 15th & "F" Sts., Washington, D. C.   Nov 30 1887

I concur with the within request and recommendation; I C Parker, Judge.

The Dalton Gang Family

The body of Frank Dalton, the Deputy U. S. Marshal who was murdered near Ft. Smith on Sunday morning, an account of which appears elsewhere in THE JOURNAL, was brought to Coffeyville on Tuesday and interred in the city cemetery. The remains were accompanied by his wife and a brother of the deceased. Marshal Dalton was well known here and quite a favorite among our people. He was a brave and efficient officer and deserved a better fate than that which befell him. It is to be hoped that his slayer will be caught and summarily dealt with.
**THE COFFEYVILLE JOURNAL
1 Dec. 1887**

(Retyped Newspaper Article)
**A TERRIBLE TRAGEDY
TWO MEN AND ONE WOMAN ARE KILLED AND TWO MEN WOUNDED**

THE RESULT OF TWO DEPUTY MARSHALS ENDEAVORING TO ARREST A DESPERATE HORSE THIEF

A FAITHFUL OFFICER MURDERED WHILE IN THE DISCHARGE OF HIS DUTY

We are called upon this week to chronicle another deadly encounter in the Indian country between United States Officers and lawless characters, in which Deputy Marshal Frank Dalton, a fearless and trusty officer, was brutally murdered while two other lives were lost and two men wounded, one of the killed being a woman. The facts in the case as near as we have been able to gather them are about as follows:

Deputy Marshal Frank Dalton came in last Friday with six prisoners, the fruits of a protracted trip to the territory, and turned them over to the U. S. Jailer.

His outfit struck camp on the opposite side of the river in the Cherokee nation to remain until the officer got ready to start out on

Tombstone of Frank Dalton in Coffeyville, KS. The stone gives the date of death as Nov. 27, 1888. the correct date is 1887. Photo Latta Collection. Courtesy of Christopher D. Brewer.

another trip. Dalton had a writ for one Dave Smith charging him with horsestealing, and Deputy Cole had a writ for the same party for introducing whisky in the Indian country. Learning that Smith was at a camp about four miles from here in the river bottom, the two officers left Dalton's camp early Sunday morning for the purpose of arresting him. They rode leisurely over to where they expected to find him, and arriving near the camp dismounted and approached the tent on foot. Dalton walked around on one side of the tent and Cole on the other. As Dalton came round toward the door of the tent Smith came out and met him armed with a pistol. Cole heard Dalton say, "Don't shoot, we want no trouble here" or words to that effect, but the utterance had scarcely left his lips when Smith fired on him inflicting a mortal wound, the brave young officer falling almost at the crack of the pistol. About the same time Smith fired, Cole came around and seeing his companion fall, shot Smith in the back, and he too fell mortally wounded. Two other men, Lee Dixon and Will Towerly, rushed out and Cole backed off, when he stumbled over a tent rope and fell, Dixon shooting at him as he fell and wounding him in the left side. He regained his feet, however, and as he retreated past Dalton asked him if he was badly hurt, but received no answer. He was fired on from the tent as he retreated and returned the fire by taking refuge behind a tree into which his assailants put several bullets, and from this shelter engaged in a single handed fight with the occupants of the tent until they ceased firing on him, when he got away on foot and reached here about 11 o'clock to report the matter at the marshal's office, when a posse of men immediately set out for the scene, where they found Smith and Mrs. Leander Dixon dead, and the husband of Mrs. Dixon badly wounded. Will Towerly had escaped, and several determined men at once set out in pursuit of him, while the wounded man, Dixon, was brought here and placed in the prison hospital. His wound is an ugly one, the ball having entered near the collarbone on the left shoulder and ranged down into the back. He says he received the shot while stopping over his wife, who had just received her death wound. Dixon denies that he did any shooting, but Cole says he is the man that shot him as he tripped over the tent rope.

Dalton was still alive when Cole retreated from the camp, and then the most brutal act of the dreadful tragedy was performed. Young Towerly came out of the tent and approaching the prostrate and helpless officer, shot him in the head with a Winchester, while Dalton was begging him not to do so as he was already killed.

Dalton was a fearless and efficient officer, and an honest, upright young man, highly esteemed by all who knew him for his many good qualities of head and heart. He was but twenty-eight years of age and unmarried, his home being with his mother at Chelsea, Cherokee Nation. His remains were brought to this city, and after begin embalmed at the undertaking establishment of Birnie Bros., were placed in a coffin and sent home by rail Sunday night in charge of his brother and Mr. Bud Heady, posse of the murdered officer.

Smith, the dead outlaw, was about the last remaining remnant of the Felix Griffin gang of thieves who made their headquarters in the vicinity of Webbers Falls. Lee Dixon, the wounded man, is a brother-in-law of Smith, the latter's wife being Dixon's sister. Dixon and some of the other men about the camp were at work cutting wood and clearing land. Towerly is a young man about nineteen or twenty years of age, and was boarding at Dixon's camp.

Deputy Cole has had several close calls since he has been on this force, being compelled about a year ago to kill a drunken bully on the ferry boat just across the river from here, the fellow firing on him for no cause whatever. Only a few days ago he and his posse came in contact with "Big Chewee," a Cherokee desperado, and his posse was badly wounded. However, he has escaped injury up to Sunday last and the wound he is now carrying is not dangerous, a fact we are pleased to note.

FORT SMITH ELEVATOR 2 Dec. 1887

NOTE: THE INDIAN CHIEFTAIN, of Vinita, Indian Territory, carried two articles about the death of Frank Dalton in the 1 Dec. 1887 issue. In this paper the brother accompanying Frank's body is identified as Robert.

(Retyped Newspaper Article)
ANOTHER MARSHAL KILLED

A note received from Atoka last Saturday informed us of the murder of Deputy Marshal Ed. Stockley by the same man who killed Frank Dalton the Sunday before—Will Towerly. On the preceding evening Heck Thomas, who was at McAlester, was telegraphed that Towerly was at Mrs. McKianey's near Atoka. Stockley who resides at White Bead Hill and is Thomas' partner, responded and with a posse went to the place indicated. When Towerly appeared he was commanded to surrender but replied with a shot which struck the unfortunate officer near the heart causing his death ten minutes later. Before falling however he fired in return as did the posse and Towerly was shot in five places, an arm and a leg being broken. The desperado was secured and the impression was that his wounds would prove fatal.
THE INDIAN CHIEFTAIN 8 Dec. 1887

GRATTON HANLEY "GRAT" DALTON

According to Lit, Grat was born 30 March 1861 near Lawrence, KS and this date agrees with census records. Grandmother Nancy Dalton supposedly named Grat for old Kentucky neighbors who were probably also relatives. Grat went to California in 1880 and worked at various jobs on ranches. It is also reported that he tended bar for awhile in Livingston in 1882. Emmett described Grat as the most pugnacious of the Daltons. He was easily stirred to wrath, and sensitive to challenge or fancied insults. In other words, he carried a chip on his shoulder. Emmett said that Grat took a wild joy in fighting and that this became an extremely dangerous trait. Grat supposedly drank heavily and was very fond of playing cards.

The files of the Pinkerton Detective Agency describes Grat as follows: "Gratton Dalton, Nativity Johnson County, Kansas. Inveterate tobacco chewer, card player and prided himself on being the best cribbage player in the country. Passionately fond of whiskey. Brags of his detective ability. When embarrassed picks

Grat Dalton as a young man. Courtesy of Western History Department, Denver Public Library.

his teeth and cleans his finger nails. ...Is left handed and generally shoots from the left shoulder although he can shoot equally well from the right."

Glenn Shirley, in his book, WEST OF HELL'S FRINGE, claims that Grat Dalton was dismissed as a deputy for conduct unbecoming an officer from both the Fort Smith and the Muskogee court for a "William Tell" type shooting incident. Grat supposedly placed an apple on the head of a Negro boy then said he would show his companions some fancy shootin'. He supposedly shot the apple dead center, knocking pieces in every direction as the Negro boy fled for his life. It is possible that this story is true but it has all the earmarks of just another tall tale about the Daltons. The same story is recorded in the INDIAN PIONEER HISTORY collection in an Interview with David O. Gillis of Tulsa, 20 May 1937. Gillis claimed Bob shot the apple off a Negro's head on the main street in Tulsa in 1883. In 1883 Bob would have been all of fourteen years old and a very short time resident in the Indian Territory as the Daltons did not move there until 1882 or 83. Still an earlier variation of this William Tell legend is told about cousin, John Younger. John supposedly displayed his marksmanship by shooting the pipe from the mouth of a half-witted person named Jim Russell in Dallas, Texas.

It is far more likely that Grat got into trouble over the incident reported in the Tulsa News Items in the 13 March 1890 INDIAN CHIEFTAIN. The CHIEFTAIN said: "Delonadale was belabored over the head with a six shooter a few days ago by Deputy Gratz [sic] Dalton, almost to insensibility."

Grat Dalton. Photo courtesy of Wells Fargo.

MASON FRAKES or WILLIAM MARION "BILL" DALTON

Littleton said his name was Mason Frakes and he was named for an old southern farmer his father stayed with for awhile in Missouri. Bill appears as Mason on both the 1870, Cass Co., MO and 1880 Bates, Co., MO census as well. His age is generally given as 29 when he was killed in 1894 which would make his birth year 1865. Census records show him as age 5 in 1870 and age 15 in 1880 also consistent with 1865 as the year of his birth. He married Jane Bliven in Merced County,

California on 15 June 1885 and he gave his name as William M. and his age as 24. He may have wanted his new in-laws to think he was somewhat older than he was to convince them he would be a responsible husband.

No matter what name his parents gave him he was generally known as Bill and he was described as the politician born. Emmett said Bill knew and commanded the adroit power of words extremely well. It was said he could talk himself into and out of anything. He was quick witted but also exercized caution and tact. He may well have had political ambitions beyond his home county in California, but according to the records of the California State Library, he never served as a member of the California State Legislature as has been widely reported. He was a talented musician and was regarded as one of the best guitar players in his area of the state.

There are more wild stories told about Bill Dalton than for all of the other Daltons combined. Bill's criminal career will be covered in a later chapter but a couple of the stories about his personal life will be addressed here.

Bill Dalton married only one time and he had two children by his wife Jane Bliven. The children were Charles Coleman "Chub" and Gracie. Chub married Emma Turner and they had six children. Chub died in Lodi, CA, 4 May 1976 and Emma also died there 24 Jan. 1969. Several of their descendants are still living.

Gracie was crippled early in life from injuries suffered in a fall. She married Leslie Rhodes of Eldridge, CA. and had one son. Gracie died in 1948 and her husband died in 1959.

After Bill's death Jane Bliven Dalton married Joseph "Bob" Adams. She and Bob had one daughter, Orva. Orva married Lloyd O. Beam. Lloyd died Oct. 1938 and Orva died September 1970.

In his book, THE DALTON GANG, Harold Preece claimed that Bill married a girl named Mary Hughes in Hugo, OK, or at least fathered her child. Mary supposedly went to Louisiana and gave birth to William Harmon or Bill Dalton, Jr. This story is clearly untrue, as the death record of William Harmon Dalton shows. William Harmon Dalton was born 28 Dec. 1880, which would mean he was conceived about March 1880. At that time Bill Dalton was only 15 years old and was living in Bates County, MO. So much for the big romance with Mary Hughes in Hugo, OK.

Bill Dalton ca. 1884 in California. Courtesy of Western History Collections, University of Oklahoma Library.

Death certificate of William Harmon reported son of Bill Dalton and Mary Hughes.

Another ridiculious story has been passed around far and wide by a family in CA, OK, and other areas. This tribe claims to be descended from Bill Dalton, the outlaw, and claim the following:

"William Marion b. 1865 d. 1894 married several times; 1. Mary Hughes, 2. Jennie Bevins, 3. ____ Adams? 4. Sarah Flinchum. Had many mistresses, went by the name Mason Wallace. Joined the Doolin Gang after his brothers were killed." This story is further embellished by a tale about how the Marshal brought the widow to town somewhere in OK after Bill's death and assisted her in obtaining a Civil War pension. Very good trick, obtaining a Civil War pension for the widow of a man born in 1865, the year that Lee surrendered to Grant at Appomattox!

A further variation on this latter story was relayed via the telephone from a woman in West Virginia. She had "Charlie" Dalton married to an ancestor of hers named Sarah York. She further claimed to have documents proving that Frank Dalton signed "Charlie's" marriage certificate after Frank was supposed to have been killed. This was all supposed to prove that Frank faked his own death and turned outlaw too. Documents

Bliven House in Livingston, California, where Bill Dalton was buried for many years. Body was later moved to Bliven family plot in Turlock, CA. Courtesy of Bill Phillips.

to prove all of this were promised but were, needless to say, never delivered.

There are other stories of Bill in Indiana, Bill in Washington D. C., etc. etc. but space is limited.

EVA DALTON WHIPPLE

Eva was born 25 Jan. 1867. There are several reports that she taught school for awhile before she married John N. Whipple in Meade, KS 25 Oct. 1887. John Whipple ran a general purpose store in Meade at the time he and Eva married. Newspapers of the period show advertisements for WHIPPLE'S HEADQUARTERS and show that groceries, feed, boots and shoes, etc. were all carried in his store. There are numerous stories connecting the Whipples with the Dalton Gang activities; these tales all appear to be complete fiction. The old Whipple home in Meade, KS is now open as the Dalton Hideout Museum. The story says the Dalton Gang hid here in a tunnel that connected the barn and the house. However, this property was sold for back taxes in 1892 and the Whipples had departed from Meade before then. From Eva's obituary it appears that she and John made the first of the Oklahoma land runs in 1889. Therefore it is very doubtful that any of the Daltons ever hid out at the Meade home after any of

Bill Dalton probably a short time before he was killed. Courtesy of Western History Department, Denver Public Library.

their crimes since all criminal activities were in 1890 or later. Further some Kansas residents claim the tunnel now in existance at the Hideout Museum was built by the WPA (Works Progress Administration) during the depression.

Eva is known to have worked as a milliner and a dressmaker. She and a friend Florence Dorland are said to have run a millinery store in Meade. She is listed as Mrs. Eva Whipple, dressmaker at 616 N. Evans in the El Reno City Directory for 1901-1902. Also the SILOAM SPRINGS HISTORY mentions that she ran a cafe right next to the post office in Siloam Springs, AR at one time.

The Whipples had two children and the 1900 census, taken 18 June 1900, for El Reno, Canadian Co., OK show the Whipples as follows:

Marriage certificate of Wiliam M. Dalton and Jane Bliven married 15 June 1885.

John Whipple b. April 1851 age 49, b. CT, occupation, Butcher.
Eva b. Jan. 1867 age 33 b. MO
Maud b. Sept. 1888 age 11 b. KS
Glenn B. b. April 1894 age 6 b. OK.

When Eva died she was survived by only a granddaughter, Mrs. W. D. Meadows, of Houston, TX. John Whipple reportedly died in 1932 and after his death Eva made her home with her sister Leona in Kingfisher. Eva and Leona sold a piece of property in Siloam Springs, AR, in July 1933. This is probably about the time she went to live with Leona. There is a bit of a mystery about the death of both the children and John.

Death records have not been found for any of them so it is uncertain when and how they died and where they are buried.

(Retyped Newspaper Article)
WEDDING BELLS

The home of Mr. and Mrs. Geo. DeCow, who live four miles south of town, was the meeting place Tuesday evening of a number of the friends of Mr. J. N. Whipple, one of our most pro-minent business men, and Miss Eva Dalton, a young lady of rare beauty and intelligence. The occasion was the solemnizing of the marriage by Judge Hudson of Mr. Whipple and Miss Dalton. The bride and groom were supported by Mr. and Mrs. Robt. Harper. The ladies were dressed in wine-colored silks trimmed with lace, the gentlemen wore the customary dress suit. After con-gratulations of the numerous friends the entire company repaired to the dining room where a magnificent feast was waiting, the result of the united efforts of Medames Harper, DeCow and Black. The presents were numerous and elegant. It is with pleasure that the editor of the Press Democrat announces the marriage of these friends and we join with all in wishing them a happy and prosperous life.
MEAD COUNTY PRESS-DEMOCRAT date not given

This photo has been published and identified as Ben Dalton. It clearly is not the man in the other two photos of Ben Dalton in this book. The author believes this is Bill Dalton. Author's collection.

(Retyped Newspaper Article)
MARRIED

WHIPPLE-DALTON—At the residence of George DeCow, south of this city, Oct. 25, 1887, by Judge W. D. Hudson, Mr. J. N. Whipple and Miss Eva Dalton. Only the immediate friends of the contracting parties were present. A guest informs us that the groom appeared at his best and that the bride was a perfect picture of loveliness and beauty. Those who are acquainted with her know her to be an excellent lady, attractive and accom-plished. The groom has undoubtedly secured

a prize. Mr. Whipple is one of our leading merchants, sociable and financially prepared to fill all the demands of the new relation. The REPUBLICAN joins their many friends in wishing them much happiness.
THE MEAD GLOBE REPUBLICAN date not given

(Retyped Newspaper Article)
OBITUARY

EVA MAY WHIPPLE

Eva May Dalton was born January 25, 1867, at Belton, Mo., and passed away at the home of her sister, Miss Leona Dalton, in Kingfisher on January 28, 1939, at the age of 72 years and 3 days.

Upon completing her education, she engaged in teaching, met and was married to J. N. Whipple of Meade, Kans., on November 20, 1888. Her husband preceded her in death, passing away in 1932.

Mr. and Mrs. Whipple came to Kingfisher during the year of the opening of the old Oklahoma Territory. They resided here for some years, but Mrs. Whipple returned to live with her sister in 1934, and made this her home until her death.

At the age of 16, Mrs. Whipple united with the Methodist church at Oswego, Kans. Her membership was

Maude Whipple, Eva's daughter. Courtesy of Nancy Ohnick.

transferred to the Kingfisher Methodist church after she made her home here.

For the past four years Mrs. Whipple had been in failing health and for the past month her condition was serious. Death came as a release to the tired and weary body.

She is survived by her sister, Miss Leona Dalton of Kingfisher; one brother, Littleton Dalton of California; a granddaughter, Mrs. W. D. Meadows of Houston, Tex.; and a nephew, Roy M. Clute of Oklahoma City.

Just a few days before her death she marked a prayer in her book of daily devotion, "O God, gracious and supreme, let the power of Christ rest upon me that I may turn all living into spiritual good, for Jesus' sake. Amen."

Funeral services were held at 2:30 p. m. Sunday at the Bracken Funeral Home, Rev. H. A. Morton officiating, assisted by Rev. Everard Carter. Burial was made in Kingfisher cemetery.

(Retyped Newspaper Article)

SERVICE HELD FOR EVA MAY WHIPPLE

Final rites for Mrs. Eva May Whipple were held at 2:30 p. m. Sunday at the Bracken Funeral Home. Rev. H. A. Morton officiated, assisted by Rev. J. Everard Carter. Interment was made in the Kingfisher cemetery, Bracken Funeral Home in charge.

Mrs. Whipple had been in failing health for the past four years, and her condition had been serious during the past month. She passed away on Saturday, January 28, at the home of her sister, Miss Leona Dalton, with whom she had made her home since 1934. She and her husband came to Kingfisher at the opening of the old Oklahoma Territory and resided here a number of years. She was 72 years old.

Surviving Mrs. Whipple are Miss Dalton, one brother, Littleton Dalton of California, a grandaughter and a nephew. Mr. Whipple died several years ago.

Her obituary appears elsewhere.
KINGFISHER FREE PRESS 23 Jan. 1939

ROBERT RENNICK "BOB" DALTON

Bob was born 13 May 1869 and Littleton said Bob was named for a Methodist Minister who was a Chaplain with General Jo Shelby of the Confederate Army. There was a Confederate Chaplain from MO by that name but it is possible that Bob was named for an older Robert Rennick. The Rennick family was captured by the Indians in VA around 1765 and the father, Robert, was killed at the time. A son named Robert died in captivity and the mother shortly after gave birth to another son whom she also named Robert. The Robert Rennick born in captivity married a Letitia Dalton in 1794 and a daughter of Robert Rennick and a previous wife also married a Dalton. A sizable number of these Rennick and Dalton families moved on west and settled in Jackson, and Johnson counties, MO. How or if this Rennick-Dalton family is connected to the Dalton Gang family is unknown. Both the names Gratton and Hanley are associated with this family and these names, of course, appear in Grat Dalton's name.

Note: Bob's birthdate was given by Emmett in a newspaper interview shortly after the Coffeyville disaster.

Bob was about six feet tall, had blue eyes and sandy hair. Emmett said Bob was perhaps the most handsome of the Daltons. Emmett also said Bob shared some of Grat's pugnacity but was also cool, deliberate, tenacious, and fearless. It was said that Bob knew where he would land before he leaped. (This did not appear to be true at Coffeyville.)

A Southern Pacific Railroad Reward Poster described Bob as follows: "About twenty-three years of age (but might be taken for 25); height, 6 ft. 1 1/2 inches; well built and straight; light complexion, but florid and healthy looking; boyish beard and mustache; light hair and eyes; weight, 180 to 190 lbs.; large, bony, long fingered hands, showing no acquaintance with work; large nose and ears; white teeth; long sunburned neck, square features. ... Is a good poker and card player; drinks whisky in moderation, but does not chew tobacco; smokes brown paper cigarettes occasionally."

Bob was the leader of The Dalton Gang and he died during the Coffeyville Raid on 5 Oct. 1892. There are many tales about Bob and a variety of women. There is no foundation in fact for any of these stories. The book THE DALTON BROTHERS written by a supposed "Eyewitness" shortly after the Coffeyville Raid claimed that Bob was in love with a cousin, Minnie Johnson, and shot a man named Charley Montgomery in the back when Minnie took up with Charley. Bob never had a cousin named Minnie Johnson, and there is no evidence whatsoever for the existence of any such girl. Bob killed Montgomery in the line of duty as the article from the Coffeyville paper which follows plainly shows. Emmett added a girlfriend for Bob in his books apparently just to add

Quit claim deed made by Mrs. E. D. Whipple and Leona Dalton for real estate in Siloam Springs, AR 10 July 1933.

The Dalton Gang Family

romance to the story. He said Bob was in love with Eugenia Moore and that Moore collected information and assisted the Gang in other ways. Moore then supposedly died of some dread disease right before the Coffeyville robbery. Not one shred of evidence can be found for the existence of Eugenia Moore either. The third tale is that the female outlaw Flo Quick, often called Tom King, was Bob Dalton's woman and Flo was supposed to have been part of the Gang. All versions of this preposterous tale can be traced to the fertile imagination of U. S. deputy marshal Chris Madsen. Numerous variations of the Tom King story are found in Latta's DALTON GANG DAYS, Preece's THE DALTON GANG, Croy's TRIGGER MARSHAL, THE STORY OF CHRIS MADSEN, and in other books and articles about the Daltons. However, Flo Quick/Tom King, who was quite a hot item in the Twin Territories for awhile, did not begin her career in crime there until mid 1893. By this time Bob Dalton had been a'moldering in his grave in Coffeyville for several months. In addition to the story of Bob shooting Charley Montgomery in the back, another fable has made the rounds about how Bob shot a completely innocent Indian boy, named Cochran, in Claremore. Even Emmett repeated the Cochran tale. However, newspapers of the time put the shooting of both Montgomery and of young Jess Cochran in a completely different light.

(Retyped Newspaper Article)
KILLED BY A MARSHAL'S POSSE

On Wednesday evening, about 7:30 o'clock, a young man named Charley Montgomery, was shot and killed by the members of Deputy Marshal Grat Dalton's posse, in the Indian Territory, about seven miles Southwest, of this city. The body of the dead man was brought to Coffeyville during the night and buried here on Thursday. The particulars of the killing and the circumstances which led thereto, as near as we can come at them, are as follows: It appears that Montgomery, who appeared in the Nation about a year ago, had been playing some unwarranted games since his advent there. For instance: About a month ago he came to Coffeyville and represented himself as a U. S. Marshal, and had to be arrested and disarmed. He was suspected of being engaged in running off horses from the Osage Country and various petty crimes were charged up to him by the citizens of that section of the Territory. Lately he had appropriated two revolvers that did not belong to him, and had secured a horse that

Most of the photos that have been published of Bob Dalton when he was living made their way into the N. H. Rose Collection. Rose heavily retouched all of these photos (following pages). A recently discovered photo of Bob Dalton (shown here) in the John Tackett Collection has not been retouched. Courtesy of Herb Osborne.

was not his own, but which got away from him before he could get it into the State. Marshal Dalton was after him, and had ordered his posse to locate and arrest Montgomery, as he was aiming to leave the country that night, whilst he came to town, expecting to find Montgomery here. In the meantime Bob Dalton had located their man at June Brown's in the Timber Hills, and as he could not find the Marshal, he took the guards and went after Montgomery. The party consisted of Bob Dalton, Al. Landis and Bill Griggs. They did not anticipate any trouble in getting the man. They found Montgomery sitting on the porch, and before they could reach him, he opened fire on Landis, whom he recongnized, with a revolver. His first shot went through the guard's hat and the next took away a small portion of one of his ears. About the time he fired the second time, Landis let go with his revolver, the shot taking effect in Montgomery's breast. At this he wheeled and started to run in the direction of young Dalton with his pistol presented at an aim. The latter called to him to stop, but was answered by a shot at such close range that some of the powder lodged in his face, but the ball passed over his shoulder. Bob Dalton was armed with a shot gun and he quickly replied to Montgomery's shot with a charge of buck shot, that took effect in the right side and stomach of the victim. He fell in his tracks and expired without a word. The men engaged in the affair very much regret the necessity for the killing. They did not anticipate any resistance on Montgomery's part, but it seems that he had given it out that he would never be taken alive. His associations were those of the criminal class, and he was accused of introducing whiskey into the Territory. His life's ending was a tragic one, and sad. He was about twenty-eight years old.

THE COFFEYVILLE JOURNAL 16 Aug. 1888

Bob Dalton, as he appeared at the age of 21 years.

Bob Dalton age 21. Courtesy of Western History Collection, University of Oklahoma.

(Retyped Newspaper Article)
THEY STOOD THEM OFF

ALEX AND JESS COCHRAN, JR, HAVE A ROUND WITH THE OFFICERS

Near Claremore last Saturday morning, at the house of a man named Hightman, a fight took place between the Cochrans and the officers in which Bob Cox, a posse man, was disabled and compelled to retire. It seems that during the preceding day Deputy Floyd Wilson was telegraphed to come to Claremore, the object being to effect the arrest of Bud Maxfield and a man named Halm, who recently escaped from the Little Rock penitentiary. When the officers reached Claremore on the evening train Wilson was suffering with an ague chill and at once went to bed and endeavored to persuade Cox to give up the raid until he was able to accompany him. This the latter did not like to do and about nine o'clock, in company with Charley Canon started for the house named, where a dance was to be held. On arriving, the officers took part in the dance and conducted themselves the same as the other guests, even to purchasing a quart of liquor which was offered them and which they found was procured of Halm, who was conducting a saloon in the loft of the barn. The whisky was purchased of Ed. Louthers, a boy who was acting as a sort of go-between. About three o'clock in the morning a pair of handcuffs were slipped upon Louthers and preparations made for an attack on Halm. As Cox was taking his Winchester from a closet, Jess, the younger Cochran, said to Alex, his father, "Let's take him (Louthers) away from them." In an instant a gun cracked and Cox reeled back against the wall with a shot through part of the neck and shoulder. A dozen or more shots were fired on both sides, another of which took effect in the officer's thigh. Cox and his partner were compelled to retire, minus even their prisoner with the hand

Bob Dalton age 21 with an unidentified woman. Courtesy of Western History Collection, University of Oklahoma.

cuffs, for he took occasion to run away during the fight. After riding a mile Cox became weak and put up at a house to wait on

a hack and a doctor to be brought from town. His wounds were not serious and a month will probably see him able for duty again. The fight occurred in the lower story of the house and the dance was in progress in the upper. Saturday evening the younger Cochran went to town after cartridges and on his way back was hailed by Dalton, another officer. Refusing to halt the other opened fire killing the horse and shooting the boy through the leg.
THE INDIAN CHIEFTAIN [Vinita] 17 April 1890

EMMETT DALTON

Emmett was born 3 May 1871 and according to Littleton, Emmett was named for an Irish orator, Robert Emmett. This name has been cited as evidence of Irish ancestry by several authors, but so far no proof of any Irish ancestry has been located for this Dalton family. (Robert Emmett was an Irish rebel who led an attempted insurrection against the British. He was convicted of treason and hanged. His namesake, Emmett Dalton, narrowly escaped the same fate at the hands of irate citizens of Coffeyville.)

Emmett was badly injured at the Coffeyville Raid and was sentenced to life imprisonment. He was pardoned after serving almost fifteen years in the Kansas State Prison. On 1 Sept. 1908, he married Julia Johnson Gilstrap Lewis of Bartlesville, OK. The story of Emmett and Julia will be the subject of a later chapter.

LEONA RANDOLPH DALTON

Leona was born 17 July 1875. She never married and cared for her mother, her nephew, and other members of her family for much of her life. She worked as a seamstress and dressmaker for many years. She did very fine work and a beautiful wedding dress she made is on display at the Chisholm Trail Museum in Kingfisher, OK. Leona was born with a cleft palate and had a serious speech impediment as a result. Leona was bedfast for some time before her death and she died in the Hukills Rest Home in Kingfisher of acute bronchial pneumonia. Due to some sort of mixup, both Leona's death certificate and her obituary give the name of her father as William Dalton. This information is incorrect as there is no doubt whatsoever that she was the daughter of Lewis and Adeline Dalton. Leona was very

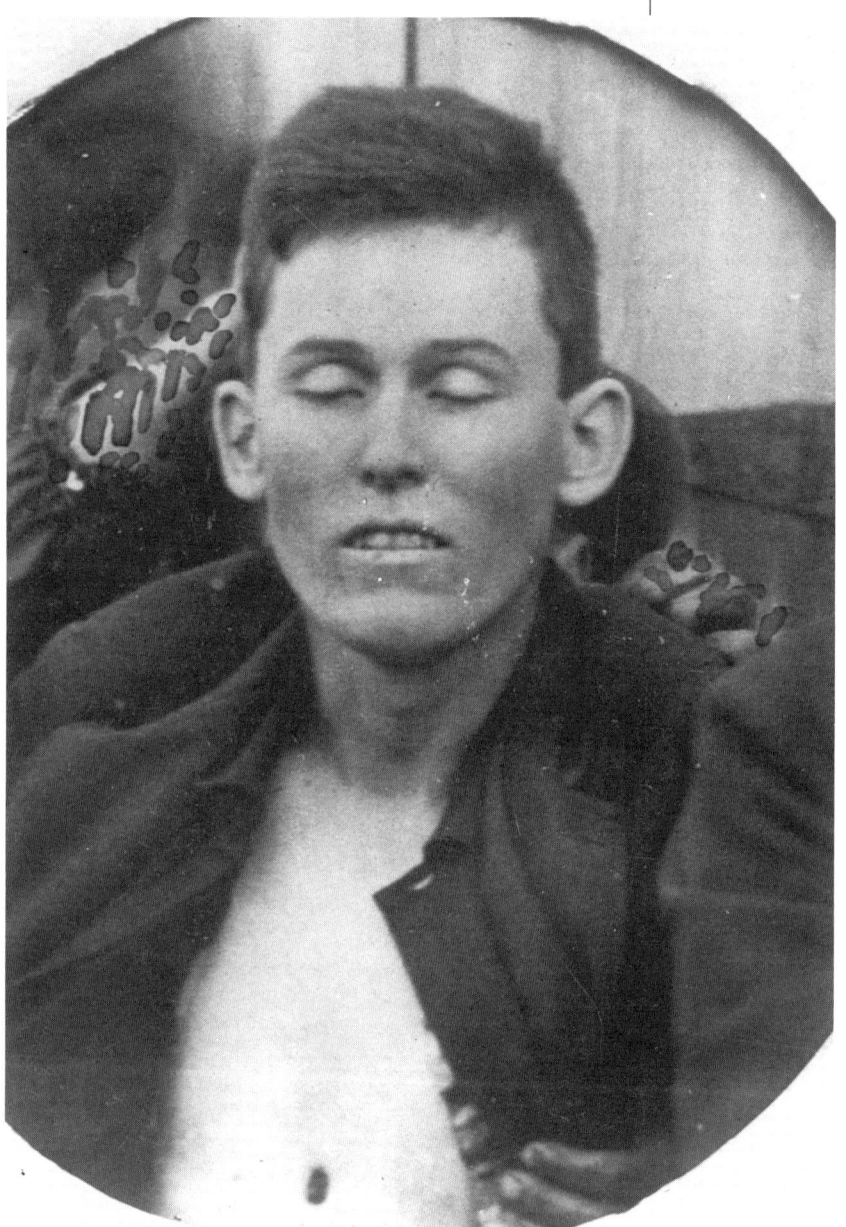

Bob Dalton in death. Courtesy of The Kansas State Historical Society.

respected and a much loved member of her community. She was a reticent woman and would not discuss what she referred to as "The Dalton Tragedy" with anyone. She is still spoken of with great affection and has been described as a truly Christian woman.

"Leona remained single and was the mainstay of the family in the later years. She stayed on the farm with her mother until Adaline gave up the school quarter in 1909. Here she was the cook and housekeeper and assisted with the farm chores. In addition, she did dressmaking for the women of the area. She was an expert seamstress and had all the work she could do. She was loved and respected by the entire community. ... [in 1909 Leona moved to Kingfisher] Here she hung out her dressmaker's shingle.

In those days, stores sold mostly piece goods, and women stitched clothing from them as best they could. About the only women's ready-to-wear garments sold in addition to the unmentionables were the mother-hubbards. A mother-hubbard was an outer garment that resembled a shift or a sheath, except it was more voluminous. In fact, it was described as a dress that covered everything and touched nothing. Hence, a woman skilled with needle and shears was in demand. Sometimes a dressmaker lived with a family till she had made wardrobes for the mother and daughters. This sometimes took a month or six weeks. Mostly, women brought bundles of cloth to a dressmaker and came every day or two for fittings. At this time, Nelle Forney, a competent dressmaker who later became Mrs. Lee Boecher, joined forces with Leona at her sixth street address. The partnership lasted a year and the two ladies were friends thereafter.

Roy Clute lived at Leona's while he attended high school. Occasionally on Friday evenings he accompanied the George Foster children to their home near the Gould bridge. He would then wade the river and walk to his grandmother's cabin. On Sunday evening, he would return with the Fosters to Kingfisher. About once a month, Adaline, now in her late 70's, would drive the mules and wagon to Kingfisher, a distance of 18 or 20 miles. She would have dinner with Leona while the mules munched hay at the wagon in the street. After doing her shopping, she would make the long trip home. Following each trip, Leona received bills from the grocery, drygoods and feed stores. ...

In 1919, Adaline—then 83—bought a small house at the corner of Fifth and Miles in Kingfisher, to which she and Ben moved. The next year, she deeded the house and the farm to Leona, who cared for her till her death in 1925. In the early 30's Ben, who had become senile, was committed to the hospital at Fort Supply. Now it seemed that Leona who had always been responsible for one or more members of the family, would be free. But, her freedom did not last long. The sister, Eva May Whipple—in poor health—came to live with her till her death in 1939. Emmett had died July 13, 1937. Now there were no Daltons left except Leona, and Nannie's son, Roy

Leona Dalton. Courtesy of Bill Phillips.

Clute. Roy loved and respected Aunt Leona, who had cared for him during his childhood.

With the passing of the years, Leona's little house on Fifth street, which had never been modern, became quite dilapidated. In 1947 she gave Roy Clute title to the property. He immediately razed the house and replaced it with a modern cottage. Here Leona lived till she entered the Hukills Nursing Home in 1958. During these remaining years, her friends visited her frequently and celebrated her birthdays. Occasionally she attended services at the First Christian church, of which she had been a member since 1902. She died April 18, 1946, and was buried in the family plot in the Kingfisher cemetery. Here she rests beside her mother, Adaline; her sisters, Nannie and Eva May, and her brothers, Ben and Simon."

Lee Boecher, "The Daltons I Knew", SHORTGRASS COUNTRY

(Retyped Newspaper Article)
LEONA DALTON DIES

FUNERAL SCHEDULED TUESDAY MORNING

Miss Leona Randolph Dalton, 88, a local resident since 1890, died Saturday in the Hukills Rest home, where she had been a resident for several years. Funeral will be held at 10 a. m. Tuesday in the First Christian church, of which she was a member. William Imhoff will officiate. Interment will be made in the Kingfisher cemetery. Langley-Mason Funeral Home is in charge of arrangements.

Miss Dalton was born July 17, 1875 in Kansas, a daughter of Mr. and Mrs. William Dalton. She came here with her parents in 1890, and they resided on a farm six miles northeast of Kingfisher.

She was a dressmaker during her early years. Survivors include two nephews, Roy M. Clute of Estes Park, Colo., and Charles Dalton of Lodi, Calif.

**KINGFISHER FREE PRESS
20 April 1964**

NANCY "NANNIE" DALTON CLUTE

Nannie was born in March 1876 according to her obituary and her tombstone. She died in Kingfisher two days after Christmas, 1901 of lockjaw that resulted from a smallpox vaccination. There was an epidemic of the disease in the area at that time. Nannie was first buried in the corner of the garden at the Dalton farm. Her body remained here until Adaline disposed of her school land lease in 1909, then Nannie's body was moved to a lot in the Kingfisher cemetery. The inscription on her tombstone was written by her mother and it reads: "Beautiful spirit freed from all pain/ours the loss, thine the eternal gain." There is another inscription on the side of the tombstone too. This one says simply: "John Phillips Guthrie OT". It is believed that Nancy's nephew John Phillips helped pay for her tombstone and had his name placed there when the stone was erected.

Wedding dress made by Leona Dalton now on display at the Chisholm Trail Museum at Kingfisher, OK. Photo by Nancy B. Samuelson.

Nancy married Charles M. Clute in Kingfisher. They had one son, Roy, who was about five years old when his mother died. Roy was raised by Leona and he died 12 April 1978 in Tulsa, OK. Roy and his wife operated motels for a number of years. Roy had one daughter.

Note: The birthdate of either Leona or Nancy must be wrong. It is very unlikely they were born only eight months apart. Since other information on Leona's

The Dalton Gang Family

CERTIFICATE OF DEATH
STATE OF OKLAHOMA - DEPARTMENT OF HEALTH
008378

- Place of Death County: Kingfisher
- City, Town, or Location: Kingfisher
- Name of Hospital or Institution: Hukills Rest Home
- Usual Residence: Oklahoma, Kingfisher, Kingfisher
- Street Address: 123 East Admire
- Name of Deceased: Leona Randolph Dalton
- Date of Death: April 18, 1964
- Sex: Female
- Color or Race: White
- Never Married
- Date of Birth: July 17, 1875
- Age: 88
- Usual Occupation: Dressmaker
- Birthplace: Kansas
- Citizen of: USA
- Father's Name: William Dalton
- Mother's Maiden Name: Adeline L. Younger
- Was Deceased Ever in U.S. Armed Forces: No
- Informant: Roy M. Clute, Estes Park, Colorado
- Cause of Death: Bronchial pneumonia, acute — 12 hrs.
- Due to: Undetermined etiology
- Due to: Aged, bedfast female
- I attended the deceased from 1959 to 4/18/64
- Kingfisher, Oklahoma
- Burial: Rural, April 21, 64, Kingfisher Cemetery, Kingfisher, Oklahoma

State Department of Health
State of Oklahoma
ROGER C. PIRRONG
STATE REGISTRAR OF VITAL STATISTICS
OKLAHOMA CITY, OKLAHOMA 73152

CERTIFIED COPY MUST HAVE EMBOSSED SEAL

death certificate is incorrect it is possible that the date of birth is also incorrect.

(Retyped Newspaper Article)
MARRIED—CLUTE-DALTON

Married, at the residence of Rev. J. C. Calnon, Miss Nannie Dalton and Mr. Chas. M. Clute, on Wednesday, the 22nd inst. Miss Nannie is one of Fairview District's most popular young ladies, and will be greatly missed in its society. Mr. Clute, before coming here two years ago, was a resident of Chicago, where he was engaged in the hardware business for the past ten years.

After the ceremony, Mr. and Mrs. Clute returned to the home of the bride's mother, four miles north of town, where they partook of a bountiful dinner, and then returned to their home six miles northwest of town.

On Friday evening quite a number of their friends of Fairview and their neighbors, gathered in to serenade them, when a delightful time was had. All left wishing them a long life of happiness and joy.

[Note: Fairview was the name of the school district. Leona, Nannie and Simon all attended the Fairview rural school.]
THE KINGFISHER FREE PRESS 30 Jan. 1896

(Retyped Newspaper Article)
OBITUARY

MRS. NANNIE DALTON CLUTE

Miss Nannie Dalton was born near Belton,

a small town in Cass county, Missouri, March 21, 1876, and died at her home in Kingfisher, Oklahoma, December 27, 1901, aged 25 years, 9 months, and 16 days. A few years ago last spring her widowed mother brought her family Emmett Dalton, now in Kansas, being a son, into this new country and settled on the claim now occupied by them five miles north east of this city. On this farmstead, made sacred by many memories sweet and bitter. Nannie made her home, the joy, the comfort, the light of her loving mother's life. Five years ago Charles M. Clute won her love and they were joined together in one until death did them part. Four years ago this winter while attending special services in the Methodist church in this city, conducted by the pastor, Rev. J. W. Sherwood, and Evangelist B. E. Shawhan, she kneeled at the alter by her husband's side and gave her heart to God. She was a lovely christian woman. To know her was to love her. But she has been called to her long home and the mourners go about the streets and we fondly believe that her soul has gone to live forever with God. The funeral was held in the first M. E. church, her pastor, Rev. W. E. Woodward, officiating and the interment was made on her mother's farm near the city.
THE KINGFISHER FREE PRESS 2 Jan. 1902

SIMON NOEL "SAM" DALTON & HANNAH ADELINE DALTON

The twins were born 6 July 1879, and the girl died at or shortly after birth. A number of writers have claimed Simon was a sickly youngster and died at age fourteen. This is not true.

Simon was a witness to the killing of a Mert Rickey in Kingfisher in the spring of 1899 and was arrested during the investigation of this case. No records have been found of the final outcome of the case aginst Simon (the records were probably destroyed in the fire that burned the Kingfisher courthouse in Aug. 1900). Simon however, enlisted in the U. S. Army 14 Nov. 1899 and he served in the Philippines in the hospital corps for most of his enlistment. He was discharged in California 15 Dec. 1902 and returned to Oklahoma soon after.

Simon was described as handsome and more than six feet tall, but his military record says he was 5 feet 7-1/2 inches with blue eyes, light brown hair, and a ruddy complexion. Simon acquired a reputation as a never-do-well who was not overly fond of work. He was working in the oilfields as a construction worker when he applied for a disability pension from the Army in Sept. 1925. His application was rejected because he had only minor medical problems. He needed to wear glasses to read, had some teeth that needed to be pulled and suffered from hemorrhoids.

Simon married Minnie (Mamie) McDaniel on 30 July 1910, at Nowata, OK. She must have died before he did as his death certificate lists him as a widower. No record of her death has been located. It is known that Minnie had a son before she married Simon but no further information has been found about the child, other than his name, Jean [Gene?] F. According to Cherokee nation records for the Cooweescoowee district the McDaniel family were part Indian. Additionally, testimony given by Minnie's mother, Mary, before the Commission to the Five Civilized Tribes, 29 Jan. 1903, Mary McDaniel was of mixed racial heritage. She was part Negro as well as Indian.

Simon was badly injured when the car he was driving was hit by a train in June 1928. He died in the University Hospital, Oklahoma City, on 13 Sept. 1928, from pneumonia and from fractures and internal injuries suffered in the accident in June.

"Simon, the youngest in the family, seemingly had no outlaw tendencies, but grew up to be irresponsible. He had handsome features, was more than six feet tall and would have made a great football player. Having no stomach for chopping cotton or other farm work, he spent his time in the saloons and pool halls of Kingfisher, and in 1899 was arrested for a boyish prank that resulted in a murder. On being released on bond, furnished by his mother, he joined the army and was sent to the Philippines. ...
After serving his army enlistment, Simon came home. Adaline, hoping to encourage him to take over the farming, bought for him a team of mules, harness and wagon and a beautiful, blazed-faced, sorrel saddle mare, together with a new saddle and bridle. But Simon still had no stomach for farm work. Cockleburrs choked his corn and crabgrass smothered his cotton, while he spent his time in Kingfisher in the saloons and other resorts. As for the saddle mare, a high-

strung, nervous animal, he beat and abused her till he could no longer control her. He soon gave up trying to ride her and Adaline sold her to a neighbor.

It was during this farming period of his life that Simon, exhibiting his courtly manner, nightly accompanied his mother and sister to the revival conducted by "Preacher" Higgins at the Fairview schoolhouse. Adaline, a stauch Presbyterian, and Leona, a Campbellite, hoped to convert and reform him, but he successfully resisted all entreaties. He then became a drifter. For a time, he was seen in the saloons of Tulsa. Later it was reported he operated an establishment in a tent at Cushing during that city's oil boom. At the time of his mother's death, he was living at Okeene. Two years later, his car collided with a train at a rail crossing. After being hospitalized for a short time, he died and was buried in the family plot at Kingfisher."

Lee Boecher, "The Daltons I Knew", **SHORTGRASS COUNTRY**

(Retyped Newspaper Article)
A NOTORIOUS WOMAN SHOOTS MERT RICKEY

INSTANT DEATH THE RESULT

She Calls Him Out of His Office
and Fires the Fatal Shot
Looks Like a Premeditated Conspiracy

Last Saturday night about ten o'clock, Annie E. Bowery, alias Greenfield, shot and instantly killed Mert P. Rickey. The shooting occurred in the livery stable of R. J. Kester, where Mr. Rickey has been working for the past few months. He with Henry Mott, John McElbraith and W. J. B. Hix, were sitting in the office at the time. Hix had just a moment before come in with his hot tamales, and was preparing to sell some to the three boys, when Mrs. Greenfield knocked at the door and asked for Mert. He stepped out into the stable near where she was standing. She called him a vile name and told him that she was going to kill him, at the same time drawing a revolver. His answer was, "You will, will you?: and started for her, when she fired, killing him instantly. When Henry Mott heard the cursing of the woman, he ran out, but was too late—Mert had fallen to the floor. Mott grappled with the woman, but she struggled so fiercely for the possession of the gun that it took the combined efforts of McElbraith and Mott to secure it. During the struggle, the woman was badly bruised about the right eye.

Now comes the interesting part of the story. When John McElbraith secured the gun, he saw two men standing behind a wagon, who started to run, and fired two shots at them.

Now, W. J. B. Hix, in his rounds, passes the house where this woman lived, and recognized Mrs. Greenfield, Eva Young, Simon Dalton and an unknown person walking up the street toward the stable. He had passed them and was in the office when the woman arrived. Miss Young, in her testimony before the coroner's inquest, says: "When we were near the stable, I turned back, and was at my front gate when the first shot was fired."

The two men ran to the street just north of the barn and ran east, stopping that night at Lyman Parson's, about two miles north of town.

Annie Bowery was arrested and put in jail.

The body of Rickey was taken to the residence of R. J. Kester.

Sunday morning, subpoenas were issued for Henry Mott, John McElbraith, W. J. B. Hix, Maud Miller, Eva Young, Simon Dalton, Arthur Phillips, Bob Porter and a man by the name of Pierce to appear at the coroner's inquest, which was held in the district Court room Sunday morning.

All the witnesses appeared except Dalton and Phillips. Deputy Sheriff Hart went to Dalton's home, north of town, and not finding them, returned home.

By this time, a great crowd of excited people thronged around the jail and demanded that Dalton and Phillips be found and brought to town. Sheriff Kelley deputized three men, and they, with Deputy Sheriff Hart, started on the search. The two boys were finally captured at the home of Mr. Clute, northwest of this city, who, by the way, is a brother-in-law of Simon Dalton. During this time, a complaint was made and a warrant issued for Eva Young, Simon Dalton and Arthur Phillips. When they were brought to town, they were immediately lodged in jail.

Annie Bowery waived preliminary examination Monday morning.

At the perliminary examination, Simon Dalton and Eva Young were bound over. Arthur Phillips preliminary is set for tomarrow.
KINGFISHER FREE PRESS 23 Mar. 1899

(Retyped Newspaper Article)
WOMAN SHOOTS HER LOVER

Guthrie, Okla, March 20—Last night a woman by the name of Greenfield, whose sobriquet is "Battle-ax" shot and killed her lover at Kingfisher. The man killed is Mert Rickey, and he is well known in Oklahoma, Kansas and Missouri among sporting men. He was the driver of the fleet-footed 2-year-old pacer, Kittie Kesler.
EL RENO NEWS 24 Mar. 1899

(Retyped Newspaper Article)

Simon Dalton, charged with being an accomplice of Mrs. Greenfield in the killing of Mert Rickey, at Kingfisher, is a brother of the notorious outlaws of that name. The mother lives a mile or two north of Kingfisher. Young Dalton is about 20 years old, and seems to have had an itiching to follow in the footsteps of his brothers. He has been an intimate friend of Arthur Phillips, who is also wanted in the Rickey case. Thomas Phillips, father of Arthur, was chief office deputy under United States marshal Pat Nagle. The two boys started to run away once to join the Daltons, but were overtaken and made to return home. Simon Dalton applied to U. S. Marshal Harry Thompson about a year ago for a commission as deputy marshal. Mrs. Dalton wrote a pathetic letter to Mr. Thompson, asking him not to encourage her son, as she did not wish to see him engaged in a business that would strengthen his inclinations toward a reckless life.
EL RENO BELL 7 Apr. 1899

(Retyped Newspaper Article)
COURT PROCEEDINGS

The following cases were disposed of: ...
Territory vs. Eva Young, indictment, murder. Plead not guilty. Case continued. Bonds fixed at $500. Released upon her own recognance. F. P. Whistler attorney for defendant.

Territory vs. Simon Dalton, indictment, murder. Pleads not guilty, Case continued. Bond fixed at $500, with mother and sister as surities. John T. Bradley attorney for defendant.
Newspaper not given probably KINGFISHER FREE PRESS 4 May 1899

(Retyped Newspaper Article)
DISTRICT COURT NOTES

The cases of Simon Dalton and Eva Young, for complicity in the murder of Mert Rickey, continued for the term.
Newspaper not given probably KINGFISHER FREE PRESS 2 Nov. 1899

(Retyped Newspaper Article)
THE ANNA BOWERS CASE

Anna Bowers, charged with the murder of Mert Rickey, was tried in the district court, on change of venue to Canadian county, at El Reno last week, Judge Irwin presiding. The case has attracted widespread attention, and much interest was felt in the result. The defense was ably conducted by Hon. J. C. Robberts, and the prosecution by County Attorney Noffsinger. No criticism attaches to the attorneys on either side. The testimony developed important facts in the woman's favor, that did not accord with the general understanding prior to the trial. The jury brought in a verdict of manslaughter in the first degree. The minimum punishment for this crime is four years in the penitentiary, that being the sentence of the court. It is only fair to assume that Judge Irwin's sentence was modified by the law and evidence. Of course, this seemingly light sentence is a disappointment to the people of this community, but it must be remembered

that the testimony of witnesses under oath, and irresponsible street gossip, very seldom correspond, and this case seems to have been no exception to the rule. In fact, the FREE PRESS has been greatly surprised, and its views materially modified by a statement of what the testimony was.
KINGFISHER FREE PRESS 28 Dec. 1899

(Retyped Newspaper Article)
PASSING ON AN "89er

Simon Nolan Dalton was born July 6, 1879, at Belton, MO. and died at University Hospital, Oklahoma City, September 13, 1928, at the age of 49 years, 2 months, 7 days, after an illness of over four months—as the result of an automobile accident at Davenport, Okla., June 1st. Mr. Dalton was in the employ of an oil company. He was going to work in a borrowed car, and started across the Santa Fe tracks, colliding with a freight train. His right leg was broken two inches below the hip and one break in the ankle, besides internal injuries.

Mr. Dalton was the youngest of thirteen children, and is survived by three brothers, Emmett, Lit and Ben living in California; two sisters, Mrs. E. D. Whipple of Siloam Springs, Ark., and Miss Leona Dalton of Oklahoma City.

Only Miss Leona Dalton and Mr. and Mrs. Roy Clute of Oklahoma City were able to attend the funeral.

Simon was reared in Kingfisher county, and lived here until he was 25 years of age. At the outbreak of the Spanish-American war he enlisted and served until the close of the war.

Funeral services were held at the Bracken Funeral Home, Friday afternoon, at 3:30, by Rev. Chas. Schwab, pastor of the Christian church. Pall bearers were chosen from among those who knew him most intimately here during his early life and were: C. P. Wickmiller, Charles Brown, John Phillips, Clyde Smith, Hal Mead and Ed Ingram.

Interment in Kingfisher cemetery by the side of his mother, who preceded him to the life beyond about three years ago.
KINGFISHER FREE PRESS 20 SEPT. 1928

Hospital records for Simon "Sam" Dalton

Death certificate of Simon "Sam" Dalton

Note: All descriptions of the Daltons, except where otherwise noted; were compiled from information in Emmet's books and from Latta's interviews with Littleton.

IV. When The Dalton Brothers Wore Badges

In time the name Dalton became almost a generic term for outlaws in the Oklahoma and Indian Territories. Why this is so is still somewhat of a mystery as the criminal career of the Daltons was so brief. Less well known is the fact that three of the outlaw Daltons as well as the older brother, Frank, all served as U. S. deputy marshals, or in Emmett's case, at least as a posseman.

In 1872 William Story was appointed as Federal Judge at Fort Smith, Arkansas. He was corrupt and apathetic toward law enforcement. In 1874 Story resigned in the face of impeachment proceedings and in 1875 Isaac Charles Parker was appointed judge of the Fort Smith Court. Parker's court was the only law in the area until 1883 when part of the Indian Territory was assigned to the U. S. District of Kansas. Other courts were later established as well, but for a long time Parker's court was the law in the area and Parker became known far and wide as "The Hanging Judge".

Frank Dalton was the first of the brothers to "ride for Parker". The job of a deputy marshal at that time was tough anywhere but in the Indian Territory it was brutal. The area had become a refuge for fugitives from justice, bushwackers, guerrillas, and every other undesirable one could imagine. There were few laws in this territory to regulate things and what laws did exist were often confusing. The federal court had jurisdiction over whites and the various tribes had jurisdiction over the Indians. When disputes involved both whites and Indians the situation became completely muddled.

There were as many as 200 deputy marshals at a time who rode for Parker. They covered a territory of 74 thousand square miles, and sixty-five of these deputies were killed in the line of duty and many others were wounded. Frank Dalton died in the line of duty and Grat Dalton was wounded while assigned to the Fort Smith territory. According to the 21 March 1889 INDIAN CHIEFTAIN Grat's arm was shattered by a bullet on 15 March at the Berryhill house about ten miles northwest of Tulsa. Deputy W. A. Moody, also in the posse, was killed at the same time. A young Indian, Wm. Bruner, shot both Moody and Grat when the posse attempted to arrest Jeff Berryhill.

Frank was probably the financial mainstay of the large Dalton family when he took the job as a deputy. Father Lewis was too busy following his ponies around all of the racing circuits to bother with the mundane task of providing a living for his family. By the time Frank became a deputy, four of the brothers, including Bill, had gone to California and were living and working there.

After Frank's death Grat became a deputy for the Western Arkansas District and Bob too served as a deputy in this district. Bob and Grat held commissions in at least one other district as well. Emmett was probably never a deputy but he did serve as a posseman or as a guard along with his brothers. Records for the deputies of this period and their service are few and far between. Some of the best documentation about the service of Grat, Bob, and Emmett was the result of the furor raised by Senator Vest after the Coffeyville raid. Vest somehow got the idea that Bill Dalton had been appointed as a deputy after his brothers were killed and wounded at Coffeyville. The senator evidently made a rather impassioned speech about the selection of deputy marshals on the floor of the Senate. His speech, in turn, caused a flurry of letters, telegrams, and newspaper articles on the subject of Daltons as deputies. The correspondence and telegrams of the marshals involved are all located in the National Archives in Washington D. C. Not all of what the marshals had to say agrees with other records concerning the Daltons as lawmen. It is obvious that all of the marshals were rather eager to wash their hands of Daltons at this point in time.

Marshal Jacob Yoes of the Western District of Arkansas, Marshals Dickerson at Paris, Texas; Grimes at Guthrie, I.T.; Needles at Muskogee, I.T.; and Walker of Kansas all wired or wrote to the Attorney General to make it clear that Bill Dalton was never a deputy marshal. Their communications did give some details about the service of the other Daltons. Yoes said that Grat and Robert were both deputies under his predecessor, Mr. Carroll. He further said the Daltons were all considered good and fearless officers but that he had only appointed Grat as Robert and Emmett seemed to him too young for deputy work. Robert and Emmett had been employed as possemen by deputy Floyd Wilson to assist him in arresting criminals that had escaped from prison. Yoes further reported that he had discharged Grat for being drunk and conducting himself badly at Tulsa, but provided no details of Grat's behavior. Yoes also reported that Robert, Emmett, and Grat had been charged with horse stealing in September 1890 and that Grat was arrested by citizens at Claremore but discharged after the preliminary examination. There had been no evidence connecting Grat with the theft, though the evidence was conclusive as to Robert and Emmett. (This last statement does not agree with the Fort Smith court records.)

R. L. Walker of Kansas said that Bob and Emmett were deputies under Col. Jones (Walker's predecessor) and that he retained them for a few months, but removed them in the fall of 1889.

Records, primarily in the Kansas City branch of the National Archives, show the following: (1) Grat and Bob were sworn in as deputies in the District of Kansas on 10 January 1889. (2) In 1889 Bob was employed as a detective by the Osage Indian Agency. He was shown on several records for that Agency from April through September of 1889 (records past that date have not been found). (3) Several documents, subpoenas, warrants, etc., for the Kansas District show Robert Dalton as a deputy in that district throughout the months of March through September 1889. Bob was serving under two different U. S. Marshals during this time, W. C. Jones and R. L. Walker. (4) One document, dated in August 1889 has been found for Grat Dalton as a deputy in the

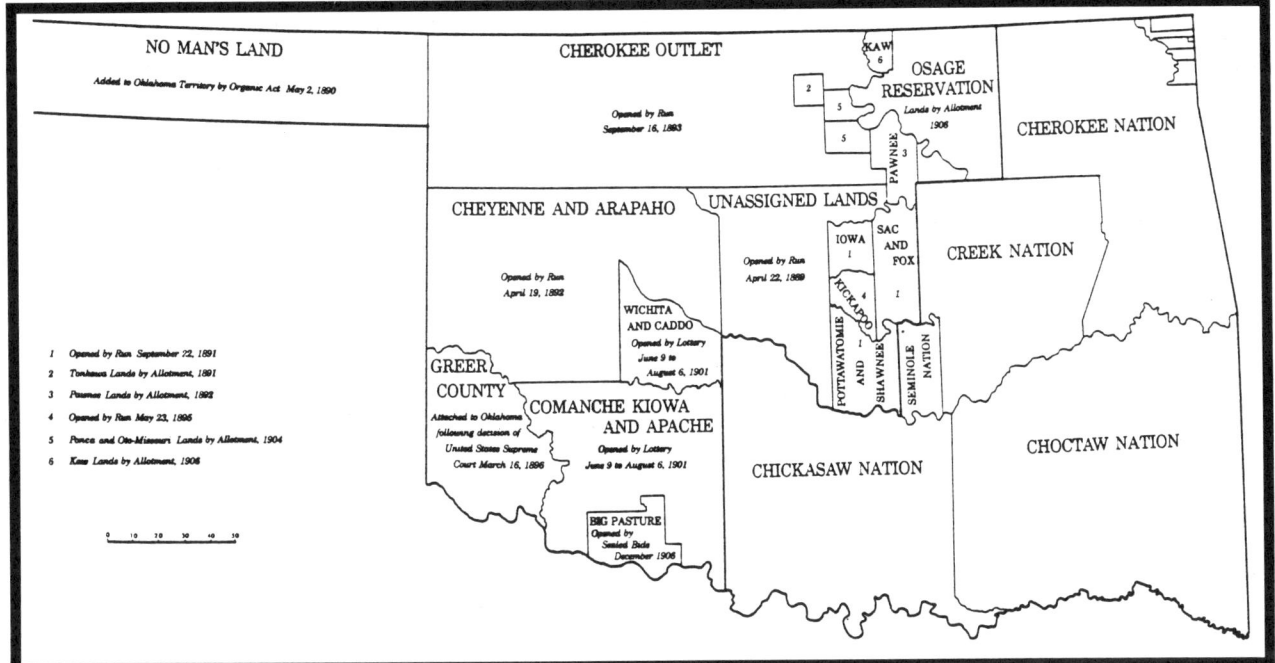

The Oklahoma and Indian Territories where the Daltons served as U.S. Deputy Marshals. Source: Historical Atlas of Oklahoma.

District of Kansas. This was a warrant of arrest served by Grat on John Poor for stealing a gun. (5) Emmett Dalton's name is found on two documents dated June 1889 for the District of Kansas. One is a receipt of pay for guarding prisoners. The other a complaint sworn by Emmett against two men for introducing and selling whiskey in the I. T. (6) On 16 June 1890 a J. C. Johnston made out a power of attorney to George Purcell for Purcell to "ask, demand and receive from the United States the sum of twenty dollars that Johnson was owed for guarding prisoners for deputy marshals Robert Dalton and Henry Roberts of the District of Kansas".

There are all kinds of stories about what the Daltons did while they were lawmen. Several of these stories can be proved to be outright fiction and others are very questionable. One such tale is the "William Tell" story. Glenn Shirley repeats this one in his book WEST OF

HELL'S FRINGE and credits Grat with shooting an apple off the head of a Negro boy in Tulsa. According to Shirley this is why Yoes dismissed Grat for conduct unbecoming an officer and further says the Muskogee court canceled Grat's commission over the incident too. The INDIAN PIONEER HISTORY series at the Oklahoma Historical Society contains another version of the story that says Bob is the one who played "William Tell" on the main street in Tulsa in 1883. In 1883 Bob Dalton was only fourteen years old and was a very short time resident in the I. T. (the

Documents from the Kansas City Branch of the National Archives for some of the service of Grat, Bob, and Emmett Dalton in the District of Kansas.

Daltons moved there in 1882 or 1883). Still an earlier version of the "William Tell" story has cousin John Younger shooting the pipe from the mouth of a half-wit named Jim Russell in Dallas, Texas. This "William Tell" story seems to be another standard tale much like the "outlaw saves the widow's farm" story. Some version of it has been told about almost every outlaw in history.

Grat was a heavy drinker and may well have been an alcoholic. He certainly had a reputation as a brawler too. He may well have gotten into trouble because he used his fists too often. However, if Grat was fired it seems more likely that it was because of the following incident reported in the 13 March 1890 INDIAN CHIEFTAIN: "Delondale was belabored over the head with a six shooter a few days ago by Deputy Gratz [sic] Dalton, almost to insensibility." This article also leads to the conclusion that Grat was still a deputy as late as March 1890.

No records of the firing of any of the Daltons have been located. There have been no records located for the Daltons serving as deputies in the Muskogee court district either.

The stories of how Bob Dalton shot Charley Montgomery in the back and how he shot the young and completely innocent son of Alex Cochran at Claremore were addressed in an earlier chapter of this book.

In April 1889 the Oklahoma Territory was opened to white settlers and on the 22nd of that month thousands of settlers rushed into the area. Liquor traffic had always been and continued to be one of the major problems in the area. There are numerous stories about the Daltons connected with liquor. One of the most often repeated tales is that Grat, Bob, and Emmett took to hiding bottles of whiskey in settlers' wagons. Later they reportedly would approach the settler, search the wagon and demand payment of a fine on the spot. This sort of tale about deputy marshals in the Territory was common. According to Shirley's HECK THOMAS: FRONTIER MARSHAL, Heck Thomas reported that such stories were stock tales in the Territory but that he never knew of a single case where a deputy actually did this. According to Heck there was simply no need for an officer to go to such expense and trouble when plenty of whiskey could be located without such effort.

The records in the Kansas City Branch of the National Archives do reveal that Bob and Emmett Dalton were charged with "Introducing" while they were still lawmen or shortly after they had left their law jobs. This is the first documentation of any misconduct on the part of the Daltons. The records that survive about this incident leave some room for doubt about their guilt. In fact, the case against Emmett was dropped but a true bill was found against Bob and he was released on bail. Bob did not show up later for trial and both he and his bondsmen were sued by the United States for the $1000 in bail and for the expenses of the trial. There have been no records found concerning the outcome of this suit.

One Henry Roberts, another deputy, filed a complaint against Robert and Emmett Dalton, Harry Callahan, and Jasper Riddle for Introducing intoxicating liquor into the Osage Nation on 25 December 1889. A warrant for the arrest of the four men was issued. A return on the warrant was filed by L. Shadley, deputy on 22 March 1890; he had arrested Bob and Emmett at Pawhaska on the 21st of March. (Shadley was later killed in the gun battle at Ingalls in September 1893. There are claims that he was killed by Bill Dalton.) A hearing was held on 26 March 1890 and seven Indians from the Osage Agency were called as witnesses. Charges were dropped against Emmett but Robert Dalton was held to appear at the next regular term of the district court at Wichita, 1 September 1890.

There are two sets of statements by witnesses and neither are dated. It appears that these were given at two different times. The writing is different so they were not recorded by the same individual. The evidence given in both sets of statements is basically the same. Several Indians were camped near the home of Chu-sho-wah-hah on Christmas Day. Late in the afternoon a wagon came into the area with two men, Riddle and Callahan, in it. The men in the wagon were dispensing whiskey to the Indians. Bob Dalton was on horseback and was riding around the wagon and around through the camp. Emmett Dalton was also in the area, but some distance away from the wagon. Here is a brief summary of statements by the witnesses: Chu-sho-wah-hah said he did not buy whisky [sic] or see anyone else buy whisky, but saw another Indian carry a jug away from the wagon. He thought Bob Dalton was under the influence of liquor. Shap-pe-nah-she said he never saw Bob get off his horse but that he [Bob] had a can with whisky in it and was giving it out to Indians. He thought Dalton was a marshal and had captured a load of whisky and was giving it away. Ho-ne-a-go said he did not know either of the Daltons and did not buy whisky of either of them. He said he bought one jug and a tea cup full of whisky from a man in the wagon. Big Road said he knew the Daltons and that Bob Dalton rode around the camp. Emmett Dalton was not there. Hul-ah-shu-tse said he knew both Bob and Emmett Dalton. Bob came up to where the wagon was with the whisky but Emmett stayed out on the road. He did not see either Dalton have any whisky. In his second statement he said Jasper Riddle was in the wagon with a young man who's name he did not know. He bought whisky from the men in the wagon. He did not see Dalton handle whisky or receive money. Pah-hah-ne-gah-hle said he did not buy any whisky. Bob came around the wagon while Emmett stayed out in the road. In his second statement he said he did not buy liquor of Dalton but that Harry Callahan and Jasper Riddle gave him liquor.

There is another list of witnesses that was filed 5 September 1890 that include the above witnesses plus three others, one Indian and apparently two white men. There are no statements by the additional three men. It appears that these witnesses were to testify during the trial but since Bob Dalton did not appear there was no trial. Other documents show that Robert Dalton and Jasper Riddle were charged with selling whiskey to Ho-ne-a-go and Hul-ah-shu-tse but these are shown as the second and third counts against Dalton and Riddle. There is no first count in the records. There is no indication that Riddle was ever arrested or tried and no indication as to what happened with the initial charge against Callahan. Except for the mention of his name by witnesses there is no further record of Callahan in this entire affair. It appears that only the case against Bob Dalton was pursued.

It is difficult to draw any definite conclusions about Bob Dalton's guilt from the documents that still exist. Other documents may be missing that would shed more light on the matter. However, there was no testimony by any witness that Bob Dalton actually sold liquor to anyone. It is entirely possible that Bob had indulged in the "fire water" himself to the point he was in no condition to arrest anyone else for selling the booze that day. It is also possible, that since it was Christmas Day, Dalton may have believed that the law should also take a holiday. He may have thought that the presence of a deputy marshal in the area would insure that the party did not get out of hand. As all remained peaceable, when the wagon with the whiskey left, Bob left the area too. What is obvious is that Bob Dalton would still have been wanted on the Introducing charge and for failing to appear for trial when trouble again arose for the Daltons in September 1890.

There are all kinds of stories about the Daltons stealing horses, but most of these stories appear to have no basis in fact. Right after the Coffeyville raid, several newspapers printed highly inaccurate accounts of both the raid and of the Dalton's previous criminal acts. On 6 October 1892, THE NEW YORK TIMES claimed that Bob Dalton had long been known as a cattle thief and had stolen cattle in the Cherokee Strip and sold the cattle in Colorado. Grat supposedly assisted in these activities until the cattlemen organized and drove them from the Strip. Bob then had supposedly been selected for his job as a deputy marshal because of his peculiar fitness to deal with desperate characters.

"Eye Witness" made a sizable contribution to the literature on the Daltons as horse thieves too. He had the Daltons running a large and systematic ring of horse thieves with a reputation for audacity that was unequaled in the Territory. One officer had even been killed during an attempted raid on the lair of the Dalton robber band according to "Eye Witness".

Numerous other writers have borrowed from "Eye Witness" or fabricated other stories of the Dalton's horse stealing activities. A lot of writers got their material from the 8 May 1891 issue of the FORT SMITH ELEVATOR.

(Retyped Newspaper Article)
THE DALTON BROTHERS
$3600 Reward for Them in
Tulare Co., California

A Brief Review of Their Exploits
Since June, 1890

Few criminals ever turned out in the Indian Territory that have made such a record of desperate deeds as have Bob and Emmett Dalton during the past ten months, and none have been more successful in eluding arrest. Up to the 20th of June last these boys were either acting as deputy marshals or posse, and were instrumental in bringing to justice some of the most noted criminals in the Creek and Cherokee Nations.

Emmett was with Deputy Floyd Wilson when they captured Carroll Collier and Bud Maxfield, both escaped convicts who are now in the Arkansas penitentiary, Collier for thirty years and Maxfield for thirteen. Prior to working for this court Bob had been a deputy marshal for the Wichita, Kansas court, and also held a lucrative position in the Osage Nation as chief of police there. He lost this place and got into trouble by taking whiskey into that country.

They made their last trip for this court with deputy Wilson, and were paid off on or about June 20th, 1890. They left here and went to Claramore, [sic] where they remained until after the 4th of July, when they visited the Osage country and stole sixteen or seventeen head of ponies and a pair of fine mules. This stock they brought to Wagoner and one, or both of the boys, came down here and tried to sell the stock to local buyers in this city, proposing to deliver it at Wagoner or opposite this city in the Cherokee Nation. They failed to make any trade, and then started to Kansas, trading the mules to Emmett Vann, in the Cherokee Nation, and disposing of the ponies in Kansas.

They next showed up in the neighborhood of Claramore, [sic] and boldly rounded up and drove away some twenty-five or thirty head of horses belonging to Frank Musgrove, Bob Rogers and other citizens. This stock, or most of it, they sold at Columbus, Kansas, to a horse trader named Scott, referring him to some of the best men in the Territory as to their standing. He gave them a check for six or seven hundred dollars which they had cashed, endorsing it with their proper names. Scott took the stock to a pasture near Baxter Springs, where the owners afterward found it. In the meantime the boys had gathered up another bunch of horses, and on the very day Rogers and others were at Baxter Springs for the purpose of recovering the stolen property, the Dalton brothers arrived there with them. A posse was hurriedly gotten together for the purpose of capturing them, when they hurriedly saddled fresh horses out of the stolen bunch and lit out with a crowd in hot pursuit. Emmett's horse gave out, and meeting a man driving a team, they took one of his horses, leaving him the jaded steed and Emmett's saddle, bridle and coat which was tied to the saddle. They were being so closely pressed that they had no time to transfer the saddle, etc., from one horse to the other. They made good their escape, however, and their brother Grat was arrested while taking them fresh horses. Grat was lodged in the U. S. jail here, where he remained for several weeks, and in the meantime, Emmett and Bob escaped to California, where they had one or two brothers residing. There being no evidence here implicating Grat in the horse stealing business with his brothers he was released and also went to California. The following circular, dated San Francisco, March 26th, 1891, show what the boys were doing while out there.

$3,600 REWARD

Supplementing circular letter of W. E. Hickey, Special Officer Southern Pacific Company, dated San Francisco, February 26, 1891, wherein is offered a reward of $5000 for the arrest and conviction of all parties concerned in the attempted robbery of train No. 17, on the night of February 6th, 1891.

The grand jury of Tulare county have indicted Bob and Emmett Dalton as principles in said crime, and William Marion Dalton and Gratton (or Grafton) Dalton, as accessories; the two latter named being now in jail at Tulare county awaiting trial.

The Southern Pacific Company hereby withdraw said general reward in regard to Bob and Emmett Dalton, and in lieu thereof offer to pay $1,500 each for the arrest of Bob and Emmett Dalton, upon their delivery to any duly authorized agent or representative of the State of California, or at any jail in any of the States or Territories of the United States.

In addition to the foregoing the State and Wells, Fargo & Co. have each a standing reward of $300 for the arrest and conviction of each such offender.

About 8 o'clock in the evening of February 6th, 1891 two armed men attempted, unsuccessfully, to rob the south bound train, No. 17, near Alila, Tulare county, California. The express messenger offered a gallant resistance, and during the interchange of shots the fireman, G. W. Radcliff, received a wound, from the effects of which he died the following day.

It is now known that the attack was made by two brothers, viz: Bob and Emmett Dalton. On the 2nd of March they left San Luis Obispo county, on horseback, and on the 8th disposed of their horses at Ludlow, a station on the A & P Railway, about 100 miles east of Mojave, and there took passage on the East-bound train, since which time no trace of them has been obtained.

It is now known that after the escape of Bob and Emmett, as related in the above circular, they made their way directly to their old haunts in the Indian country. Their mother lives at Kingfisher, and there they spent one night, after which they secured horses and went to the Cherokee Strip. They have also been seen not more than two weeks ago at Tulsa. The country up there is full of detectives and officers, who are endeavoring to secure the big reward. Parties from there state that Bob Hughes is now with the Daltons, and that they range up in the Turkey Track ranch neighborhood, which is in the Sac and Fox reservation.

No one lives in that section, it being 35 to 50 miles from one habitation to another. Deputy Marshal Heck Thomas is out there, and all manner of rumors reach Tulsa and Red Fork as to the movements of the fugitives and those in pursuit of them. It is thought that news of an encounter will be heard of soon. The Dalton's are desperate, are thoroughly acquainted with the country, and have friends who will keep them posted. Bob Dalton is recognized as one of the best shots with a Winchester rifle in the Indian country, and that they will never surrender without a fight is a foregone conclusion. Bob Hughes is a brother of the late Tom Hughes, who was killed in Van Buren last September by Felix Houck. Bob spent last summer in jail at Fayetteville, where he is now under indictment for robbery, but we understand was released on bond.

FORT SMITH ELEVATOR 8 May 1891

Note: The 15 May 1891 issue of THE ELEVATOR retracted the part of the story about Bob Hughes; Hughes had been tried and sentenced to three years in the penitentiary. He was in jail, not with the Daltons.

Harold Preece in THE DALTON GANG, and Frank Latta in DALTON GANG DAYS as well as several other writers repeat the story from THE ELEVATOR with variations. However, there are official records that survive about the charge of horse stealing and the records of the Fort Smith Court DO NOT agree with THE ELEVATOR article.

The Fort Smith Court records are located in the Fort Worth branch of the National Archives and are summarized as followed:

On 8 September 1890 one C. V. Rogers, of Claremore, I. T. sent a telegram to the prosecuting attorney at Fort Smith. The telegram said, "Grat, Bob and Emmett Dalton are stealing horses here by the drove. Grat is here under arrest have writ sent here to W. B. Killion, U. S. Marshal for the three Daltons." A writ was promptly issued for only Grat Dalton a white man (later race seems to be an issue in some of the testimony) for stealing, in the Cherokee Nation on 10 July 1890 fourteen head of horses valued at $500, from Frank Musgrove and Clem Rogers. The next day Grat was placed in the Fort Smith jail by B. F. Cox, Deputy. On September 15 and 16 subpoenas were issued for ten witnesses, and on the 18 and 19th of the month a hearing was held at Fort Smith. Only six of the ten witnesses testified at the hearing. All six lived in the Cherokee Nation. The witnesses were Clem Rogers, Zul and J. W. Mitchell (husband and wife), Frank Musgrove, T. Burnett, and Rhoda Rogers. Rhoda was not Clem's wife but a neighbor living about ten miles from Clem.

Clem Rogers testified that he did not know the defendant, Grat Dalton. He had lost one horse the later part of July but did not miss the horse until he and Musgrove went to round up and brand colts on August 15. Musgrove then found he had twelve or fifteen horses missing. The two men heard that a lot of stolen horses were at Columbus, Kansas, and went there. They found the horses had been sold to a man named Scott. They went on to Baxter Springs to see Scott. Scott had a couple of their horses. They found some of their other horses in possession of a man named Dillon [? very difficult to read this name] and one colt in possession of a colored man named Cab Rogers who lived eight miles from Clem Rogers.

Just as Rogers, Musgrove, and Scott came into the edge of town at Baxter Springs they met Bob Dalton and two other men with twenty head of horses. Dalton and the other men took off and rode southwest when they saw the Rogers party. (Remember that Bob Dalton was still wanted on an Introducing charge and for failure to appear for trial.) These horses left by Dalton, were put in Scott's barn and they supposedly belonged to four other men from near Claremore. Horses, brands, etc. were described in detail by Rogers. Rogers could not identify Grat Dalton as one of the men with Bob Dalton. There is no mention of a posse or chase after Bob Dalton and his party. There is no mention of a check or any other such evidence either.

Musgrove stated that he did know Grat Dalton, when he saw him. He identified Emmett Dalton as one of the men with Bob but could not say who the other man was. Stated he could not tell if he was a white man or a nigger, but was sure the man was not Grat Dalton. All of Roger's and Musgrove's horses were out on open range when they were stolen or lost.

The Mitchells' testimony was lengthy and was mostly concerned with various visits the Daltons had made to their home and horses in possession of the Daltons when they had been at the Mitchell residence. Both stated that they knew Grat, Bob, and Emmett Dalton. Bob and Grat had been at the Mitchells around 20 July 1890. They were each riding one horse and leading one horse. The Daltons stated that they had just come from burying their father and they had gotten the extra horses from their father's estate. (Lewis Dalton died 16 July 1890.) There was also some discussion about a horse the Daltons were missing. One thought the horse had broken its rope and strayed and the other thought the horse had been stolen. Bob and Emmett had been at the Mitchells between midnight and dawn of July 31 and had had twenty-five to thirty head of horses that they turned out to pasture near the Mitchell place. The Daltons said they were taking these horses to Fort Scott, Kansas, for some gentleman (the Mitchells had heard the name but could not remember it) and that the man was to meet them at Lenepah. The Daltons were to get $60 from this man for making the trip with the horses.

The Mitchells had seen Grat Dalton on 4 August at a picnic or some such celebration at Goose Neck Creek. On 5 August all three Daltons had visited the Mitchells. While visiting, Grat had played the piano and Bob a harp (apparently a mouth harp). Bob had also paid Mrs. Mitchell $5 that he owed her. She had placed the money in a silver pitcher in the parlor and shortly after the Daltons left she checked on the money and found it gone. A Mitchell child said he had seen Bob take the money from the pitcher.

T. Burnett was a guard on duty at the Goose Neck picnic. He stated that he knew all three Daltons. He had seen all three Daltons at the picnic, Grat first, who had left before he saw the other two. He said there was a darky with Bob and Emmett and that Bob and Emmett were drinking a good deal during the evening. There was no mention of horses in Burnett's testimony.

Rhoda Rogers first testified that she knew all three Daltons, but on cross examination she said she had seen Bob only twice, and had never seen Emmett to know him. She also said she had never seen Grat until August 4th when he and Bob had dinner at her house. She said Grat had a white beard or mustache all over his face on that occasion. (Grat was about age 29 at this time and appears in all of photos to have had dark hair). The Daltons had said they were looking for a roan horse and had asked if she knew who the bunch of ponies out on the prairie beyond belonged to. She said she did not know until Bob described the brand; then she said they belonged to her husband. The Daltons then asked to see the branding iron and said they would know the brand anywhere when they saw it. Shortly after this the Rogers missed eight head of horses.

Commissioner Brizzolara decided the above testimony was satisfactory evidence to believe Grat Dalton guilty and ordered he find bail of $1000 or that he stand committed for trial on 15 October 1890. Grat could not make bail and was returned to jail.

There is nothing further concerning this incident in any official records found to date. On 25 September THE INDIAN CHIEFTAN reported that Grat was still in the Fort Smith jail in default of $1000 bail. It appears that later the charges were dropped and he was released. There is no record at all of charges against Bob or Emmett for this supposed horse stealing incident.

The U.S. District Court records for Muskogee, I.T. of 13 Nov. 1890 show that Grath [sic] Dalton entered a plea of guilty to a charge of disturbing the peace. No further information is given in the court records about this incident.

By this time it seems obvious that the Daltons have decided to give up on the lawman business for one reason or another.

However, one last story about why the Daltons departed from the right side of the law bears some scrutiny. Emmett always claimed that Bob handed in his badge because he was owed a large sum of money in back pay and had been unable to collect wages for some time. Records in the National Archives in Washington D. C. support Emmett in this case. Only a few of the Emolument Returns for the U. S. Marshals survive for this period, but the one for Marshal W. C. Jones of Kansas for 1 January through 27 May 1898 is one of them. These records show that Robert Dalton had earned $181.80 for this period, but the marshal's office had received only $136.35 of this amount from the federal government. The record further shows that the marshal had retained the entire amount received. Bob Dalton had not received any pay at all from Marshal Jones for that five month period.

Later, in 1889, R. L. Walker became the marshal for the Kansas District. The federal records show that as late as 1895, after Walker had left the marshal's job other deputies were still trying to collect the fees that Walker owed them. A former deputy, John Jones, had written to the Attorney General about $550 in back pay for services over a period of four years that was still owed to him. Walker had written to the Attorney General himself several times concerning the matter of money still owed to his deputies. On 4 January 1895 he said. "The records of my office show that during my time of office the earnings of the office have been $64,000. I was compelled to employ an attorney in Washington, ... to prosecute an investigation. ...I am just as anxious to close accounts with my deputies as they are to get their money, for it is humiliating and embarrassing to me to receive such communications as the one from Mr. Jones, and greatly embarrasses me financially. I desire to assure you that no time will be lost by me in closing my accounts with my deputies upon receiving my money from the government." It could not be determined from the records if the government ever did pay Walker what was due him and if he was ever able to settle accounts with his deputies. But as far as Bob Dalton was concerned, the subject was academic anyway. Bob Dalton settled his accounts with everyone on this earthly plain on 5 October 1892 in Coffeyville.

V. The Daltons Versus the Southern Pacific Railroad

"RAILROAD. v. t. 1. To send a person directly to prison without proof of guilt, due process of law, or a fair trial; to send to jail by false evidence or by cheating, tricking, deceiving, or framing. 2. To force or speed up an action without due process, in disregard of regular or accepted procedures, or without the consent of others concerned; to force one's opinion or schemes upon others."

It was the age of Robber Barons. Graft, bribery, and all sorts of corruption was commonplace. In California it was the Southern Pacific (SP) Railroad and the Republican Party that led the way in the 19th century game of "Monopoly". "The Big Four", Leland Stanford (or £eland $tanford or Stealing Lanford), Collis P. Huntington, Mark Hopkins, and Charles Crocker ran the SP and had founded the Republican Party in California. By the late 1880s the SP had a virtual monopoly on the entire transportation industry in California and a strong hold on many other enterprises as well. Stanford had served as Governor of California and two terms in the U. S. Senate. He did an outstanding job of looking out for the railroad's interest while in both positions.

The railroads obtained huge land grants from the federal government, openly bought elections, controlled the state and many local governments, and in fact, used any and every method known to mankind to advance their financial gain.

The Railroad was despised for a number of reasons but in the San Joaquin Valley the feelings against the SP were especially strong. For a number of years the Railroad had encouraged settlers to move on to the SP land grants before the company actually took title to the land. (The government foolishly expected the Railroad to pay taxes on the land once they had the title.) The Railroad promised when they obtained a good title then the land would be sold to the settlers at a price of $2.50 to $10.00 an acre. Improvements made in the meantime would not be taken into consideration in setting the price, and the settlers would be given the first chance to buy. Settlers came by the drove, went to work and turned previously sterile land into productive and prosperous farms. In 1877 the SP began to take title to the land and then reneged on every promise made to the settlers.

A Settlers League was formed and the case was sent to Congress. There was no action. (The Railroad had plenty of influence in Washington.) The League went to the courts and the cases were found in favor of the Railroad. (The judges had been bought and paid for by the SP.) Violence broke out when federal marshals arrived in Hanford county to eject settlers. The incident became known as the Battle of Mussel Slough; seven men were killed and one wounded. Several of the settlers were arrested and served jail sentences. From this time on hostility toward the SP was very strong.

Then came what some historians have called the SP War. Between February 1889 and August 1892 five SP trains were robbed. All five robberies were committed by two men, usually masked and the method of operation was basically the same for all. On 22 February 1889 it was train No. 17 at Pixley, 20 January 1890 train No. 19 at Goshen, 6 February 1891 train No. 17 at Alila (the town is now called Earlimart), 3 September 1891 train No. 19 at Ceres and on 3 August 1892 train No. 17 at Collis (now named Kerman).

There was not a clue as to who the robbers were during the first two hold-ups. The Lawmen and the SP detectives rushed to the scene, rushed here, rushed there, and found nothing. The public in the San Joaquin Valley was very closed mouthed. There was a general feeling that the SP had appropriated settler's land and that someone had set out to even up the score a bit by taking Railroad money.

After the Alila robbery things were much the same at first. Over 100 officers and citizens were out searching for robbers. Search parties went west, went south, went toward Costal Mountain range, went every which direction, and in no direction at all. Various sets of tracks were followed here and there. Others searchers were out with bloodhounds sniffing for the robbers. The newspapers all rehashed the two previous train robberies. The opinion was widely held that the Alila robbery had been committed by the same men that robbed the trains at Pixley and Goshen.

The robbers got nothing during the attempted Alila robbery. C. C. Haswell, the express car messenger or guard, had quickly realized that a robbery attempt was under way. He put out the lights in the express car and did battle. The car was fired on several times and Haswell returned the fire. During the fight the train fireman, George S. Radliff, was wounded. Radliff died the following afternoon. Haswell was struck in the forehead by something, probably buckshot, and was very slightly wounded. Haswell reported that the robbers fired at him with both a shotgun and a pistol. He also said he saw the man who shot him and he fired at him. Haswell was confident that he had wounded the robber. He later testified that the robber threw up his hands and said, "I'm hit.". Haswell also stated that he was confident that he did not fire the shot that killed the fireman.

On 21 February the WEEKLY DELTA gave the first description of the robbers. This description appeared to have been supplied by the train crew. The description matched the same general description from other robberies and was basically: "one tall and very straight robber, one short and heavy set robber."

Within a few days SP detectives learned that one William Dalton lived near Cholame and that his brothers Gratton, Robert, and Emmett from Oklahoma were visiting. The detectives had also learned that the Daltons were related to the notorious Younger brothers who were serving time in the Minnesota State Prison for bank robbery. Almost immediately a new description of the robbers was circulated. On 26 Feburary the TULARE COUNTY TIMES said, "One man fully six feet high, weight one hundred and ninety pounds, very fair complexion, very small mustache, blue eyes and was an expert at poker. He wore new square-toed calf boots and was about twenty-eight years old; was well built, had a full face, and rode a dark bay horse about sixteen hands high and weighing about 1,050 pounds. The second man was about five feet ten inches in height, dark complexion, small dark mustache, which looked as if it had been dyed; full face weight about 175 pounds and about twenty-nine years old. He rode a light bay horse about fourteen hands high and which would weigh about nine hundred pounds. The third man was about twenty-one years old, of light complexion, no mustache, and his weight was about one hundred and sixty pounds."

Two men have suddenly become three and there is now explicit knowledge about the age of the boots they wore, their card playing abilities, and the horses they rode! (During the Alila robbery the bandit's horses had been tied some way off from the train and the train crew never saw a horse.)

From here on the story line can be compared to the plot of a comic opera; however, the results were anything but funny to the Daltons. Several arrests were made. Sheriff Kay followed two sets of horse tracks. Two tracks became three, the two tracks were lost so Kay followed the single set of tracks and arrested a Mexican on the highway to San Luis Obispo. This man was questioned and released. Then W. E. Hickey (it later turns out that he was a SP detective), Grat Dalton, Cole Dalton, and Jack Parker (or Carter) were all arrested. Grat was released, then arrested and released again, then arrested for the third time, and jailed at Visalia. Bill Dalton was arrested and put in jail in Visalia. Cole was released after he was questioned by the grand jury. After this the newspapers lost interest in anyone that was not named Dalton and no one seemed to know or care about what happened to Parker (or Carter).

C. C. Haswell quickly got his reward for protecting the treasure in the express car. According to the DELTA and the Tulare County Court Records, he was indicted for manslaughter for killing Radliff. A true bill was found against Haswell on 11 February. On 12 February he was arrested and released on bail. On the 19th of March the newspapers reported he he was arraigned in the superior court in Tulare County and his counsel was W. A. GRAY (dear reader please remember this name.) Various sources say that Haswell was acquitted or that the charges were dropped, but there is no evidence in the Tulare court records that any further action was ever taken on the case.

On 28 March 1891 the MERCED EXPRESS reported that the widow of Fireman Radliff had been given $2500 by Wells Fargo and Company. Wells Fargo was, of course, owned and controlled by the SP.

On 9 March a grand jury convened in Tulare County. The TULARE COUNTY TIMES of 12 March reported. "The gentlemen summoned to appear as Grand Jurors answered to their names as the roll was called, with the exception of one or two who had forwarded physicians certificates certifying as to their ill-health and inability to attend Court. Several others were excused on account of sickness, and it was found necessary to issue a venire for ten more jurors so that the jury could be filled and duly empannelled." The same epidemic of illness was still raging when it came time to seat a jury for Grat's trial.

THE TIMES further reported, "A TIMES reporter attempted a little interviewing on behalf of the readers of this journal, but with very unsatisfactory results. The officers are close mouthed, and nothing could be obtained from them. Not a witness was found who expressed the opinion that the Daultons [sic] were the guilty parties, though nearly all entertained the belief that they had a knowledge of the men who attempted the robbery."

On 17 March 1891 the Tulare County Court records show that ROBERT, EMMETT, GRATTON and WM. M. DALTON were indicted for: ASSULT WITH INTENT TO COMMIT MURDER UPON ONE C. C. HASWELL and ASSULT WITH INTENT TO COMMIT ROBBERY. Forty-three witnesses were called before the Grand Jury. Only three of these witnesses can be identified as actually present at the scene of the robbery. A significant number of the witnesses were Railroad employees. Five were SP or Wells Fargo detectives or special agents. Three were other lawmen, the Sheriff of San Luis Obisbo County, the Sheriff, and a deputy of Tulare County.

Most of the literature concerning this case states or implies that the Daltons were indicted for the murder of the fireman, Radliff. It is also stated that only Bob and Emmett were indicted for the actual deed and that Grat and Bill were indicted as accomplices or as accessories to the crime. Even the SP Reward poster says Bob and Emmett are principals and Bill and Gratton are accessories, but that is not what the court record says.

On 16 March 1891 the WEEKLY DELTA reported: W. A. Gray received a telegram last

This page and the following two pages: Records of Tulare County, CA showing that Robert, Emmett, Gratton, and Wm. M. Dalton were all indicted on two counts each: Assault with Intent to Commit Murder and Assault with Intent to Commit Robbery.

The People
vs
Wm M. Dalton
} Assault with intent to Commit Murder.

The Defendant appeared in Court without Counsel. And Stated that he was unable to procure Such Counsel. Whereupon the Court appointed E. O. Larkin Esqr as Counsel for the Defendant. Thereupon defendant by his Counsel waived the reading of the Indictment filed herein and the Clerk delivered him a Certified Copy thereof. Defendant upon being asked if Wm M. Dalton was his true name he replied in the affirmation.

Whereupon the Court Ordered that Monday March 23rd 1891 at 10 oclock A. M. be set as the time for the defendant to plead.

And it is further Ordered that the said defendant be admitted to bail in the Sum of $15000."

The People
vs
Wm M. Dalton
} Assault with intent to Commit Robbery.

The Defendant appeared in Court without Counsel and Stated that he was unable to procure Such Counsel Whereupon the Court appointed E. O. Larkin Esqr as Counsel for the defendant. Thereupon defendant by his Counsel waived the reading of the Indictment filed herein and the Clerk delivered him a Certified Copy thereof. Defendant upon being asked if Wm M. Dalton was his true name he replied in the affirmation.

Whereupon the Court Ordered that Monday March 23rd 1891 at 10 oclock A. M. be fixed as the time for defendant to plead.

And it is further Ordered that the said defendant be admitted to bail in the Sum of $15000."

The People
— vs —
Grattan Dalton
} Assault with intent to Commit Murder

The Defendant appeared in Court without Counsel and Stated that he was unable to procure Such Counsel Whereupon the Court appointed E. O. Larkin Esqr as Counsel for said defendant. Thereupon defendant by his Counsel waived the reading of the Indictment filed herein and the Clerk delivered him a Certified Copy thereof. Defendant upon being asked if Grattan Dalton was his true name answered in the affirmative. Whereupon the Court Ordered that Monday March 23rd 1891 at 10 Oclock A. M. be Set as the time for the defendant to plead. And it is further Ordered that said defendant be admitted to bail in the Sum of $1500.00

The People
— vs —
Grattan Dalton
} Assault with intent to Commit Robbery

The Defendant Came into Court without Counsel and Stated that he was unable to procure Such Counsel whereupon the Court appointed E. O. Larkin Esqr as Counsel for said defendant. Thereupon defendant by his Counsel waived the reading of the Indictment filed herein and the Clerk delivered him a Certified Copy thereof. Defendant upon being asked if Grattan Dalton was his true name he answered in the affirmative. Whereupon the Court Ordered that Monday March 23rd 1891 at 10 oclock A. M. be fixed as the time for the defendant to plead. And it is further Ordered that the defendant be admitted to bail in the Sum of $5000.00

Saturday morning to the effect that he had been appointed as *AN ADDITIONAL SUPERIOR JUDGE FOR THIS COUNTY* [emphasis added]. ...Judges Gray and Cross have made no arrangement, as yet, as to how court business will be disposed of, but it is probable one of them will take the civil cases and the other the criminal and probate business, and alternate the order every six months."

W. A. Gray had been defense counsel for C. C. Haswell just a few days earlier, and the Haswell case disappeared into thin air. Gray was appointed as judge *BY TELEGRAM* in the middle of March. Further the biography of the Judge Wheaton Andrew Gray in the HISTORY OF CENTRAL CALIFORNIA informs: "In politics he has been an active Republican, and has frequently stumped the county in favor of Republicanism and the candidates of the party. He was chairman of the Republican Central Committee in the last campaign, and was efficient in helping to secure the election of Governor H. H. Markham. In 1891 he was appointed Superior Judge of Tulare County by Governor Markham." The not so fine hand of the SP was clearly at work here.

On 2 April 1891 the VASALIA WEEKLY DELTA announced: "Grattan and William Dalton were arraigned in department No. 2 of the superior court, JUDGE GRAY PRESIDING [emphasis added]."

In the meantime Bob and Emmett had made their escape and returned to the Twin Territories. Several California lawmen and Railroad detectives reportedly went to the Territories and made various unsuccessful attempts to capture them. Soon Bob and Emmett were writing some new pages into the history of old Oklahoma. In the meantime Grat Dalton went to trial, with Judge W. A. Gray presiding.

Grat was tried ONLY on the attempted robbery charge. The trial began on 17 June and ended on 9 July 1891. The only official records that were kept of the trial is a list of the witnesses that were called. The reason for this will be shown a bit further on in the story. The TULARE COUNTY TIMES, however, reported the trial in a considerable amount of detail. [Author's single spaced typescript of the newspaper account is fifty-seven pages long.] There are a great many irregularaties in the trial procedures, and the evidence against the Daltons is only circumstantial and even that is extremely weak. The chain of evidence is a joke. All actual items presented in evidence had been in the hands of the SP or Wells Fargo employees for weeks or even months before the trial.

The trial opened in the absence of the attorney of record for the defense as he was still involved in a murder case in another town. Several material witnesses had failed to obey the summons of the court and were also absent. Motions to delay the trial were filed because of the absence of the above. Judge Gray denied the request for delay.

Jury selection followed much the same pattern as did the selection for the grand jury. Thirteen jurors were excused at their own request in front of the clerk. Four jurors for whom subpoenas were issued had not been found by the Sheriff and some jurors did not appear but forwarded affidavits from their physicians that they were unable to attend. After only a portion of the jury had been seated one juryman returned drunk from the noon recess. This occured on Tuesday and the Judge excused the drunken juror until Thursday morning. The request was made for another venire for an additional forty to fifty jurors. There was considerable discussion about who could properly serve the venire. The Judge then permited the Coroner to summon an additional forty jurors. This procedure was promptly challenged by the defense attorney of record, J. W. Breckinridge, when he arrived and took charge of the case. Breckinridge stated that the Coroner and his deputy were biased against the defendant. The jury was finally seated at the end of the forth day of the trial.

Both the district attorney and the defense counsel requested that a complete transcript of the trial be kept by a court reporter. Judge Gray denied this motion, thus the only official records that survive of the trial is a list of the witnesses called. Defense attorney Breckinridge then requested that the witnesses be put under the rule and excluded from the courtroom. The prosecution objected and the court sustained the objection.

The opening statement by the prosecution stated that the robbery had been attempted by TWO men but that he proposed to show by CIRCUMSTANTIAL EVIDENCE that there was a CONSPIRACY between the FOUR [emphasis by author] persons in the case.

Three crew members from the train were the first to testify. Their testimony was confusing and contradictory. A photo of Bob Dalton was identified as one of the robbers. One man identified Grat as one of the robbers but did so only on cross examination. Bill was brought into court and could not be identified by any of the crew. No picture of Emmett or any of the other Daltons was ever presented throughout the trial. The testimony of one witness was that the robbers had only pistols. Another witness was sure the robbers used both shotguns and pistols. Haswell testified that he was positive he shot one of the robbers in the fleshy part of the left shoulder and that it was not his shot that wounded Radliff.

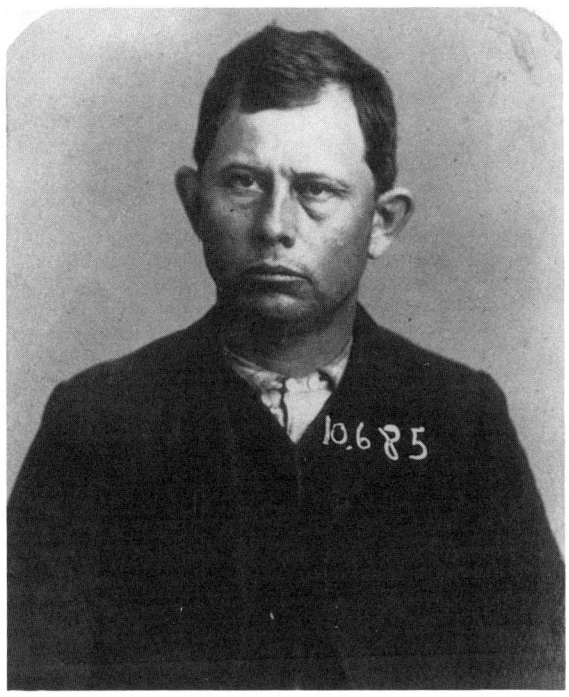

Mug shot of Grat Dalton when he was arrested for the Alila train robbery in 1891. Courtesy of John E. Boessenecker.

Two passengers on the train were called and both testified they heard shotgun and pistol fire during the shooting.

Next various neighbors and acquintences of Bill Dalton were called. They testified about horses, saddles and other tack, either owned by Bill Dalton, or borrowed by Bill from neighbors.

Next came a large group of witnesses from Traver, Delano, Tulare, Paso Robles, and Merced. They established that two or three men had been in the area on horseback and had visited their business establishments. The men described had been drinking and playing cards in some places. The men had also bought food to take with them and grain for their horses, some spurs and spur leathers at various places along the route. The men observed by this group of witnesses may or may not have been the Daltons. Descriptions varied a great deal, though some of these witnesses did identify the photo of Bob Dalton. None of the witnesses reported seeing shotguns in possession of the men they had seen.

Then came testimony of various lawmen, SP, and Wells Fargo detectives and agents. Much of this testimony had to do with tracking the robbers and finding grain, pieces of bread and meat and various bits of saddles and other tack not far from the scene of the robbery. There was an attempt to prove that the grain, and the pieces of bread and meat found near the robbery site were the remains of items sold to the (maybe?) Daltons before the robbery. (The robbery was in February and this material was presented in court in July; must have smelled great!).

There was also an attempt to establish that various common bits of saddles, harness, spur leathers, and etc. had belonged to equipment that had been loaned to Bill Dalton or that the (maybe?) Daltons had purchased a few days before the robbery. Here the chain of evidence became completely ridiculous. One of Bill Dalton's neighbors testified that he had sold one of the saddles in question to SP detective Bill Smith before or during the trial. Another witness Frank Meisenmeimer, a constable and marshal at Paso Robles, testified that he had removed the stirrups and stirrup leathers off a saddle presented as evidence before he turned the saddle over to SP detective Hickey. ALL ITEMS SHOWN IN EVIDENCE HAD BEEN IN THE HANDS OF THE RAILROAD OR WELLS FARGO PERSONNEL FOR SOME TIME, MOST OF IT FOR SEVERAL MONTHS, BEFORE THE TRIAL.

Several witnesses testified they had talked with SP detectives during the trial and that the detectives had reminded them of things they had forgotten when previously giving testimony. Several witnesses testified that their expenses for attending the trial were being paid by the SP and still others admitted that they were traveling on SP passes.

When the prosecution rested the defense counsel made a motion that the court instruct the jury to bring in a verdict of acquittal on the ground of the insufficiency of the evidence. The motion was promptly denied by Judge Gray.

The defense presented its case and TWELVE witnesses testified that Grat Dalton had been in Fresno in a hotel drinking and playing cards at the time the Alila robbery occured. Some of these witnesses were not of completely sterling character; one was a pimp and a professional gambler and a couple of others were race track hounds and gamblers. However, other witnesses were hotel clerks, bartenders, and salesmen who were staying in the hotel. The dated hotel register was introduced as evidence and the hotel clerk and one other witness had watched Grat sign the register.

Bill and Grat Dalton both testified as did Littleton, and Mother Adeline was even put on the stand. It was clear that Bill and Grat Dalton had both lied to SP detectives during the investigation. Both clearly considered the SP detectives as some kind of a joke, at least they had early in the investigation. They clearly considered changing the stories they told the detectives more of a matter for sport than anything else. Grat said at one point he had only corroborated Smith's statement to get rid of him rather that to talk two weeks more about it.

Near the end of the trial it was discovered that Grat had a key in his possession that supposedly unlocked the doors of the jail. There was actually testimony by Sheriff Kay and a couple of others to the effect that the key had been tried and that it would not unlock all of the doors or other locking devices within the jail. It is not recorded, what happened to the key; Grat may well have kept it in his possession.

Haswell's indictment for manslaughter for the death of Radliff was not mentioned during the trial, or if so the newspaper did not report it. There were, however, several speeches during the course of the trial by the prosecution about the death of Radliff, with the implication that the Daltons had killed the man.

The jury deliberated for twenty hours and returned a verdict of "Guilty".

Both Grat and Bill had been held on bail of $30,000 each ($15,000 for each charge) until this time. Bill's bail was now reduced to $5000 and he was released on bond. Bill's trial was set for 5 October 1891 and Grat was held over for sentencing. Sentencing was fixed for 29 July but later there were delays or postponments to this.

On 3 September another SP train was held up at Ceres. Again it was a tall and a short man. The detectives were off and running again. A Swede coming from Mariposa was arrested then released. Two or three other men were arrested but they proved to be tramps who had nothing to do with the robbery. A young couple named Graham had been camped near the robbery site. It was reported that the robbers had stopped and got a drink of water from the campers and supposedly the Grahams could identify the robbers. It was painfully obvious this time that Bob and Emmett were back in Oklahoma and Grat was in jail so they could not be guilty of this job. However, the SP went after Bill and a man named Riley Dean (Wiley Dean in some newspapers).

Southern Pacific Railroad's William Smith. He was severely criticized for his handling of California train robbery cases and greatly disliked by fellow lawmen. Courtesy of John E. Boessenecker.

Now even the newspapers were openly expressing their opinion of the work of the detectives. On 7 September the SAN FRANCISCO EXAMINER said, "Evidently a direct motive influenced detectives to make the facts indicate that the Daltons were not concerned in the attempt to commit the train robbery at Ceres last Thursday, for now that William Dalton and Riley Dean have been arrested, every one of them says with emotion, 'Of course Bill Dalton was the smaller of the two robbers. We knew that all the time. We have been looking for him.' Yet only last Friday the descriptions given of the Dalton brothers made them all imposing giants of towering height and vast breath of back. Now Bill Dalton appears a man under the average height and exactly fits the description given by the engineer and others of the lesser of the two robbers. "

On 13 September the UNION announced, "Dalton and Dean Discharged for Want of Evidence." Immediately after Bill was released he was again arrested and taken back to Vasalia and placed back in jail because a bondsmen in the Alila case had withdrawn his bond.

Now Bill Dalton sounded off. The TULARE COUNTY TIMES of 17 September published his comments to a newspaper reporter. Bill was asked "How do you account for your recognition by the Grahams?" he replied, "They did not recognize us. When brought face to face with us they could not identify us as the men they had seen. Now just consider how improbable a story that is. Here every one says I am a desperate and shrewd man. I have the ability to plan a train robbery and the courage to execute it. Yet I would be such a fool as to go in broad daylight, and be seen within a few miles of the scene of the robbery. I go there for water when I know every foot of the country and can find water anywhere without being seen. Does this story strike you as probable. ...The train was robbed on Thursday. We had till Sunday to escape, three full days, yet we are found within a comparatively short distance of where the robbery was done and in our old haunts. The whole story is so absurd that no one but a Southern Pacific detective could ever conceive it."

On 24 September the TIMES published a card Bill sent to the newspaper. In this he said he and his family were victims of unscrupulous railroad machinations. Other comments were: "My life has been an open book, whose pages the world—or I challenge any man—to search my life's record and recall an illegal transaction or a disgraceful act; my chief crime being probably the non-accumulation of wealth. ...They [the SP] have manufactured testimony and even gone so far as to openly perjure themselves in order to secure the coveted prize. But when I say 'they' let it be here understood I mean the detectives and not Mr. Kay, or any of his officers, for he is a man I esteem too highly, and is possessed of too high a sense of self respect to be a party to a shady transaction. I think." Bill went on to say that the detectives had him arrested in order to keep him from securing bond for his brother pending his appeal. He was especially vehement in his denuciation of detective William Smith. Dalton claimed Smith admitted when he had him arrested that Smith knew he was not guilty of the Ceres robbery. "Yet this same man, whose mind seems only a cesspool of abominations, goes and attempts to coerce my wife into giving false testimony against me, something even prohibited by law, in order to strew his path to fame and renown with one more rose. "

Bill Dalton meanwhile was back in jail along with Grat. Then Grat Dalton broke out of jail. The stories are legion about how this was accomplished and who assisted in the break. But no matter who assisted, Grat and two other men were free. Bill stayed in jail, and later played his guitar and sang, "You'll Never Miss My Brother Till He's Gone." for the benefit of all that cared to listen. Grat hid out in the mountains and at Christmas time a posse located him and Riley Dean in their mountain camp. Dean was captured but Grat spotted the posse before they caught up with him and escaped on a plow horse from the nearby Elwood ranch.

According to Frank Latta in DALTON GANG DAYS, Grat went to the home of W. W. Gray (not related to the Judge) a Merced County ex-supervisor. Grat was now suffering from pneumonia and the Gray family hid him until he was well enough to travel. The Gray's also provided Grat with a horse and saddle. Grat, along with his brother Cole, according to Latta, then made the long trip back to the Indian Territory on horseback.

Bill Dalton's trial for "Assult With Intent to Commit Robbery" was held in October. Both the public and the newspapers appear to have lost most of their interest in the whole affair by this time. The trial lasted several days but the TULARE COUNTY TIMES did not report on the event until the day it ended. The coverage in the paper was brief.

Some of the significant testimony that the TIMES did report is as follows: Bill Smith, the SP detective, did testify that he had told Bill Dalton a number of falsehoods and that he considered this one of the means a detective could use in the interest of justice. SP detective Hume testified that he went to Dalton's bondsmen and asked them to withdraw their bond in order to place Bill Dalton in jail again. Hume claimed their business would be safer with Dalton locked up than at large, he also said he considered it his duty to his company to get the bondsmen to withdraw.

Thirteen prominent citizens of the community appeared as character witnesses for Bill Dalton. All stated that Dalton was of good character and had a reputation for honesty and integrity. Most had known Bill Dalton since 1884 when he first moved into the area. W. W. Gray, who latter hid Grat, was one of the character witnesses for Bill.

The jury was out for approximately fifteen minutes and returned a verdict of, "Not Guilty". The charge "Assult With Intent To Commit Murder" was dropped on grounds that the evidence would not warrant a conviction. Bill Dalton was discharged and his bail was exonerated, according to the court records.

A few more bits of information contribute further to the evidence that the Daltons were indeed RAILROADED for the Alila robbery. A closer look at the history of Attorney Breckinridge and W. W. Gray provides more evidence of this. These two men were both prominent men in Merced County and they were married to sisters. Breckinridge was the son of John C. Breckinridge who was Vice President of the United States under Buchanan. Breckinridge had served as the prosecuting attorney of Merced County and in the California State Legislature. W. W. Gray, in addition to serving on the Merced County Board of Supervisors for seven years, had been an officer in the Union Army during the Civil War and had also served as the Chief of Police in Oakland, California. Both Gray and Breckinridge were also prominent in the Democratic Political Party, the party that opposed the Railroad. Why did this family hide Grat and assist him to escape from California? Could it be because they knew for certain that he was not guilty of the crime for which he was convicted?

Note: Information concerning Breckinridge and W. W. Gray was obtained primarily from obituaries of both men in THE MORNING CALL, May 10, 1892 and the MERCED EXPRESS April 19, 1902, respectively, and from Breckinridge's marriage record.

In summary of this matter, Littleton Dalton's statements to Frank Latta also need to be addressed. Littleton makes a very convincing case to Latta for the guilt of his brothers. But as previously pointed out, Littleton had not been near any of his family for over forty years and he was somewhat senile at the time Latta interviewed him. Here are specifics of Littleton's story that do not agree with the evidence in the trial:

1. Littleton told a story that Grat's horse went lame, and that Grat came to him to get another horse just before the Alila robbery. At the trial Littleton said he saw Grat in the hotel in Fresno the day of the robbery and that was the first time he had seen Grat for three years.

2. Lit claimed Bob and Emmett had bought two quarts of whiskey along with sandwiches. The boys drank heavily all day the day of the robbery and the whiskey bottles were found along with the remains of the sandwiches, the saddle parts and other items. Lit further said the remains of the sandwiches were wrapped in a newspaper with the restaurant owners name written on it. During the trial there was no mention of whiskey bottles found with the other items. Neither was there any mention of any name on the newspaper. What was stated during the trial was the fact that the newspaper found with sandwich remains was dated 7 Feb. 1891, THE DAY AFTER THE ROBBERY OCCURRED.

3. Lit also said that all kind of evidence about the bullets from the robbery was presented during the trial. Supposedly bullets had been dug out of the express car and compared with the bullet in Radliff's body. The newspaper account of the trial never mentioned any such ballistic evidence.

What Littleton told Latta just does not agree with the evidence brought out during the trial.

After Coffeyville Ben Dalton expressed his views on why his brothers had turned to crime. His statement too should be considered and here it is, interwoven with the reporter's history of the Dalton's entire career in crime.

(Retyped Newspaper Article)
WERE NOT AT ALILA

BEN DALTON DEFENDS HIS BROTHERS

They Lived Honest Lives in California

Victims of the Express Company's Persecution—Their First Crimes

As late as June, 1890, the three Daltons who became outlaws were in the United States service. The Alila (Cal.) robbery occurred February 6, 1891, eight months later, and then followed the series of train robberies in the Indian Territory in quick succession and the culminating tragedy at Coffeyville, Kas.

Ben Dalton's story of how the outlawry came about, told to a St. Louis GLOBE-DEMOCRAT reporter, is a strange one. He said false swearing and persecution in the California affair started the boys in the train-robbing profession. But they had begun to go wrong in other ways before that. "The Government service," said Ben, "was their eternal ruin. They got into bad associations. The United States Marshals didn't pay up. The court at Fort Smith owed Bob several hundred dollars, and so did the one at Wichita. He never did receive it. The boys couldn't get their money when they needed it, although they had earned it, and they took ways which were wrong to raise it. That was the beginning of their going astray and that was the cause of all that followed."

Ben is the oldest of the Daltons. One of the brothers died in infancy. The third is Cole Dalton, now living in Oklahoma. Nothing is charged against him. Then came Frank Dalton, who was killed in Government service. Next in the line is William Dalton, who settled in California, married and was doing well until the Alila trouble cast a cloud upon him.

After these older brothers come the three—Grat, Bob and Emmett—who led and fell in the Coffeyville raid. These were the outlawed members of the family. All of them were under 30 years, Emmett was just 21, of athletic build, to the saddle born by their Kentucky blood, splendid marksmen, raised on the border, it was not strange that one after the other of the boys entered the Government service as Deputy Marshals for the Indian Territory. That was the life that called into play the qualities the Daltons possessed. Frank Dalton entered the service first. He went out with a posse from Fort Smith to help arrest horse thieves. He came back bringing in a wagon the body of the leader of the posse, who had been killed by the Cherokee outlaw, Bill Pigeon. For his conduct on that occasion Frank Dalton was made a Deputy Marshal with full powers. He became one of the best officers of the Fort Smith court. In "riding the district"—that is, looking for horse thieves, illicit whisky sellers and other violators of the Indian Territory laws—Frank was accompaned by Bob, at that time scarcely more than a boy.

One November day Frank Dalton and Bob brought six prisoners into Fort Smith. The second morning after Frank started with another Deputy Marshal for a woodchoppers' camp four miles out of town to get a horsethief named Dave Smith. The two deputies dismounted near the camp and walked in. They were fired upon. In the fight which followed four were killed, including Frank Dalton. The body of the deputy was shown all possible honor. It was embalmed and sent to the sorrowing mother, who was then living in the Cherokee Nation. Very different was the unceremonious burial of the two Daltons who died in the alley at Coffeyville last week. It was the difference of a good cause and a bad cause.

After Frank Dalton fell in trying to execute the law, Bob stepped into his official shoes, and for several years he filled them worthily. First Grat and then Emmett joined Bob in this Federal service. Grattan Dalton, after being trained by Bob, was attached to the Wichita district. After some time Bob and Emmett were "riding" the Fort Smith district. Emmett was three or four years under age. The others were not 25. They were too young, Ben Dalton says, for such service. Recklessness, rather than depravity, led to official crookedness. The deputy marshals are dependent on the United States Marshals for their pay. The latter draw compensation through fees, which must be allowed by courts and passed upon at Washington. Sometimes accounts are months behind. Unless the marshals have credit or capital the deputies must wait for their pay. These Dalton boys, with hundreds of dollars owing them, found themselves short.

They had arrested some men who had smuggled whisky into the Territory. These prisoners offered money for freedom. The arrests had not been reported. The boys took the money and turned the prisoners loose. This was the beginning. Worse offenders were treated in the same way for larger consideration. Such doings could not go on long without discovery. Information reached superior officers. Complaints were filed in court. The boys gave themselves up, agreed to stand trial and were let out on bond. But after getting out they concluded that conviction was certain. They repudiated their bonds and took to the brush in defiance of the Government. This was two years and three months ago. Horse-stealing was the next step. Their operations were characterized by that boldness which made the Coffeyville plan feasible in their minds. A bunch of ponies and a team of mules were run out of the Osage nation, where Bob Dalton had for a time been chief of police. The stock was taken all the way to Kansas City and sold. Then thirty head of horses were gathered up from various owners, driven out of the Territory and sold at Columbus, Kan. The boys took a check in payment, indorsed it with their own names and cashed it.

By a curious coincidence the purchaser of the horses, the former owners of them and the Dalton boys arrived in the vicinity of Baxter Springs on the same day. There was a hurried unraveling of the plot. Bob and Emmett Dalton had just time to transfer their saddles to fresh horses when the angry crowd started for them. Then ensued a great man hunt. Down through the Territory the outlaws fled, hard followed. The Daltons left the roads and went through pasture after pasture, jumping off their horses and snapping with nippers the wire fences as often as they came to them. Emmett's horse gave out and he forced an exchange with the first farmer he met, but the pursuit was so hard that there was no time to saddle. Emmett went on bareback until he met another man on horseback. He offered him twice what his saddle was worth, transferred it and told him a party of friends would be along in a few minutes to pay for it. The chase lasted all day, and the Daltons escaped. That was the last seen of Bob and Emmett in the Indian Territory for many a day. Grat Dalton was arrested for supposed complicity in the horse stealing and locked up. He was a prisoner a couple of months, and was then turned loose because there was no evidence against him. He too, disappeared. This is the story of the Daltons up to the time and they were first accused justly or falsely of train robbery.

"The boys" said Ben Dalton, "went to California. They were looking for work at the time of the Alila train robbery and they intended to lead honest lives. Now I will tell you the way they came to be charged with that crime." Ben Dalton stooped down and drew a diagram on the floor, "Here" said he, "is Tulare lake and here is Alila. After the train robbery which was done by two men, the Sheriff and his posse found a trail leading away from the place. They followed in the direction of Old Mexico down toward Sonora for many miles until they lost it. Then they came back and went to looking in all directions. They came upon the trail made by my brothers on their way through the country. It was not anywhere near the train robbery, but it passed at one place where the boys had bent down in their course to go around the lake within four or five miles of the train robbers' trail. The officers took up the trail and followed it to the vicinity of where my brother William was living. I have all of these facts from the officers themselves. The Sheriff told me that the trail of the robbers led from the robbery down into Old Mexico, "but", he said, "there appears to be evidence against your brothers."

"After they had failed to overtake the robbers in Old Mexico," continued Ben Dalton, "the detectives of the express companies went to work to swear the crime on my brothers, Bob and Emmett. With only the fact that the trail my brothers made as they passed through was at one point within four or five miles of the robbers' trail the whole case was constructed. Two men (Ben Dalton gave the names) procured a witness who would swear to anything. (The name of the witness was also given.) They paid this man $500 for his testimony. They even wrote out the story to which he made oath. My brother Cole was in California. He went before the Grand Jury and pleaded with the members two days. He told all of the circumstances. He explained that the boys had come to California to look for work, and had not been at the train robbery. The Grand Jurors were not inclined to find any indictment, but the influence of the express companies and the railroad was too strong. I am satisfied the Sheriff and the other officers did not think the boys had anything to do with the robbery. My brother found that he could not save them; that the express companies were determined to swear the job on them. So he said to them, 'Boys you had better take a couple of horses and get out of the country.' And they went. There was no claim that Grat Dalton was at Alila. Fifty men were ready to swear to an alibi for him. When the robbery took place he was playing cards in a crowd many miles away.

"Now, this is the true story of that Alila business," continued Ben Dalton. "My brothers had nothing to do with it, but the crime was sworn on them by bribery and perjury, and then they entered on the life which ended here at Coffeyville—not a word, but those two men who hired a perjurer in California to swear that train robbery on the boys I believe are responsible for what has happened since."

"Had you seen the boys recently?"

"No, not for nearly two years. They hadn't been home and we had seen nothing of them. After things began to go wrong they didn't come to us and didn't send us any word about themselves. They knew it might cause us trouble. My mother and I were talking about them only two or three days before this thing happened at Coffeyville. We agreed that they had probably left the Government. We rather thought they had gone to South America. Right after that came the telegram from Coffeyville."

Bob and Emmett left California when they found their brother's plea before the Grand Jury could not save them from indictment. Grat made no effort to get away. He was arrested as accessory. Then came the Lillieta train robbery, on the Missouri, Kansas and Texas Railway. Whatever the truth about the Alila affair there is no doubt the Dalton boys, Bob and Emmett, were at Lillieta. Emmett Dalton, since his capture at Coffeyville, has admitted these later train robberies. It is said that the Lillieta robbery was undertaken to raise money for the benefit of Grat, who was still in jail in California. Soon after Lillieta the door of the jail where Grat was confined opened one night and Grat walked out. He returned to the Indian Territory and joined Bob and Emmett. The train robberies of Red Rock, Wharton and Adair followed. It was the avowed purpose of the boys to make a large stake and leave the country. They expected the raid on Coffeyville to be their last, and it was.

SAN FRANCISCO CHRONICLE 27 Oct. 1892

VI. The Dalton Gang

While Grat and Bill were in California doing battle with the SP Bob and Emmett were back in the Indian Territory. It wasn't long until these two Dalton brothers, along with some of their friends, did start robbing trains. Emmett confessed to four train robberies in all. Exactly what all the Daltons did do, and who did it along with them will never be established with exact certainty at this late date. It is a safe bet that the "Dalton Gang", as they were quickly dubbed by the newspapers, were guilty of the four robberies for which Emmett claimed credit.

The Gang, again according to Emmett, consisted of Bob, Emmett, Grat, George Newcomb, Charley Bryant, Bill Power, Charley Pierce, Dick Broadwell, William McElhanie and Bill Doolin. Who participated in what robbery is not known for sure with some exceptions. Grat could not have been at the first two robberies which took place in May and September of 1891 because he was still in California when those events took place. Charley Bryant could not have been present at any but the first robbery, because he was killed in August 1891.

Very little information has been found on the background of any of the other members of the gang. Emmett always claimed it was Will McElhanie in California with Bob, but there is no evidence to support this. Many researchers and writers have reached the conclusion that McElhanie was purely a creature of Emmett's imagination; however, there is evidence that such a man did exist. Dr. Pickering who kept a record of the Ingalls battle in his diary also mentions Mc Elhanie in the diary. Pickering says, " McIlhiney (Narrow Gauge Kid) skipped his bond and is gone for good. Some think he went to Cuba." There is also a mention or two of McElhanie in newspapers and he was wanted for stealing livestock. No further records of him have been found, likely because the court house burned where the records on him should have been. How much Mc Elhanie participated in the Dalton Gang activities is a matter of pure conjecture.

Charley Bryant was supposedly a member of the crew when the gang robbed the train at Wharton in May 1891. He was often referred to as Black Faced Charley because he supposedly had powder burns on his face acquired in a duel of some kind. There are numerous claims that Charley was a real bad actor and had been involved in a lot of criminal activities before he joined the Daltons. No evidence has been found to support any of these stories. There are several tall tales about Bob Dalton and a Daisy Bryant who reportedly was either Charley's sister or his former mistress. There has been no evidence found for the existence of Daisy. She appears to have been a completely fictional character. Charley was widely reported to have been from Wise County, Texas. A check of the 1880 census records for that county show three Bryant families living there, but there is no Charley (or any version of that name) or Daisy Bryant in any of these families. In HANDS UP! Fred Sutton claimed he went to school with Bryant in Atchison, Kansas, but a lot of Sutton's claims are untrue. Emmett said Charley had a brother Jim in Mulhall, Oklahoma who claimed Charley's body. For now Charley Bryant remains a mystery man. The only thing known for sure is that he and Ed Short killed each other in a gun battle on a train near the end of August in 1891.

Some background information has been located for Bill Power. Power is the correct spelling of the name though it generally appears as Powers in most of the literature. A relative of Power has done some research on the family and shared the information. Power's full name was William Todd Power and he was the son of James R. and Sarah O. Power. The parents were both born in Indiana but Bill and his siblings were all born in Missouri or Illinois. Bill's mother died when he was young and his father then married a woman named Mary. Mary was not kind to her stepchildren and both Bill and another brother left home at around age 13 because of the way their stepmother treated them. Bill reportedly filed on some land in the area now known as Cowboy Flat in Oklahoma in May 1891 but sold the land in December of that year. Nothing further is known of his activities until he died at Coffeyville.

After Dick Broadwell was buried at Coffeyville his brother George came from Hutchinson, Kansas to claim his body. The grave was opened and Broadwell's body was taken to Hutchinson and reburied. Most of the sketchy information about the rest of the gang members that has appeared in print is probably open to question and no further information has been located on any of them.

The numerous stories of Bob Dalton's women and female's involvement with the gang can be disposed of at this point too. Cousin Minnie Johnson, that Bob reportedly shot Charley Montgomery over, is a figment of the imagination of "Eye Witness". Eugenia Moore was also a fictitious character and she must have been invented by Emmett and Jack Jungmeyer, along with the stories of Emmett's childhood romance with Julia Johnson (more about that later) when they wrote WHEN THE DALTONS RODE. Romance was almost entirely lacking from Emmett's first book, BEYOND THE LAW. The women and the romance were likely added to the later volume in order to increase sales of the book. The Bob Dalton and Flo Quick a/k/a Tom King stories all seem to have originated with Chris Madsen. Tom King was a very real person and she was arrested and jailed several times. She was very adept at breaking out of jails too. The newspapers contained a variety of stories about her, and the records of Johnson County, Missouri revealed further factual material about Miss Tom King. She was Flora Quick, the daughter of Daniel Quick who died during the first half of 1890. A guardian was appointed for Flo on 15 July 1890 and on the same day she married John O. Mundis with the consent of the guardian. The final settlement of Dan Quick's estate was made in May 1892. Mundis appears to have stuck around to help Flo spend her inheritance; then he probably left her. It was not until May 1893 that Tom's horse stealing and jail breaking proclivities first became news. Tom's escapades were then hot news in the Territories until sometime in 1894 when it was announced that Tom was released from jail because of her delicate condition. Her jailors had no desire to act as midwife it seems. Tom was for a time associated with Earnest Lewis, who later married Julia Johnson. Julia, in turn, made Emmett Dalton her third husband after he got out of prison. By the time Flo Quick/Tom King became an outlaw Bob Dalton had been a'molderin' in his grave for some time.

The stories of the train robberies vary widely and there is no way to prove exactly what happened at these events. No official records have been found for any of these robberies, and the accounts that have been left by such people as Chris Madsen, Fred Dodge, etc. vary a great deal and the accuracy of such accounts leave much to be desired. The newspaper accounts vary widely too, but they are perhaps the best way to give the reader a sense of place and atmosphere of the time and the events. There are numerous stories of one robbery or the other that claim the Daltons killed a station agent or a telegraph operator. This never happened as the newspaper accounts which follow will show. One man was killed and several others were injured during the Adair robbery, but it should be pointed out that there was a carload of policemen and guards involved this time and the shooting must have been so indiscriminate that it was impossible to tell who did what to whom on this occasion.

Here is how the newspapers of the day told the Dalton Gang story of the train robberies.

WHARTON

(Retyped Newspaper Article)
BOLD TRAIN ROBBERY

**A SANTA FE TRAIN HELD UP IN OKLAHOMA
THE ROBBERS NEATLY FOOLED**

GUTHRIE, Ok. May 11. The south bound passenger train on the Santa Fe road was held up Saturday night at about 11:30 o'clock by five masked men, supposed to have been the notorious Dalton boys, who have been seen in this neighborhood recently

The men boarded the train at Wharton and detached the engine and express car and then proceeded two miles south and robbed the express car of all the money in it.

The passengers were not molested but a more frightened lot could not be imagined. The boys informed them when they procceded with the engine and car that they were to remain with the coaches in order to secure themselves. They obeyed.

(Retyped Newspaper Article)
ACTIVE PURSUIT

GUTHRIE, Ok. May 11—A large posse of well armed men left this city early yesterday morning in pursuit of the Dalton gang, who held up the Santa Fe passenger train's express car.

It is known that the men are carrying a large sum of money on their persons taken from cattlemen and settlers heretofore.

The robbers succeeded in getting only $500 Saturday night, and this was brought about by the shrewdness of the express

messenger who secreted a large sum in the stove and fooled the thieves by pointing to a pouch and telling them that it contained a large sum of government money, when in fact it contained some papers of no value to them.
THE MUSKOGEE PHOENIX 14 May 1891

(Retyped Newspaper Article)
TRAIN ROBBERY

THE DALTON BOYS SAID TO BE "IN IT" AND PROBABLY ARE

On Saturday last the south bound passenger train on the Santa Fe was held up at Wharton station, sixty miles north of the Kansas line in the Indian Territory, the robbers being disguised with handkerchiefs tied over their faces. A special from Guthrie gives the following account of the Robbery:

"When the robbers boarded the train at Wharton the messenger was looking out of the door of his car, and , seeing what was going on, immediately apprehended danger. He closed and locked his door and then commenced to hide the money and valuables in his keeping in places of safety where they would escape detection by the robbers. While the bandits were detaching the engine and express car from the rest of the train and were running it to the place where the robbery occurred, two miles distant, the messenger disposed of most of the valuables in places of safety. Then he locked the safe.

When the robbers appeared at the door of the express car he made a show of resistance, but finally admitted them. They immediately made for the safe and demanded that it be opened. With feigned reluctance the messenger opened it, and at the command of the leader handed over the contents, among which was a package of worthless papers which he told the robbers was a valuable package of money. Most of the money had been hidden in the stove, which was not being used for its legitimate purpose. In the search which the robbers made of the car, they overlooked that hiding place, but tumbled upon a package of $500, which they secured. Finding nothing more of value, they made their escape.

A dispatch from Topeka says: An official report of the robbery has been made to the headquarters of the Santa Fe railway. The details made public are very meager, but coincides with the report from Guthrie. The amount secured by the robbers is given out by the Santa Fe as $1,500. A large force of United States deputy marshals was organized at Guthrie last night as soon as the news of the robbery had been received, and pursuit of the robbers was immediately begun. There seems to be no doubt that the bandits were the notorious Dalton boys."

In publishing a brief history of the career of the Dalton boys last week, we stated that Bob Hughes was with them. In this, however, we were misinformed, as we have since learned that Hughes was tried at Fayetteville a few weeks ago for robbery, was convicted and sentenced to three years in the penitentiary. The party with the Dalton's that was supposed to be Hughes is said to be a fugitive from No-Man's-Land, and an exceedingly tough character.

Deputy Marshal Heck Thomas, accompanied by Burl Cox and an officer from California named Smith were close on the trail of the Dalton's—so close in fact that the outlaws abandoned their camp, leaving their packhorse and camp outfit, which fell into the hands of the officers. When the robbery occurred last Saturday Thomas and his companions were at Tulsa, where they learned of the robbery. While there is no certainty that the Wharton robbery was committed by the Daltons, it is nevertheless more than probable that they were in it, as they are known to be in that country, and since their California escapade are ripe for anything.
FORT SMITH ELEVATOR 15 May 1891

(Retyped Newspaper Article)
WHO THE DALTONS ARE

The Dalton family are originally from Missouri. There were some six or seven of the boys. Their mother was a sister of the notorious Younger boys, and their father was a well-to-do man, though he indulged to some extent in horse-racing. Some years ago Mr. and Mrs. Dalton separated, and the old gentleman died about a year ago in Kansas, while the mother resides at Kingfisher, in the Indian Territory.

Frank Dalton one of the elder brothers, was a deputy marshal, here years ago, and was killed just across the river from this place November 27, 1887, while in the discharge of his duty. He was with Deputy Marshal Jack Richardson, when that officer was murdered by the Cherokee outlaw, Bill Pigeon. Frank Dalton was recognized as a faithful and efficient officer, and an honest, upright man, with nothing of the braggadocio tinge about his make-up, which has characterized his younger brothers.

From the way Emmett and Bob are starting out, they bid fair to outstrip their Uncle Cole in criminal exploits, and will end their career in the same manner he has, if they are not killed.

FORT SMITH ELEVATOR 15 May 1891

Note: This article and the one that follows, appear to be the source of the story that Lewis and Adeline Dalton divorced.

(Retyped Newspaper Article)
THE DALTON BOYS

LEADERS OF A GANG OF TRAIN ROBBERS

Our readers in this immediate locality will remember the Dalton family that resided near this city during 1888 and 1889. It consisted of Louis Dalton and wife, two daughters and three sons at home and two sons in the Territory. The elder of those in the Territory was a Deputy U. S. Marshal, and was killed near Ft. Smith in 1888. Three of his brothers subsequently became Marshals and were known throughout the length and breath of the Cherokee and Osage nations, for their reklessness and daring. They were not generally trusted as officials, and in 1888 they killed a young man named Montgomery near this city, as they alleged, because of his being a well known horse-thief and an attempt on his part to allude arrest. He was shot by Ben [sic] Dalton, the next to the youngest boy of the family. A great many people believed at the time, and do yet, that young Montgomery was killed because he knew too much about the plans and acts of the Daltons. He was an inoffensive but reckless young man who came to the Territory from Steelton, Pa. His remains were brought to this city by the Daltons and "buried with boots on" in the Potter's field. The Dalton family did not get along well in the home circle, and finally broke up and left the city. Old Louis located near Dearing where he died last fall. Mrs. Dalton was a full cousin of the father of the notorious Younger boys, and the Daltons seemed to be bred to the Younger side of the family. They run from bad to worse until the name became a synonym for horse-stealing, robbery and rascality all over the Indian Country. They took horses by the herd and cattle by the drove, and the officers were powerless to prevent them. Laterly [sic] they have been hovering near the east line of Oklahoma and hiding in the dense forests of the Iowa reservation. They always have plenty of money, and friends at every point. It is vaguely hinted that they have confederates near this city who keep them posted and share the spoils with them. They run much of the stolen stock to Texas, and recently they were arrested and indicted but were released on bail. They forfeited their bonds, but it is understood that they have reimbursed their bondsmen, getting the money from their extensive transactions in horse flesh.

On Saturday night a south bound train on the Santa Fe, was held up at a point about twenty miles north of Guthrie, and the express car robbed. The Dalton boys and a desperado named Six Shooter Jack and a young fellow named Norton were known to have been loafing in that locality for several days and they were at once suspected of being the robbers. The men who perpetrated the robbery are described by the conductor as ranging from 28 to 35 years of age. All were masked and roughly dressed. They left the train at the coal chute near Wharton where they had horses waiting. The description fits the Daltons in age and size. The robbers succeeded in getting only $500, and this was brought about by the shrewdness of the express messenger, who secreted a large sum in the stove and fooled the thieves by pointing to a pouch and telling them that it contained a large sum of government money, when in fact it contained some papers of no value to them. Twenty-four hours prior to the robbery $80,000 passed over the road in charge of the express company for parties in Texas. It is believed that the gang had knowledge of this shipment, but miscalculated trains. This is substantiated by the fact that after holding up the express messenger and securing all in sight they then asked him for his watch, which he handed over with this remark: "Boys you should not take my watch. I have to work hard for all I get here and you have a large sum of money in that pouch you have taken."

After robbing the train the gang went in the direction of the Cherokee Strip. A large body of Marshals and Sheriffs are in pursuit. The robbers will never surrender alive. They are desperate men and know that to surrender means life imprisonment or death, as large rewards have been offered for them before this last theft and the inducement to follow them by detectives, cowboys, and brave men is very great.
COFFEYVILLE JOURNAL 15 May 1891.

Note: It appears the JOURNAL had a short memory of their own story in 1888 about the killing of Charley Montgomery.

(Retyped Newspaper Article)
GENERAL MUSKOGEE NOTES

It is reported that about two hundred men are out searching for the Dalton gang. The rewards offered by them for the Santa Fe robbery and the robbery and murder in California aggregate $6000.
THE INDIAN CHIEFTAIN 21 May 1891

(Retyped Newspaper Article)
UNTITLED ITEM

The Dalton boys and their gang are supposed to be hiding in the Sac and Fox country.
COFFEYVILLE JOURNAL 22 May 1891

(Retyped Newspaper Article)
GENERAL NEWS ITEM

The Dalton gang of desperadoes in the Indian Territory recently succeeded in eluding the officers in the Creek mountains and are now safe from arrest for a time at least. The gang is wanted in California for two train robberies.

(Retyped Newspaper Article)
THE DALTON BOYS GET AWAY

SAC AND FOX AGENCY, O.T. June 1—Chief of Police Alex Connelly and his posse of Indian scouts, have just returned from a ten days' fruitless ride after the Dalton brothers. He says they had the train robbers at bay on the 18th instant, but that an Indian living in the neighborhood piloted the boys out over an unknown and supposed impassable road through a dense swamp, before sufficient help arrived to enable him to close in on them. The gang now numbers seven, including the most desperate characters in the Indian Territory. The robbers are now safely ensconced in the mountains on Tiger creek, in the Creek nation.
INDIAN CHIEFTAIN 4 June 1891

(Retyped Newspaper Article)
UNTITLED ITEM

Sunday night a deputy marshal named Ed Short arrested at Hennessy, Okla., one Charles Bryant, said to be a member of the Dalton Gang. As he was taking him to Wichita next day the prisoner, who was in the baggage car, got possession of a pistol and a fight ensued in which both were killed.
INDIAN CHIEFTAIN 27 Aug. 1891

(Retyped Newspaper Article)
UNTITLED ITEM

Charlie Bryant who was killed by Ed Short near Hennessey, was a native of Decatur, Wise county, Texas, where his parents and relatives still live. They are said to be highly respected and wealthy. For the past ten years

Bryant has been on the Strip and joined the Dalton band of desperadoes about a year ago. Ed was fearless and dangerous and had killed several men.

(Retyped Newspaper Article)
ED SHORT'S CAREER

The west has produced many such characters as Ed Short. His class was a shade higher than than of a desperado, yet he was a bad man. He was a bad man in the sense that he was a dangerous man. There was little of the bravado about him. Small in stature, quiet in manner, dudish in dress, he was not a man to inspire fear. He was totally unlike the dime novel hero, yet he reveled in deeds of blood and more than one man in Oklahoma will breathe easier now that he is dead.

Of this latter class Judge Theodosius Botkin probably comes first. Some weeks ago Short added much to his already notorious name by openly avowing that he intended to kill Botkin if the latter persisted in sitting as judge at the trial of James Brennan, accused of the murder of Colonel Sam Wood.

Short was Wood's friend and he shared the popular opinion that Botkin was in a measure responsible for his death.

When Sam Wood established the town of Woodsdale, in 1886 he chose for his town marshal Sam Robinson, a man with a justly earned reputation as a killer. Wood and Robinson finally disagreed and the latter went to the rival town of Hougoton. Then Wood sent for Ed Short and installed him in office to succeed Robinson.

Subsequently Short went to Hugoton on a fast horse with a warrant for the arrest of Robinson on the charge of assaulting with intent to kill a Woodsdale man at Voorhees. Two other Woodsdale men accompanied him in a buckboard.

Robinson was standing in the door of his office, on the west side of Main street, keeping close watch of Short, when the latter rode quickly up to him and thrusting his revolver toward him, fired, at the same time crying, "I have a warrant for you." He missed his mark and Robinson jumped inside the door and pushing the barrell of his gun through a broken window pane returned the compliment paid him by the Woodsdale officer. Short rode away to the north firing as he ran. Half a block down the street was J. B. Chamberlain, chairman of the board of county commissioners, standing in front of his grocery store. As Short rode by he sent two balls crashing through the front of the store, but neither took effect on Chamberlain, at whom they were aimed.

The poor marksman and his race horse kept right on down the street and across the prairie to Woodsdale. His companions in the buckboard didn't linger in Hugoton a minute after Short began his fight and they, too, struck out across the prairie. Pursuit was given by Robinson and others. Short had a good lead as did the men in the buckboard, but the latter paying little attention to the road ran into a plowed field and found their progress retarded. Seeing that they were likely to be captured they cut the traces and mounting the horses rode into Woodsdale with short tugs.

THE NEUTRAL STRIP MASSACRE

Not long after Robinson, Charlie and Orrin Cook and A. M. Mc Donald, with their wives and children, went down into the Neutral strip for a pleasure trip, expecting to hunt and fish. Short hearing of their departure started down with a posse to arrest Robinson. He overtook the party while they were preparing dinner at the Patterson ranch, and surrounding the house sent word that unless Robinson was surrendered in ten minutes he would fire on the house. Robinson felt that he could expect no mercy from Short. His friends were not willing to surrender him, but they did not wish to begin a fight which would endanger the children. Robinson was the owner of the fastest running horse in Stevens county and he proposed that he go out, mount his horse and ride away, hoping to draw the attention of Short and his party to himself and give the Cooks and McDonalds a chance to get away with their families.

Short, after surrounding the house sent a courier to Woodsdale with a message to Sam Wood asking for "ten good men and true" to come to his assistance. This reduced his party to seven. The man who was guarding the south side of the house galloped around to the north side to parley with Short. This gave Robinson his opportunity and he rushed out and mounted his horse and rode away to the south. Short and four men gave chase, firing at the fleeing horseman. After following him all day they abandoned pursuit and returned to the Patterson ranch to find that the others had escaped.

Meanwhile news of Robinson's danger had been conveyed to Hugoton and a large party hurried into the strip. They overtook Sheriff Cross and party, who had come in response to Short's message, at the hay meadows, and surprising them at night killing all except a boy named Toney. Owing to the fact that the forces of Short and Cross had not had time to unite the former escaped.
OKLAHOMA CITY TIMES JOURNAL 25/26 Aug. 1891

Note: See WHEN KANSAS WAS YOUNG by T. A. Mc Neal for further information on Short, Sam Wood, Robinson and the Stevens County war.

LILLIETTA

(Retyped Newspaper Article)
SUCCESSFUL TRAIN ROBBERY

THE PACIFIC EXPRESS COMPANY AGAIN SUFFERS

The south bound passenger train on the Missouri, Kansas & Texas road was stopped by six men at Lillietta, forty miles south of this city, Tuesday night and the express car robbed. It is thought that a large amount of money consigned to the Lehigh coal companies was secured but of course no one knows but the express officials. Engineer Russell, on arriving at Wagoner told the story substantially as follows: They had just taken water and were pulling out when two men appeared at the cab with Winchesters and commanded them to "hold up". The engineer and fireman were taken back to the express car and an entrance effected: two of the men got inside, two remained outside and two guarded the train. Whenever anyone came out of the cars they were quietly taken charge of and kept until the work was accomplished. The messenger opened the "local" safe and after taking its contents the robbers demanded that he open the "through" safe. This he could not do and finally satisfied them that such was the fact. The train was not detained but a short time and very few persons knew what had happened.

There is a story to the effect that $25,000 was secured, $2,500 of which was in silver. It is also said the agent at Lilletta went out in the direction the robbers left and came upon them dividing the plunder; also that they kept him prisoner until the job was finished. Two blood hounds were brought up from Atoka yesterday morning and an organized pursuit is being conducted. It is needless to say the Dalton's are supposed to be implicated and it is said that one of them was seen in that vicinity on Wednesday of last week.
INDIAN CHIEFTAIN 17 Sept. 1891

(Retyped Newspaper Article)
TRAIN ROBBERY
THE EXPRESS ON THE M. K. & T.
TOUCHED FOR TWO OR THREE THOUSAND DOLLARS

The Daltons are, of course, Accused of Being In It

On Tuesday night last the southbound passenger train on the M. K. & T. was flagged at Lillietta, a cattle station a few miles north of Wagoner, and the express robbed of about $2,500 or $3,000. The robbers did not molest the passengers and only detained the train a few minutes. So quietly did they do the job that the passengers did not know the train had been robbed until after they had pulled out and were nearly to Wagoner. Reports are conflicting as to the number of the robbers, one being that there were only three and another that there were seven.

Of course it is the general opinion that the job was done by the Dalton boys, and it is more than probable that they were "in it", though this is a mere matter of conjecture at this time. We got the above information from a passenger who was on the train, and what we have stated is all that he knew about it.
FORT SMITH ELEVATOR 18 Sept. 1891

(Retyped Newspaper Article)
THE CALIFORNIA DALTONS

While Bob and Emmett Dalton are worrying the officers out on the Cherokee Strip, or at least are supposed to be there, their brothers in California are making it lively for Tulare county officers. Last week we mentioned an attempted train robbery at Ceres, Cal., in which considerable shooting was indulged in, a detective named Harris being badly wounded. William Dalton and Wiley Dean are now in jail at Visalia, Tulare county, charged with being the robbers. In the same jail lies Gratt Dalton, well known in this section, who was recently convicted as accessory with Bob and Emmett in the attempted robbery sometime since in the same county. Gratt is endeavoring to get a new trial, and were he able to give $5000 bond would be released, but he can't make it. The Tulare Register gives a long account of the successful capture of Will Dalton and Wiley Dean, and asserts that there is no question about their being the right men, and says: "When the news was spread in Visalia Thursday night that a train had been held up at Ceres, Sheriff Kay asked Capt. Byrnes of Company E. N. G. C. [National Guard or State Militia] to guard the roads leading into town. Within an hour after the request was made every thoroughfare leading out of the town was guarded, and they remained guarded during the balance of the night. It was thought the robbery was committed to call out the officials at the county jail, and in their absence confederates would overpower Jailer Williams and release Gratt Dalton from the prison.

It is now known, however, that William Dalton's purpose was to rob a train, furnish bail for his brother and then the two to skip the country, but the effort was a dismal failure."

The last California legislature made attempted train robbery a capital crime punishable by death or imprisonment for life, as the jury may elect. Pryor to the attempted robbery at Ceres, Bill Dalton was in Visalia, and made threats that if his brother Gratt was sentenced it would take the entire State militia to get him to San Quentin.
FORT SMITH ELEVATOR 18 Sept. 1891

Note: No California newspaper ever reported the calling out of the National Guard or State Militia when Bill Dalton was taken to jail. Neither is there any evidence that Bill made such threats if Grat were sentenced.

(Retyped Newspaper Article)
UNTITLED ITEM

The Dalton boys have been seen recently near the Sac and Fox agency. Special Agent Dodge, sent out by the Wells Fargo Express company, had his horse shot from under him by the gang Monday last, and had a narrow escape himself.
The COFFEYVILLE JOURNAL 18 Sept. 1891
This issue of the JOURNAL also repeated the INDIAN CHIEFTAN article of 17 September.

Note: See UNDER COVER FOR WELLS FARGO by Fred Dodge. He never mentions the Lillietta robbery and never claimed the Dalton's shot a horse out from under him at anytime.

(Retyped Newspaper Article)
APPARENTLY THE DALTONS

Charley Laflore, chief of the Indian police told a reporter for this paper last week that the train robbers had been heard of twice only and there had been no fight nor anything approaching one. Twenty miles from the scene of the robbery, about two o'clock the same night, four men were seen riding northwest and leading two horses. The next night a woman who is acquainted with the Dalton boys saw two of them and two others west of Redfork, riding in the direction of the mouth of the stream of that name. They also had two lead horses and the outfit corresponded with that seen the night of the robbery. The use of the blood hounds with safety the morning after the hold-up was rendered impossible because so many persons had been trailing around there. Captain Laflore is satisfied the Daltons were the robbers.
INDIAN CHIEFTAIN 8 Oct. 1891

(Retyped Newspaper Article)
THE TERRITORY

Muscogee Phoenix: There is a rumor afloat to the effect that the California detective who came to this country to hunt the Dalton boys, and Marshal Heck Thomas, together with a posse of Uche [Yuchi] Indians, have cornered the Dalton gang in the western part of the Creek Nation. They captured their supplies and it is said trailed them to their rendezvous. A note addressed to Heck Thomas from one of the Daltons was picked up. It warned him not to try to capture them on peril of his life and stated that they (the Daltons) could have killed him more than once during the past day or two, thereby showing that the parties have been in close proximity.

COFFEYVILLE JOURNAL 23 Oct. 1891

RED ROCK

(Retyped Newspaper Article)
WORK OF THE DALTONS

A BOLD EXPRESS ROBBERY COMMITTED IN THE TERRITORY

THE DALTONS CHARGED WITH THE CRIME. A BIG HAUL MADE

The Santa Fe passenger train was held up Thursday morning of last week at Red Rock, in the Cherokee Strip, and the Wells-Fargo Express Co. robbed of a large amount of money.

It was 1 o'clock when the train reached Red Rock, in the northwest corner of the Otoe and Missouris reservation in the Cherokee Indian strip. Just as it was pulling out a few minutes later two men, with black masks covering their faces, jumped suddenly into the engine's cab from the tender, and covering the engineer and fireman with revolvers, commanded them to run the train down to the stock yards and to stop there at a given signal. Mack, the engineer, and Frank Rogers, the fireman, obeyed the command. To have resisted would have meant their death. When the train stopped the two robbers were joined by five masked companions. Their leader commanded the engineer and fireman to walk back to the express car, and commanded the fireman to break open the door with his coal pick.

E. C. Whittlesy, the messenger, and J. A. Riehl, the guard, anticipating what was going on when the train came to a standstill, had blown out the lights in their car and refused to allow any one to enter. The bandits then opened fire upon the car from all sides, and the two men responded promptly, aiming all their shots at the door. The highwaymen shot into the car from all quarters, even getting under it and shooting through the floor. Their firing, however, was all to no effect, for the messengers bravely stood their ground. In the meantime one of the robbers had chopped a hole in the door of the car large enough to admit a man's body, and the fireman was told to crawl through it into the car. This placed him literally between two fires, and Engineer Mack, seeing that it meant death to his companion, explained the situation to the messengers within and told them to cease firing. When the robbers at last entered the express car they covered those within with their guns, and with a sledge-hammer and chisel broke open both the way and through safes and robbed them of everything of value. They also took $50 and a gold watch from the guard of the express car. Messenger Whittlesy had hidden his money and watch, and the robbers got nothing from him.

The robbers are described by several of the passengers who talked with them as being well dressed and of gentlemanly appearance and bearing. This is especially true of the leader, who apologized to the engineer for a rough remark made by one of the crowd, and promised him that it should not occur again. The leader, in conversation with a passenger, asked for some smoking tobacco. The passenger reached into his coat-tail pocket for it, when the robber told him if it was in his hip-pocket he had better not attempt to get it. Afer the robbery the men mounted their horses and rode off to the southwest. The Daltons are charged with the crime, and judging from the descritpion given of the robbers by those who are acquainted with the Daltons, it was undoubtedly the notorious gang. A detective and posse had been on the latter's track for some time. Only a day or

so ago one of the gang bought eighteen boxes of cartridges at Oklahoma City, and afterwards escaped the vigilance of his pursuers. The train proceeded to the next station and the news was telegraphed along the line. It is claimed that the robbers secured the Sac and Fox annuity money, about $70,000, which was to be expressed to the Sac and Fox Agency for payment to the Indians. The express company is silent on the subject and will not say how much was stolen. This is the third attempt that has been made to secure the Sac and Fox money. This is the second time Engineer Mack has been held up by express robbers. A few months since his engine was stopped at Wharton, and he had to enter the express car.
FORT SMITH ELEVATOR 10 June 1892

(Retyped Newspaper Article)
UNTITLED ITEM

U. S. deputy marshal C. Madsen, of El Reno, was seen at the Santa Fe depot this morning. He has been acting marshal in the absence of Marshal Grimes at Washington. He was on his way home from the Pan Handle, Texas, where he has been posting detectives for the Red Rock robbery thieves. Mr. Madsen is a genial gentleman to converse with and he talked freely of his experience on the trip. There are many items concerning the matter which, as detective officer, he could not divulge. In his opinion it was not the Dalton gang. From all indications the parties were not "well up" in such business. He says the whereabouts of the fellows is known, but it is a difficult matter to corner them. His labors in the Pan Handle were attended with considerable difficulty. It was almost impossible to secure help, horses or provisions. He was finally obliged to ship horses from Kiowa. Refugees have the advantage in that section in knowing the country and having rallying points and provision stations. Mr. Madsen posted a large number of detectives and Indian scouts in that region. [from the Arkansas City Traveler.]
THE KINGFISHER FREE PRESS 16 June 1892

Note: This is the only article found so far where Madsen is mentioned in connection with the Daltons.

ADAIR

(Retyped Newspaper Article)
THE ADAIR TRAIN ROBBERY

ONE MAN KILLED, FOUR WOUNDED AND THE EXPRESS CAR CLEANED OUT

Last Thursday night's Missouri, Kansas & Texas train from the south was stopped at Adair, the express car robbed, Dr. W. L. Goff killed and several other persons wounded. The particulars of the affair as given below were chiefly obtained from a gentleman who had an excellent opportunity for observing and we believe the account is substantially correct.

As the train on the night in question whistled for the Adair station, sixteen miles south of this city, four men confronted night operator Heywood and ordered him to "flag her down," presenting their Winchesters. He agreed to do so and they got behind the depot, keeping him in range to see that he did, while the balance of the gang three or four in number stationed themselves at convenient places. As the train came to a stand-still the engine was boarded by two men while others took the conductor and train men in charge. The information published in last week's CHIEFTAIN that the Dalton boys and their associates, numbering in all about eight men, were rendezvousing in that vicinity had reached the railroad officials and as a consequence the train had been carrying guards between Muskogee and Vinita for some nights. There were eight of them on this occasion, among them being J. J. Kinney, special detective of the railroad company, Capt. Charley Leflore, Alf McCay and Bud Kell of the Indian police and Sid Johnson, a deputy marshal. Pryor Creek had been looked upon as the place of attack but still a watch was kept at all stopping places in that vicinity. Bud Kell, looking from the smoking car window, saw what was happening, gave the alarm and the officers stepped out on the east side—the opposite side from the depot. Such a move had evidently been anticipated and several of the outlaws were here to meet them and a brief fight took place, the officers using a coal house standing there as a fort. Why this fight did not last longer is accounted for in several ways, but the general belief is that it got altogether too warm for the guards. The robbers however took care to shield themselves with train men and to fire was to endanger the lives of the latter as much as the former. Simultaneously with the stopping of the train the night operator went to the express car as ordered and called the messenger but that party, glancing out of the window, saw what was "on" and jumped back. The fireman with his coal pick was next pressed into service and telling the messenger who he was and not to shoot he began battering on the door. It was not long in being opened and the express car was soon rifled of all its contents of value, including what there was in the "through" safe. This is guarded with a combination lock and the messenger is not supposed to know the combination. Messenger Geo. P. Williams got the safe door open in a very short time however, but how, he does not know. While the robbing of the car was going on the night operator was taken into the depot and told to open that safe but convinced the robbers he could not do so and they contented themselves by taking the change out of the ticket drawer. A sackfull and a half of plunder was taken from the express car, but how much money was secured is not known. The express folks say very little, as the raid was expected and shipments of value were not made by the night trains.

When the work of the raiders had been finished and they were retiring from the scene, the most unfortunate occurrence of the evening took place. Dr. W. L. Goff, who has of late been residing at Fredericktown, Mo., but was back at Adair on a visit, and Dr. T. S. Youngblood, engaged in practice at Adair, were seated on the porch of the Skinner store building, some sixty five yards from the track. In leaving the train three or four of the robbers passed through the street in front of these doctors and as they got opposite fired a volley of eighteen or twenty shots at them. Both were shot in each leg and Dr. Goff fell forward exclaiming "I'm killed." Dr. Youngblood started to run around the building when he was struck by another ball which brought him down. He then made his way as best he could to the depot and told what had happened, and the train men went after his companion. The train, which had been detained forty minutes, now proceeded upon its way, bringing the two unfortunate doctors to this place. Drs. Fortner and Bagby had previously been notified by wire that their services were needed, and as soon as the train arrived they took charge of the sufferers and rendered all possible aid. It was plainly to be seen that Dr. Goff's principal wound which was in the knee, was of a dangerous character, and it was determined that the only hope for him was to amputate the leg. The operation was carefully performed and the patient recovered from the influence of chloroform, but he had lost too much blood and died next morning at half past five. The body was embalmed and sent home to Frederickstown, on Friday night's train.

Dr. Youngblood's wounds were temporarily dressed as speedily as possible and also the wounds of the three officers. A bullet went through the flesh of Mr. Kinney's shoulder, another struck Johnson's watch and imbedded itself in his arm, while Charley Leflore had the stock of his gun struck with a shot and the slivers driven into his arm. The officers all went south on the four o'clock morning train.

On an examination of Dr. Youngblood's condition, when daylight came it was discovered that his right foot was badly shot and it was taken off at the instep. If nothing unforseen happens he will recover. Dr. Youngblood came from Taney County, Mo., six weeks or two months ago and located at Adair. The night of the robbery he and Dr. Goff were in the office when the latter insisted on going over to see the operation but reluctantly gave it up and sat down at the place named. The robbers separated, part of them going east and the balance west, as stated. The opinion is that all of them went towards the east finally, but nothing definite is known. There have been reports of them in all directions. One was that they camped a few miles from Adair and were seen cooking breakfast, another man saw them near Blue Springs, east of Grand river, where they were caring for one of their number who was wounded. Saturday two men supposed to belong to the party, one, a whisky peddler called John Green, were seen at Catoosa. These men were heavily armed and were riding fagged-out horses.

While the battle was raging, one of the outlaws was heard to cry out, "I'm shot; help me on my horse! help me on my horse!"

The railroad and express companies have joined in an offer of $5,000 each "for conviction, the aggregate sum not to exceed $40,000." Under these terms there will be no pursuit by men of experience in the country. Those who know the Dalton boys, and there can be no doubt but that they were in this hold-up, know they cannot be captured alive. To kill them does not comply with the terms and will not secure the reward but it will expose whoever does so to prosecution in the U. S. court at Fort Smith. The experience of Sheriff E. Sanders in the Kep Queen case is proof sufficient of this statement. A call for volunteers Friday to make up a pursuing party met with so few responses the project was abandoned.

A surprise party was in progress at D. S. Cumming's residence the night of the robbery and it was a vehicle from there bringing the agent's sister in, which was mistaken for the plunder wagon of the robbers.

The latest intelligence is that Gaskell's sawmill hands ran on to a gang of eighteen men in the Grand river hills who had a stack of Winchesters and a blanket spread upon the ground covered with six shooters. The strangers told the sawmill men they had business back the way they came and to go and attend to it. The advice was taken. A party, supposed to be the same one, had a wounded man and have been to the orphan asylum for a doctor and medicine. The rumor is that they buried their man a few days since, procuring a spade for digging the grave at Tip Mayes' place. Considerable alarm exists at Adair and below there. Another raid is feared and the town is closing up at dark as it had been for a week before the robbery.

INDIAN CHIEFTAIN   21 July 1892

(Retyped Newspaper Article)
THE TRAIN ROBBERY

PUSILLANIMOUS CONDUCT OF GUARD SPECIALLY INSTRUCTED FOR THE OCCASION—FATAL RANDOM SHOTS

PARSONS, Kn. July 16.—It was the most audacious thing the train robbing Daltons have done yet—their successful attack on the Pacific express car of Missouri, Kansas & Texas train No. 2 at Adair, sixty-eight miles south of here in the Indian nation, Thursday night.

They whipped a special guard of nine men, left behind them one man killed by a random shot, loaded their booty of unknown amount into a wagon and drove calmly away.

For the eight men who did this daring thing rewards aggregating $40,000 have been offered.

In the smoking car of train No. 2 there were sitting nine well armed guards sent along to prevent just such an episode as was going on in the express car. These doughty guards were commanded by J. J. Kinney, chief of the road's detectives and Capt. J. H. La Flore, chief of the Cherokee Indian police, who had been told to expect a raid at Adair that very night. About the time the robbery was all over these guards became dimly aware of what was going on, and they opened a rapid fire at the freebooters through the car windows. The robbers replied with promptness and much vigor. Bullets whistled everywhere. However, the robbers loaded their wagon and drove merrily off toward the wood, firing as they went.

After the robbers had disappeared in the dark it was found that their fire had been deadly.

In a drug store near the depot Doctors W. L. Goff and Youngblood had been sitting. Many stray bullets tore through the frame wall of the building and both of the men were struck by them. Dr. Goff died in a short time. Dr. Youngblood's condition is most serious.

The robbers' bullets wrought injury among the guards too. Capt. Kinney was slightly wounded in the shoulder and La Flore received a superficial wound on the arm while a guard named Ward was slightly wounded.

(Retyped Newspaper Article)
HELD UP THE TRAIN

ARMED MEN HOLD UP AND ROB A TEXAS EXPRESS—TWO PERSONS ON THE TRAIN REPORTED TO BE WOUNDED.

PARSONS, Kan. July 15—Word has just reached here that the Missouri, Kansas & Texas passenger train No. 2 was held up at Adair station in the Indian territory about seventy miles south of this city by the notorious Dalton gang.

The safe in the express car was blown open and robbed of its contents.

Capt. J. J. Kinney, chief of the detective force of the Missouri, Kansas & Texas, and L. A. Flore, of the Indian police, and two doctors from Adair were shot while attempting to protect the company's property, but none of them were seriously injured.

The exact amount of money secured by the robbers is not known.

The robbers made good their escape.

The train was held up at the tank just south of Adair, and when the engineer attempted to step on the footboard, he was confronted by two men with drawn revolvers and told to remain quiet or he would have his brains blown out.

There were six men in the gang, and two remained to guard the engineer and fireman while the others watched the train and broke into the express car. The fireman was compelled to go ahead of the robbers and break down the door, and came near being killed by the messenger, who shot several times at the attacking party.

Capt. Kinney and the Indian policeman were in the car as there had been a rumor of trouble, and they were prepared to make a

William Todd "Bill" Power. Courtesy of Pat Waddle.

desperate fight, but were wounded before they were able to do anything towards defending the safe.

When the robbers effected an entrance they went to work to get into the safe, and wasted no time but at once blew it open. They hastily grabbed up all the contents and then went off, telling the engineer to go ahead and not stop until he got to the next station.

When the attack was made there was a

fusilade between the robbers and the guard which sounded like a battle.

It is said that there were several large sums in the safe, aggregating over $40,000, but the people connected with the company will give out nothing definite, but say that the amount was very small.
THE KINGFISHER FREE PRESS 21 July 1892

Adair was the last train robbery for the Dalton Gang. The next step was the attempt to make outlaw history by robbing two banks at one time. This foolhardy raid in Coffeyville, Kansas proved to be the Waterloo of the Dalton Gang.

VII. The Coffeyville Affair

By 4 October 1892 the Dalton Gang had been pared down to only five members. Stories abound about why Doolin, Newcomb, and Pierce left the Gang. Emmett said those three men became too undisciplined and dangerous and were asked to leave. Others have claimed the Daltons kept too much of the proceeds of the robberies and the other three got tired of getting the short end of the stick. In any event, on the night of 4 October it was Bob, Emmett, Grat, Power, and Broadwell who camped on the farm of P. L. Davis on Onion Creek.

The three men in front, Grat, Power, and Broadwell proceded to enter the C. M. Condon & Co. Bank. The men in the rear, Bob and Emmett entered the First National Bank. As they walked to the banks one man in the street noted that part of the men were wearing false beards. He continued to watch; as soon as he saw a Winchester pointed at the cashier in Condon's Bank he sounded the alarm.

The citizens were totally unprepared but quickly

On the morning of 5 October around 9 a.m. the five men rode into Coffeyville, Kansas. The streets were already filled with people going about their normal business. Witnesses later said that when the men rode in they were mistaken for a posse. However, no arms were visible and the men rode in two ranks, three in front and two in the rear. The men hitched their horses in an alley at the rear of a lot owned by Police Judge Munn and at about the same time an oil tank of the Consolidated Company pulled by two horses was also hitched in the same area.

The men dismounted and grouped themselves into the same formation, three in front and two in the rear.

Dead bandits at Coffeyville. Left to right are Bill Power, Bob Dalton, Grat Dalton, and Dick Broadwell. Notice the state of their clothing, Bob's pants, all pockets turned out, etc. Courtesy of the Kansas State Historical Society.

went to the two hardware stores in town, armed themselves, and did battle.

The robbers found C. T. Carpenter, one of the owners, Tom C. Babb, bookkeeper, and Charles M. Ball, cashier, in the Condon Bank. The bandits demanded the money from the vault but Cashier Ball told them there was a time lock that could not be opened until about 10 minutes later. The bandits decided to wait, but in the meantime the citizens opened fire.

In the First National Bank Bob and Emmett found Thomas G. Ayres, cashier, W. H. Shepard, another employee, and B. S. Ayers, bookkeeper. B. S. Ayres collected the money for the bandits. The Daltons then marched the three bankers out in front of them, when they reached the door citizens began shooting at them. Bob and Emmett retreated and left the bank by the back door.

At Isham Brothers & Mansur and A. P. Boswell & Co., the hardware stores, guns had been swiftly handed out. George Cubine and C. S. Cox had stationed themseves at Rammel Bros. Drug Store. Charles T. Gump had been driving a team; he ran into Isham's and armed himself. He was wounded in the hand by a shot from Bob Dalton and pulled back into Isham's store. Lucuis M. Baldwin, a clerk at Read Brothers General Merchandise went to Isham's, got a pistol and started toward Bob and Emmett. The Daltons ordered him to stop; he kept walking and Bob shot and fatally wounded him. He died about three hours later. Bob then spotted George Cubine at Rammel Brothers and shot him through the heart. Charles Brown approached the prostrate man, seized Cubine's gun and began firing. Brown quickly fell, fatally wounded.

Thomas Ayres left the bank and seized a Winchester at Isham's; Bob shot him and wounded him in the face. He recovered from his wounds. Lewis A. Dietz and T. Arthur Reynolds were cusomers in Isham's when the battle started. Reynolds was wounded in the foot. M. N. Anderson, Charles K. Smith, and Henry H. Isham all did battle from the vicinity of Isham's.

Grat, Broadwell, and Power all came under fire from the guns at Isham's. Grat was wounded and found cover behind the oil tank, from there he fired several wild shots. Power received mortal wounds and fell dead at the feet of his horse.

John J. Kloehr, Carey Seamen, and Marshal Connelly (unarmed when the shooting started, he obtained a Winchester from the Swisher Brothers machine shop) all advanced on the alley. Grat shot and killed Connelly. Broadwell made it to his horse, mounted and rode away but was shot by Kloehr and Seamen. After the fight Broadwell was found dead about one-half mile out of the city.

Bob was hit from by gunfire from Isham's and staggered across the alley, sat down, and kept shooting. He got to his feet and was hit again by Kloehr. Grat again tried to get to his horse and Kloehr shot him in he throat and broke his neck.

Emmett reached the alley unhurt and attempted to mount his horse. He was carrying the money bag from the First National. Bob and Power's horses were killed by the shots fired at Emmett, as were the two horses hitched to the oil tank wagon. Emmett made it into the saddle but was shot through the right arm, left hip, and groin. Still clinging to the money bag Emmett rode back and reached down for the dying Bob. Carey Seamen shot both barrels of his shotgun into Emmett's back and Emmett dropped to the alley.

Emmett held up his uninjured hand and surrendered. The crowd suggested lynching but cooler heads prevailed and he was taken to Dr. Wells' office and given medical care.

The shooting stopped less that fifteen minutes after the robbers had entered the banks.

All of the bandits were described as closely shaven, clean and well clothed. Grat was wearing a false beard and Power and Bob were supposedly masked. The three Daltons were all armed with a Winchester and with a pair of revolvers each. Supposedly all three of their Winchesters had been repeatedly fired, but none of the revolvers had been used. Later Emmett's guns became an issue and he claimed he had never fired a shot.

The tally was eight men killed and three men wounded. The money was recovered and the next day the First National reported a surplus of $1.98 and Condon's a loss of $20.00.

Note: The account of the raid is summarized from D. S. Elliott and Ed Bartholomew's THE DALTON GANG AND THE COFFEYVILLE RAID and from the account in the 7 October 1892 COFFEYVILLE JOURNAL written by D. S. Elliott.

The news quickly spread and soon newspapers everywhere carried the story. A great deal of false information was reported in the beginning. At first there were reports that six men had been seen riding into town that morning and new stories are still appearing about the "Sixth Man". It was Doolin and his horse went lame. It was Newcomb and Bob told him to go out around town and come in another way. It was Julia Johnson dressed as a man. It was Grandpa and he held the horses while the Daltons robbed the banks. It was Uncle Charley and he rode up to the city limits with the Daltons while trying to talk them out of the whole thing. There are hundreds of stories, but there is no evidence for the presence of any sixth man. Eyewitness accounts were, as they always are, conflicting.

The most repeated story in the early newspaper accounts was that the sixth man was Allie Ogee and that he escaped. One newspaper even reported that he had been killed and his body was being brought in. Allie himself quickly laid this tale to rest when he sent a letter to the Coffeyville newspaper a few days later informing one and all that he had been living and working in Wichita since January of that year. Other people who knew Allie also sent letters to the Coffeyville paper, to the WICHITA EAGLE and to other publications in his behalf as well. Allie had been at work at Dold's Packing House in Wichita at the time of the robbery. The missing man was undoubtably Broadwell who rode out of town a short way before he died.

The shooting was over but the excitement was not. People descended on the town in droves. On 7 October the COFFEYVILLE JOURNAL reported that an estimated 2,000 people had visited the city. The bodies of the dead bandits were carried to the city jail and placed under guard, but not before many people took pieces of clothing, hair, and other items as souvenirs. The dead horses were mined for souvenirs too, manes and tails were clipped, and horse shoes were taken.

Reporters from other towns soon arrived, demanded, and were granted interviews with Emmett. At this time nobody thought Emmett would live much longer and some newspapers even reported he had died.

One paper carried a lengthy article about the affair on 7 October. Excerpts follow:

"The air was full of rumors and conflicting stories and amidst so much confusion and excitement, it would have required a reporter of years of experience to ferret out the truth. When we arrived there the citizens killed and wounded had been removed to their homes, and stretched on a platform near where they received their fatal wounds, were the four bodies of the desperadoes, surrounded by a crowd. On every corner and at every convenient point were groups of men and women, and no two would tell the same story.

There were a few who saw the men enter town positive that there were six of them. A number of ladies, living on the street by which they entered the city, and who were attracted by their ruffian appearance, said that there were only five, and Emmet Dalton stated the same fact. By those who believed there were six, it was stated that a half breed by the name of Allie Ogee, remained with the horses, and with the first report of gun mounted his horse and made for the territory. There were wild reports that Lemon's old mill was full of desperadoes the night before, and that there was an armed force of Indian Territory ruffians liable to drop down on the town at most any moment.

Through the kindness of Sheriff Callahan we were permitted to visit the office of Dr. Wells, when Emmet Dalton was under examination. We saw a young man lying on a bed who had just reached his majority. He had rather an attractive face, a mild clear eye, good complexion, regular features, and a voice as smooth and pleasant as a man often possesses. There was nothing coarse, nor brutal, nor villinous looking about him. A man would indeed have been hard hearted, who could have witnessed the ordeal through which he went without feeling a pity in his heart.

All the bodies were carried before him for identification. The first corpse was of a tall young man, rawboned, with prominent features. As it was lifted to where Emmet could recognize it, he faltered, and in quivering voice said: 'I identify that as my brother Bob Dalton.' The tears filled his eyes and for a moment it seemed as if he would give up to his feelings, but he soon recovered himself, and proceeded to answer questions.

He said Bob Dalton was 23 years old the 13th of last May. That he [Emmett] had not been with his brothers for a year and a half, until the 1st of October, when he met them south of Tulsa in the territory. Bob told him that he was in the Adair robbery, and also in the California robbery in January, 1890 [sic]. Grat Dalton, Tom Evans and Jake Moore were in Adair robbery with Bob.

The second corpse brought into the room was identified as Graton Dalton, and again he broke down. He said Bob told him that Graton was in the California robbery. He was 31 years of age.

The third corpse he identified as Tom Evans and the fourth as Jake Moore. He knew

The Coffeyville Affair

nothing about them. He first met them October 1st. He knew nothing about 'Texas Jack' or whether he was the man called Jake Moore or not.

In an imperfect manner we noted down the following statement as he made it, in regard to the Coffeyville bank robbery:

"On the 1st of October I met the boys 20 miles south of Tulsa. They asked me how much money I had, I told them about $20. I asked them the amount they had, and they replied about $900. I asked them what they were going to do. They said this town of Coffeyville had been talking about them; and some of the people at Coffeyville had been trying to have them captured. I told them it was a lie; that they used to have lots of friends there. Bob said that he could discount the James boys' record, and go up and rob both banks in one day. I told him that I didn't want any of it in mine. They said I had better go along and help, and get some of the money and leave the country; that if I staid around here by myself I would be sure and get caught, or killed.

On the morning of the 3d we were north of Tulsa, in Osage nation, and we rode twenty miles towards Coffeyville. We talked the bank robbery over as we came along that day. I tried to persuade them not to come, for the people here had never done us any harm. So they said all right, if I didn't want to go along that four of them would go and give them a round up. So I told them if that was the case I might as well go along; and I went for the love of my brothers, I knew the people would chase me just as hard if I was not along, and I had no money to get out of the country on.

We camped yesterday, the 4th, on a timbered hill on Hickory Creek, about 12 miles from Coffeyville. During the night we saddled up and rode to Onion Creek, and camped on Mr. Davis' farm. This morning we fed the horses some corn, and I asked them if they were still in the notion of coming up here, and they said they were. I told them they had better not go; that it wouldn't be treating the men right who had always defended us. I asked them how they were going

Bob and Grat Dalton after the Coffeyville raid. Courtesy of the Kansas State Historical Society.

to do it. Bob said we'd ride in here about 9:30 a. m. I asked him what his idea was for that, and he said there wouldn't be so many people here at that time—wouldn't be so many people to hold up in the morning and wouldn't have to hurt anybody. He told me he would like to have me go with him because I was quick on foot, and he and I would go to the First National bank and let the other three go to other bank. So he said we would ride and hitch north of the lumber yard. We would hitch there as people wouldn't see us until we were right in the bank. When we got out to the lumber yard we saw there were no hitch racks, so we came around near the cooler [the jail].

I am a full cousin of the Younger boys. My mother is a sister to Cole Younger's father. They and the James boys are no relation. Five were all there were of us. I have not seen Allie Ogee for two years.

Bob and I started to come out the front way of the First National bank. Bob stepped on the street and shot his Winchester south once. We then went back and went out of the back door to the alley. Met a man with a six-shooter. Bob killed him. We then went west went in back of Wells Bros. to our horses. Bob shot several times going up the street. I did not see Cubine. I know him. I could have got away, but saw Bob fall, and rode back to him. He held up his hand and I was endeavoring to get him on my horse, when I was disabled.'

He here showed signs of weakening under the questioning, and murmering something about his dead brothers, began to cry. The sheriff stopped the examination and cleared the room.

Emmet told the story several times during the day, and always the same way, except in some small details. Knowing that a man guilty of the sets he was that day could not be relied on, we heard his statements with many doubts as to the part he played in the tragedy. It seems to us, since considering it, that he was making a shrewd, careful talk for his life, as he evidently feared a mob."
STAR AND KANSAN 7 OCT. 1892.

The newspapers reported that Adeline Dalton along with Ben, Bill, Simon, and Eva all arrived in Coffeyville on 7 October. From the newspaper reports and from the documents concerning the estates of Bob and Grat it appears that considerable tension developed between Bill Dalton and the population of Coffeyville.

Here again the newspapers tell the story:

(Retyped Newspaper Article)
LAST RAID OF THE DALTONS

Send in your orders at once of "The Last Raid of the Daltons." The edition will be limited. First come first served. Mailed to any address upon receipt of twenty-five cents.

(Retyped Newspaper Article)
UNTITLED ITEMS

United States Marshal Payne of Oklahoma came up on Thursday to get a look at the remains of the Dalton gang whom he had been following for fifteen months.

The relic hunters cut off portions of the manes and tails of the Dalton horses and all the strings from the saddles. They also took pieces from the clothing of the dead robbers.

Supt. Frey, of the M. K. & T. railroad, and about fifty men armed with Winchesters came down from Parsons on a special on Wednesday to assist our people if help was needed. They made the run in thirty-two minutes.
COFFEYVILLE JOURNAL 7 Oct. 1892

Note: This is the only newspaper article found so far that mentions Payne in connection with the Daltons.

(Retyped Newspaper Article)
LOST THE DALTONS
...William Dalton arrived here yesterday (Guthrie, O.T.), he came overland from the direction of the country where his brothers had been for some time, and he wore a full beard, which he had shaved off at once. His actions are suspicious all around and are being investigated by the officers.
TOPEKA DAILY CAPITOL 8 Oct. 1892

(Retyped Newspaper Article)
UNTITLED ITEMS

Ben Dalton and his mother left for home this evening.

Mrs. Whipple, sister of the Dalton boys left for her home at Kingfisher on last Monday evening.

COFFEYVILLE JOURNAL 10 Oct. 1892

(Retyped Newspaper Article)
UNTITLED ITEMS

Emmet Dalton was taken to Independence by Sheriff Callahan on Tuesday morning. He was accompanied by his brother William, and stood the trip quite well. At last accounts, he was thought to be slowly improving.

K. C. Star: D. S. Elliott, editor of the Coffeyville, Kas. JOURNAL, is in town with a mass of reading matter, pictures, etc. intended for the manuscript of a book about to be published concerning the Daltons, their lives, deeds and tragic end. He took part in the fight and will bring out a little book just as soon as the publisher can print it. He intends it a good deal as a tribute to the brave citizens who fell.

The chestnut sorrel horse, captured from the Daltons, was turned over to Mr. Chapman of Tulsa, he having proven by several witnesses that the horse was stolen from his pasture on the 30th of September.

COFFEYVILLE JOURNAL 11 Oct. 1892

> **C. G. GLASS will furnish Photographs of the**
> **DALTONS**
> **and scenes incident to the RAID from the**
> **Original Negatives.**
> (The only good ones made)
> To any address upon receipt of price
>
> Robt. Dalton - - - - - - 35c
> Robt. and Grat Dalton - - - - 35c
> Daltons, Broadwell and Powers - 35c
> Condon & Co's. Bank - - - - 35c
> Condon & Co's. Bank Windows showing shots - - - - - - 35c
> Fence where horses were tied and and where Bob fell dead - - 35c
>
> The above Photographs are all Cabinet size.
> **ROBERT DALTON, LIVING,**
> from the only Photograph known to be in existence will be on sale on and after Oct. 28, price 35 cents.
>
> **C. G. GLASS,**
> **Photographer,**
> **Coffeyville, Kansas.**

This ad first appeared in the Coffeyville Journal 18 October 1892. This or similar ads continued to run in the Journal as did ads for Editor Elliott's booklet THE LAST RAID OF THE DALTONS.

(Retyped Newspaper Article)
A CARD

We desire to return our sincere thanks to the citizens of Coffeyville for their uniform kindness to us during our stay in their midst. We have no emnity against any one what ever on account of the late terrible tragedy. We desire to return our thanks, also to Dr. Wells for his kind attention to Emmet.

Mrs. A. L. Dalton
Ben Dalton

COFFEYVILLE JOURNAL 14 Oct. 1892

By late October it was obvious that Bill Dalton had raised a little hell because some of the citizens of the town and area had appropriated Emmett's guns and horse. Bill had obviously taken legal action to have these items returned to the Dalton family. The JOURNAL and the STAR AND KANSAN were also in a contest about some of these matters. The JOURNAL editor is very much involved and from here on the JOURNAL loses no chance to slam Bill Dalton every chance they got. Other neswpapers were in for a good bit of acid from the pen of the editor of the JOURNAL as well. A rather controversial Kansas congressman, Jerry Simpson also got "the treatment" from the JOURNAL.

(Retyped Newspaper Article)
**WILL DALTON
A BROTHER OF THE DEFUNCT DESPERADOES
HE THREATENS COFFEYVILLE CITIZENS
WITH A SUIT—A SLICK HAND AT CARDS—HIS BOLD
AIRS MAY END SORROWFULLY**

COFFEYVILLE, Kan., Oct. 26—A new feature in the Dalton affair is promised, and a most unique one it is. Will Dalton is contemplating suing the city for damages, alleging as a cause of action that while the bodies of the dead bandits were in charge of the city

Grave of Bob, Grat, and Bill Power. Note metal bar to the left of tombstone. This is part of the hitching rail where the horses were tied. This was the sole grave marker for many years. Emmett had the tombstone put up many years later. Latta Collection. Courtesy of Christopher D. Brewer.

unauthorized persons were allowed to rifle the pockets and abstract money and valuables, which have not been turned over to William or the family.

Will was interviewed in regard to the matter and acknowledged that there was a strong probability of such an action being begun, claiming, however, that one of the ablest attorneys in the state was backing and instigating the suit on a contingent fee.

Who this attorney is he refuses to state, but it is thought by the citizens that Luther Perkins, the moneyloaner, is really at the back of the affair, although the description does not fit him, as he is not allowed to practice law, although he is an attorney.

Will said that he knows one of the citizens robbed the bodies of the $900 which Emmet claims they had before coming into Coffeyville. This is in all probability the sheerest nonsense, as no one else seems to know anything about it. The chances are that it is only a bluff game, played in order to force those who took the articles from the bandit's pockets and are keeping them as relics to return them.

William is not very popular here as it is, and such a move as this and statements like he made yesterday morning when he said: "The boys were wrong in trying to rob the banks, but were right when they shot the men who were trying to kill them," are calculated to make him less so.

Emmet is still improving and will undoubtedly recover. His cell is brightened by bouquets of beautiful flowers sent him by foolish women and he is having what many people think an easy time when it is considered that three widows and one poor old mother mourn their husbands and son by reason of the Dalton raid. William declares that there will be no danger of Emmet's conviction and that there will be plenty of money for his defense is certain. Will's actions and words and his bank account are all interesting straws to watch when considering the question of his being a silent partner in the late firm of "Dalton Brothers, bandits and outlaws." whose business cards should have borne the inscription: "Train and bank robbing a specialty."

Will is a pretty smooth individual with cards, and it is said by knowing ones that Sunday night was a time which will be remembered by Independence sports on account of William walking away with $500 of their cash which they had wagered in a poker game.

In speaking of Ben, the elder brother Will says: "He is too chicken hearted and easy. Why he was scared half to death when he was here and kept begging me to keep still, but they can't bluff me, I say what I please." The statement of Ben being frightened is hard to believe, for in addition to his impressing one with a belief in his coolness and grit his actions here were quiet and gentlemanly and he was well treated by everyone. All the citizens believe in his honesty and credit him with being a good citizen, so there was no reason for his being frightened even if he were inclined to be a coward. After the conversation with the reporter Will entered the hotel office and stated that he came "very near shooting a newspaper man just now and the next one that braced him would be shot."

INDIAN CHIEFTAIN 27 Oct. 1892

(Retyped Newspaper Article)
SLANDERING SIMPSON

**HE APOLOGIZES FOR ROBBERY
AND MURDER
A DEFENDER OF BANDITS
A GRATUITOUS INSULT TO EVERY BRAVE MAN IN
KANSAS**

[A letter is quoted which appeared in the Kansas City Journal. Simpson was on a train when he heard about the Coffeyville Raid and he reportedly said] "The Dalton boys were no worse than the national bankers and thousands of others in Kansas who are engaged in pretended lawful pursuits, while really they are robbing the people. They are to be no more condemned for their acts than the bankers they robbed." [other letters followed that stated that Simpson was quoted correctly]

[The JOURNAL commented]: "Business men of Kansas, whether republicans or democrats, what do you think of a party that will put forward a man so devoid of principle as a leader and mouthpiece? The people's party is bound by the declarations of Simpson.

Will you vote to endorse doctrine like that enunciated by Simpson? Brave men of Coffeyville, rise in your might and resent the insult."

A number of Chicago Bankers had a gold medal made to be presented to John Kloehr, who killed three of the Daltons in the recent raid on Coffeyville. The metal was recently

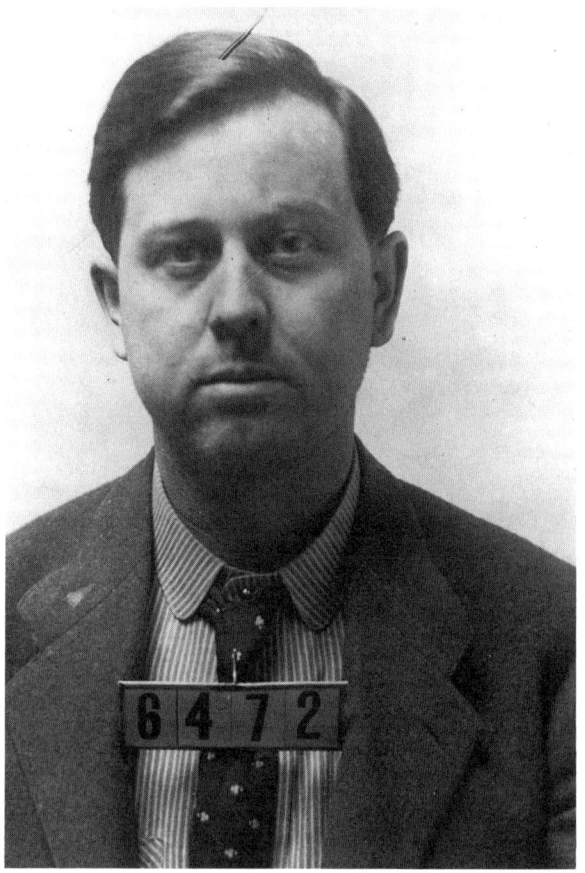 

Prison mug shots of Emmett Dalton. Courtesy of the Kansas State Historical Society.

(Retyped Newspaper Article)
UNTITLED ITEM

John Callahan has taken out letters of administration in the estate of Bob and Grat Dalton.
COFFEYVILLE JOURNAL 28 Oct. 1892

(Retyped Newspaper Article)
UNTITLED ITEMS

The story of the plot to kill Jerry Simpson is very thin.

forwarded to Mr. Kloehr. It is of gold with a large diamond set in the center. The inscription reads "John Kloehr-the emergency rose, the man appeared."
COFFEYVILLE JOURNAL 4 Nov. 1892

(Retyped Newspaper Article)
UNTITLED ITEMS

John Callahan was in town yesterday collecting the effects of the late lamented Bill Powers who passed away during the recent Dalton raid. He will sell them and apply the money towards the payment of the funeral expenses which necessarily occurred.

The theory of the people of Coffeyville that Mr. William Dalton likes to drink whiskey better than he likes shooting scrapes, is doubtless in the main correct, for it is probable that human nature is as strong in the Daltons as it is in other men, and that the desire to become a corpse, however natural the features may look, is easily controlled. While on the other hand the desire to accumulate a richly scented jag and paint Michael Aelong [Michelangelo?] frescoes on the sky, is doubtless in a low browed citizen such as Mr. Dalton is said to be, hard to supress. K. C. Star
COFFEYVILLE JOURNAL 2 Dec. 1892

(Retyped Newspaper Article)
WORKING THEIR SCHEME

EMMET DALTON'S PISTOLS GIVEN UP BY MR. ELLIOTT IN ANSWER TO A REPLEVIN SUMMONS WITH THE OUTLAWS NAME ATTACHED AS PLAINTIFF—THE OLD GANG'S WORK.

From the Daily Telegram. The sequel to the demand of Bill Dalton on the editor of The Journal, for Emmet's pistols came out this morning when constable H. C. Jewett of Independence came down and served a writ of replevin on the editor for the guns. The writ was issued on behalf of that exemplary candidate for heaven, Col. Emmet Dalton who is now visiting with Major Thos. Callahan, sheriff of Montgomery county, occupying the chamber of state in the county hotel and receiving the deferential and obsequious attentions of the many good people of Independence who deeply sympathize with him over the very unfortunate circumstance of his being charged with assisting in the murder of four of the citizens of Coffeyville and attempting in a joking way to abstract the money belonging to those robber institutions, the banks of this city.

In his hour of trouble he is greatly comforted by the hearty sympathy and assistance proffered him by Col. Charles Ehret of the Star and Kansan, and other scalawags too numerous to mention, all of them by the way being pliant tools of that angelic person who resides in Coffeyville and whose name we have agreed to ourselves, never to inflict upon our many readers again, where it can be possibly avoided. In this replevin action it was necessary for even such a distinguished and noble citizen, as Col. Dalton to give bond. Although for several years having been in open rebellion against the unjust laws of the country which, owing to carelessness on the part of lawmakers, did not give him the right to levy tribute on express companies and banks and to use his "God given right of self defense" (according to his brother, General William Dalton, of California fame) in depriving any who might object, of their lives, he in this instance had to conform to the laws which he so justly despises. This was no doubt a hard pill to swallow but Dr. Mc Cullagh and Major Grant sugar coated it by going on the bond.

The guns were given up by the editor who it must be confessed acted something nearly akin to a champ in letting this outfit take any advantage of laws meant for the protection of decent people and which have numerous clauses providing for the care of such roosters, in a thickly populated settlement, not far from Leavenworth. It is surmised, by the way, that the reason part of this gang have not long since joined the population of that busy community, is due to a hesitancy on the part of the managers, who dislike the danger of corrupting the morals of their wards.

One thing however must be taken into consideration and that is, a probable desire on the part of Callahan's distinguished guest, to pay a visit to his friends in the Territory and help his brother "Billious" search for some of the wealth which Billious and the other members of the tribe concealed at various times and places. When the time comes for him to go on this visit these revolvers will come in good play, for it may be possible some ignorant guards, (waiters, Emmet likes to consider them and it must be confessed this seems to be the right name) might object to his leaving on such short notice and these "persuaders" would help him overcome their objections.

That he will have these in his possession is certain, for the writ directs the constable to turn them over to him and when it comes to serving him the officers will of course do their whole duty.

In the meantime we would quietly suggest that there is a time coming when it will be still more unhealthy for a number of this gang that it has been in the past and now is.

The guns give [sic] this morning to Constable Jewett by the editor of the Journal, were surrendered to Mr. Elliott, (he being the first one to reach Emmet) by Emmet Dalton when he was lying in the Slosson alley. The charge that Mr. Elliott had or has anything belonging to the dead bandits, is we are requested to say by him false in every particular. It originated with certain enemies who delight in sneaking contemptible ways. They have for their tools the editor of the Star and Kansan and others who in due time will, to their sorrow, wish they had never allowed themselves to be roped in.

COFFEYVILLE JOURNAL 2 Dec. 1892

(Retyped Newspaper Article)
UNTITLED ITEM

The report sent out from Muskogee last Monday that Wm. Dalton had shot Deputy Marshal Chapman on the day previous in the Deep Fork country, over Emmett Dalton's horse, is undoubtedly false. On the day referred to Dalton was in this city, [Independence, KS] and remained until Monday."

STAR AND KANSAN 2 Dec. 1892

(Retyped Newspaper Article)
OUR FRIENDS, THE ENEMY

The Independence Reporter, is evidently trying to wrest the honor of being the official organ of "the gang" from the Star and Kansan. In commenting on our article regarding this gang, the young scissors wielder who writes such a hand that his printers mistake "took" for "stole," gives vent to the following which we select from a mass of other "stuff."

'We do not believe the ravings of D. Stewart Elliott and his echo Joe Goodykoontz of The Telegram represent the feelings of the citizens of Coffeyville, and THE SOONER THEY HAVE THEIR WIND SHUT OFF THE BETTER.

Replying to the above we desire to say that quite enough people have had their wind shut off by this gang. Charles T. Connelly, Chas. Brown, George Cubine and Lucius Baldwin were victims of this "shutting off" business, and the people of Coffeyville are in no humor to have the gang shut anybody else's wind off, regardless of what young jackanapes Sickels may advise. If this represents the feelings of the Independence people they are to be pitied. Can it be possible that they want anyone else killed by this outfit? If the editor of the Reporter were a representative citizen, we might think so, but as it is we are disposed to think a little better of them than this. Regarding the feelings of the people of Coffeyville towards the editors of the Telegram and JOURNAL, a casual glance at our advertising columns will show how the merchants feel and our subscription lists will emphasize the fact that the people are with us. Coffeyville has suffered enough, too much, from this gang already. There will be no shutting off of wind.

(Retyped Newspaper Article)
UNTITLED ITEM

The attempt of the Independence Tribune to explain the Dalton revolver controversy is worse than an open attack on the editor of The Journal. The facts in the case are known to every man who cared to inquire into them, and Charley Yoe [Yoes?] certainly did not write the article in question, because he knows how the editor got the revolvers and why he retained them. In connection with the aspersions that have been cast on the editor of THE JOURNAL, the public ought to know that every man who had anything to do with wiping out the raiders is spotted; that threats have been made openly and covertly , against the defenders of Coffeyville's honor and property of her citizens' that armed allies of the Dalton's frequent our city and by their presence threaten the personal safety of the heroes who flew to the defense of right on the 5th of October; therefore every word that is uttered against one of these men is an encouragement to the red-handed murderers to continue their work and carry out their schemes for revenge. The advice of the Tribune's baby, surnamed the Reporter, that the wind of the editors of THE JOURNAL and Telegram ought to be shut off, comes with very bad grace from a self-styled organ of law and order. The fellow who undertakes the job can only accomplish it by pursuing the same cowardly methods that the gang and their organs are following—shooting in the dark. We are not compelled to rely on the guns of red-handed murderers, highwaymen, outlaws and inhuman wretches who had no rights that any citizen was bound to respect, for defense. The scoundrel who undertakes the "shutting off" job is informed that the very same Winchester that spoke so effectually on the 5th of October is within easy reach, and it has not lost any of its efficiency or death-dealing qualifications.

(Retyped Newspaper Article)
UNTITLED ITEM

Young Sickels, who plays like he is editing a paper in Independence, while to a great extent a pair of shears furnishes the copy for the printers who work on the paper (?), would better ask the old man to give up that soft snap he has in Topeka and come down and run the paper, or send a man who can do some decent work. The young gentleman is more fitted for a skating rink master than a pen wielder. In a few remarks in last Saturday morning's paper he spilled himself over those pistols which once belonged to Emmet Dalton and said they were "stolen" by Col. Elliott. In Sunday morning's sheet he renigged, eat his words as it were, and laid the blame on the poor printers who work for him. All editors write horrible fists, generally, but it seems hard to believe that a man would write "took" in such a way that the printers would set it up "stole" and then where was proof reader Sickels? It won't wash young man. You have evidently prevaricated as you did when you said the pistols were Gratton Dalton's. If they were Grat's why is it that Emmet Dalton claims them? In a very evident desire to besmirch the character of the editor of the Journal, you have lent yourself to the gang. Repent young man, before it is too late.

(Retyped Newspaper Article)
UNTITLED ITEM

The first edition of 5000 copies of the "Last Raid of the Daltons" by the editor of The Journal, is about exhausted. Another edition will be issued at once, and the demand for this reliable account of the raid met by the publishers.
COFFEYVILLE JOURNAL 9 Dec. 1892

(Retyped Newspaper Article)
UNTITLED ITEM

Emmet Dalton's Winchester was found in the possession of an Independence citizen this week, who surrendered it as reluctantly as did the Coffeyville Journal editor the revolvers. Every shot was discharged, and the man who had it claims it was in that condition when it came into his possession.
STAR AND KANSAN 9 Dec. 1892

(Retyped Newspaper Article)
UNTITLED ITEM

We have it from good authority that Col. D. Stewart Elliott, the man who parts his name in the middle—the editorial individual who delights in his own picture—solicited an Independence attorney to take his case in procuring a return of the Dalton pistols, on the ground that they are contraband goods—that is goods which neutrals are prohibited from furnishing the belligerent party during a war. Of course the lawyer, being one of the best in the county, refused to take charge of such a case. In attempting to raise technicalities of this nature has led some to believe that Col. Elliott is the attorney for the Daltons, and all the balderdash in the Journal and Telegram about everybody who is not "mashed" on the pseudo-colonel being a Dalton sympathizer is a part of a deep scheme to blind people so that they will not catch on to the maneuvers of the gang. If he can get possession of the revolvers as contraband goods, then the plea is to be raised that Emmet Dalton is being held as a prisoner of war, and as the war is over he should be released. The latter proposition

is as sensible as Elliott's present plea.
STAR AND KANSAN 16 Dec. 1892

(Retyped Newspaper Article)
BILL DALTON AS MARSHAL

The latest farce in the dealing out of justice is the appointment of Bill Dalton as deputy United States Marshal, his commission being issued from the office of Col. Yoe [Yoes] at Ft. Smith. there have, for several days, been rumors to the effect that this was the case, but not until yesterday were we able to ascertain definitely the facts in the case.

The commission is a special one, issued with a warrant for the arrest of Ed Chapman who has possession of the horse Emmet rode into Coffeyville. It would seem that there are enough good men to enforce the laws of the land without calling on the Dalton gang. Senator Vest was right in condemning the condition of affairs which permit this and kindred appointments. There needs to be a purification in the courts as well as in some other places.
COFFEYVILLE JOURNAL 23 Dec. 1892

(Retyped Newspaper Article)
UNTITLED ITEM

On last Monday morning district court reconvened and the first case called was that of Emmett Dalton, charged with murder. He was taken from the county jail in a chair, fastened on two polls [sic], and carried by Deputy Sheriff Morgan and Baliff Hamilton. Tom Earnest and Harrison Fairleigh marched in front with Sheriff Callahan and Marshal Griffey behind. Out side of the jurors and lawyers there were but few in the court room at the time; but about 200 afterwards came up. When Dalton was placed in position he looked weary and worn. The judge asked him if he was ready for trial, and he said he was not. He was then asked if he was ready to enter a plea in regard to the information charging him with murder, and he said he was not. He was then asked if he had a lawyer, and he replied no. He said that he had consulted with City Attorney Fritch some, but it was more in regard to other matters. Mr. Fritch then arose and stated to the court that he had to leave the city on the morning train, and would be unable to look after the matter. When asked if he had money to employ an attorney, Dalton said that he could raise some, perhaps. After these preliminaries, Judge Mc Cue said, owing to the weak condition of his wife, he was unable to hold court this week; but instructed Dalton to be ready for trial at nine o'clock next Monday morning. It was the work of but a few minutes, and Dalton was taken back to jail, and court adjourned until the time above mentioned.
STAR AND KANSAN 23 Dec. 1892

Bill Dalton, of course, was not appointed as a deputy by Marshal Yoes at Fort Smith or by anyone else. He had replevin orders for Emmett's horse and and guns. Any number of people jumped to the unjustified conclusion that the official document Bill had was a commission. This is what touched off the "flap" discussed in chapter four of this book. The newspapers were full of articles where the various U. S. Marshals denied that Bill Dalton was ever a deputy.

By April 1893 Emmett has gone to prison and the entire Coffeyville affair should have been put to rest by the COFFEYVILLE JOURNAL. However, editor Elliott still had Bill Dalton under the JOURNAL gun.

(Retyped Newspaper Article)
FRANK JAMES AND BILL DALTON

A special from Guthrie O. T., to the Kansas City Journal says: "William Dalton brother of the notorious Dalton brothers, who were killed at Coffeyville last fall, and exmember of the California legislature, and at one time charged with train robbing in California has been in this city for several days and left tonight for Dallas, Tex., to meet Frank James of equal notoriety, and to complete arrangements for the opening of a saloon in Chicago at an early date, by the two. Their great notoriety will be a card which will draw the immense patronage."

(Retyped Newspaper Article)
UNTITLED

The probablility is that the report that Frank James and Col. William Dalton are to start a saloon in Chicago , is false. It is said that Mr. James is not very anxious to set foot in Illinois soon for fear of the governor of that state refusing to protect him from a requisition from the governor of Minnesota, as did the governor of Missouri. As far as Bill Dalton is concerned, he would make an ideal beer slinger—indeed, it is about all he is fit for.
COFFEYVILLE JOURNAL 25 April 1893

(Retyped Newspaper Article)
UNTITLED

Bill Dalton and his party are in Creek country. They are hard up for cash and the winter is before them.
COFFEYVILLE JOURNAL 27 April 1893

From here on Bill Dalton is connected with the Doolin Gang and they are accused of every crime in the area. Many times the Dalton Gang are still accused of crimes long after this date and even after Bill too is dead.

The settlement of the estates of Bob, Grat and Bill Power continued to make the newspapers. There is also a sizable collection of court documents about the Dalton estates that survive. Not one word has been found about the estate of Broadwell. His family may have handled it as they came to Coffeyville to claim his body.

The court documents show a number of interesting things concerning the estates of Bob and Grat. One item is a relinquishment document dated 15 October 1892 that says, "We the undersigned heirs of Gratton Dalton and Robert Dalton, deceased, hereby renounce all legal right now by law vested in us respectively to administer upon the estates of the said Gratton Dalton and Robert Dalton deceased." This statement is followed by a list of names: Adeline L. Dalton, W. M. Dalton, C. B. Dalton, H. C. Dalton, L. Dalton, Mrs. E. D. Whipple, and Leona Dalton. Adeline and C. B. Dalton appear to have signed their own names but the other names are all in the same handwriting. Bill Dalton's name has a wavy line drawn through it. It appears that Bill did not agree with the document. However, Sheriff John Callahan was appointed as the administrator of the estates.

The inventory of the estates showed that Emmett's statements about the amount of money his brothers had before the robbery must have been correct. Here is what was listed in the inventory:

```
Robt. Dalton Probable Estate
Cash                              $900.00
1 Gold Watch & chain                50.00
1 set jewelery                      10.00
1 Pr. six shooters (Colts)          26.00
1 Winchester Rifle                  20.00
1 saddle & bridle                   15.00

Total                            $1021.00

Grattan Dalton Probable Estate
1 Diamond Ring                   $  50.00
1 horse                             50.00
1 saddle & bridle                   15.00
1 Gold Watch & chain                50.00
1 Winchester Rifle                  15.00
1 Pr six Shooters (Colts)           26.00
Cash                                73.00

Total                             $279.00
```

On 6 January 1893 Callahan announced a public auction to be held on 14 January to dispose of the effects of the Daltons and Power.

(Retyped Newspaper Article)
BROUGHT FAIR PRICES
THE SALE OF THE DALTON STUFF NETTED $294.25 TO THE ESTATE WILL BE APPLIED ON THE DEBTS

Administrator John Callahan, Saturday sold the horse, saddles, guns, watch, etc., which belonged to the deceased members of the late Dalton Gang.

Quite a little interest was manifested and on a few of the articles the bidding was quite spirited, but others did not bring such good prices.

Following is a list of the articles sold, to whom and the prices.

```
Grat's horse, to John Kloehr          $90.00
Grat's Winchester, to Dr. W.C. Hall    28.00
Bob's Winchester, to W. S. Upham       60.00
Bob's revolver, to W. H. Clark         31.00
Bob's scabbard, to R. J. Mitchell       2.00
Bob's saddle, to John Kloehr           23.50
Power's saddle, to John Shaw           19.25
Grat's saddle, to James McKennan       16.00
Power's watch, to M. G. Hughes         24.00
Grat's cartridges, to W. C. Hall        1.00
Total                                 $294.25
```
COFFEYVILLE JOURNAL 20 Jan. 1893

Several creditors appeared and filed claims against the estates of Grat and Bob. Some of the bills had been outstanding for a considerable length of time. This may be further evidence that the Daltons were not collecting earned fees as deputy marshals. Bob owed Barndollar, Bartles and Gibson of Pawhuska $42.90 for items purchased from July through early October 1889. This included clothing, rope, and pasturing some mules for two and one-half months. Grat owed Barndollar Bros. of Coffeyville $28.95 for clothing items that had been purchased in January 1890. Grat and Bob also owed George Pfister of the Gold Room Loan Agency of Coffeyville $72.10. This had been borrowed in January 1889 and the due date had been April 1889. Grat had also obtained two additional loans in January 1889, one for $16.80 and another for $11.00 from E. C. Robertson. Promissary notes for these amounts plus interest due were paid by Callahan from the estate.

Bill had been successful in reclaiming all of Emmett's property. It turned out that evidence was located that the Daltons had bought the horse in question, they had not stolen it. Emmett disposed of his belongings as he prepared to depart for the Kansas State Prison. The STAR AND KANSAN of 10 March 1893 described the scene as follows:

"In taking leave of his brother Ben and other friends at the depot Emmett broke down completely and wept like a child. He took out his scarf pin and sent it to his aged mother, who lives in Oklahoma. His Winchester he gave to Sheriff Callahan, his pistols to Attorney Fritch, and his white cowboy hat to Billy Smith. ... He directed that his horse be sold and the proceeds applied to paying Dr. McCulley for his medical services."

The Coffeyville affair was now at an end, but the world had not heard the last of the Daltons. It was only a short time until the books began to appear. The first was a paperback with a yellow cover and later additions of this book were, THE DALTON BROTHERS by An Eye Witness. Here is what happened to Deputy Marshal Ransome Payne for furnishing the material for this book.

(Retyped Newspaper Article)
UNTITLED ITEM

The following dispatch from Guthrie to the daily papers, will interest the people of Coffeyville who are acquainted with Payne: A few weeks ago some flash literature publishing house published a dime-novel life of the notorious Dalton brothers, in which Deputy United States Marshal Ransom Payne figured as the hero who had trailed them for years and finally run them to the earth. This book has been the cause of a big row in the United States Marshal's office here. Marshal Grimes has revoked Payne's commission and in a published letter charged him with furnishing manuscript for the book, making himself a hero and traducing his fellow-officers, when, in fact, he never attempted to go after the Daltons, and was always sick or got thrown from his horse when there was any real danger to be met. The matter is creating a big sensation, and there will likely be some big damage suits, if nothing more serious, to follow.
COFFEYVILLE JOURNAL 3 Feb. 1893

(Retyped Newspaper Article)
GRIMES TO PAYNE
U.S. MARSHAL GRIMES SCORES RANSOM PAYNE AND DISMISSES HIM FROM THE GOVERNMENT SERVICE FOR MAKING HIMSELF A HERO IN A DALTON HISTORY.

Guthrie, OK, Ter., Jan, 5, 1893
Ransom Payne, Esq.,
Guthrie, Ok. Ter.

Dear Sir:

After having employed you for a period of nearly two years as Deputy U. S. Marshal for this district, during which time I have tried you in various places and under different circumstances, some of which required conservativeness, a great amount of energy and perseverance and nerve, such as go to make up a good officer for handling the class of criminals which have, and to some extent do yet infest this country, I have found you to be unfit for the position in every particular named.

WESTERN PUBLICATIONS • WESTERN GRAPHICS

205 West Seventh Avenue, Suite 202
P.O. Box 2107
STILLWATER, OK 74076
(405) 743-3370

FIN #73-1203943

INVOICE

0133367

DATE: 7-23-92

SOLD TO: Cash

SHIP TO:

CUST. ORDER NO.	DATE SHIPPED	SHIPPED VIA	TERMS	SALESMAN	F.O.B	OUR ORDER NO.

QTY. ORDERED	B/O	QTY. SHIPPED	DESCRIPTION	UNIT PRICE	AMOUNT
			Indian Fighters		$26.75

Thank You

INV-764-3
PRINTED IN U.S.A.

* * * * * * *

I wish to call your attention to some of the particular claims made by you in this book. [THE LIFE OF THE DALTONS, published by Laird and Lee, of Chicago.] One statement is to the effect that you were the party who was instrumental in making the capture of Charley Bryant, and the statement goes so far as to claim for you that you made the capture and turned the prisoner over to Deputy Ed. Short, with instructions, etc., as to how to convey him to jail.

This is purely a mis-statement of facts in every particular. To my knowledge, you never saw Charley Bryant. You were not directly or indirectly instrumental in his capture, and shame to the man who would credit to himself the work that was accomplished by one of the most fearless, daring

Detail of Relinquishment Document filed 15 Oct. 1892 on the estates of Grat and Bob Dalton. Note William Dalton's name has a wavy line drawn throught it. Copied from Montgomery Co. KS Court records.

and efficient officers this district ever contained, and who gave his life to the work. You know you placed yourself in a false light in taking the credit in this instance in the book referred to, as well as in most every other instance where it required nerve to make any capture of importance. It is not neccessary for me to say that the statements through the entire book, so far as they refer to you, are of such a character that anyone with common decency would have long since denounced the book and made a public statement that the stories contained therein were ficticious, and that you never performed the work credited to you in the book.

It also seems to be a studied effort on your part in furnishing manuscript for this cheap literature to speak lightly and insignificantly of some of the best officers, not only in this district, but of the West—such as Deputies C. Madsen, Heck Thomas, Tillman Lilly, Joe Severns, Frank Kliss, and Geo. Thornton (who lost his life the same as Ed. Short), and others I could mention, either one of whom have done more to put down and wipe out what was known as the Dalton gang, or the subject of your pamphlet. In the book you are continuously spoken of as "My Most Trusty Deputy," as the man, without whom, this Territory and the adjoining country, would go to destruction, as the man for whom the people called loudly in their distress, as the man who was the only one the Daltons feared, following their trail for two years and finally running them to earth at Coffeyville, Kansas. You well know that you never made a step alone to capture the Daltons, and what was credited to you is due to the people of Coffeyville and to those who went down in the fight against the lawless band, who for so long have infested this country; is robbed from them, or at least attempted to be taken from them by you who never did a thing except to go up to Coffeyville and get their pictures after they were dead, and trying to get their bodies and take them to California for the reward which had been offered for their capture by the authorities of that State; and you know as well that never were you instructed from this office to take charge of any other deputy nor to pursue with large posses any lawless band in this Territory, as stated in the book. It takes men of a different stamp to do that kind of work. On every occasion when the train has been robbed you have either been sick or taken sick very suddenly, got thrown from your horse or lost your cartridges, so as not to be endangered by going out until after the trail was too old or too many had been over it to make danger possible. For these and various other reasons I have not mentioned, your commission stands revoked, which you will please send to this office at once.

Respectfully,

Wm. Grimes
U. S. Marshal

COFFEYVILLE JOURNAL 17 Feb. 1893

VIII. Bill Dalton: Most Notorious Outlaw of All

A quick review of the literature will show that Bill Dalton was one of the most active outlaws of the Old West. However, there is no agreement between any two authors on what exactly it was that Bill Dalton actually did. Furthermore, Bill was killed several times. Newspaper reports of the Ingalls gunbattle on 1 September 1893 had Bill wounded so seriously he could not live. In April 1894 he was again reported so badly shot up that he would die; this time as a result of a gun fight with a deputy (or retired deputy) William Carr at (or near) Sacred Heart Mission. Later the same month Bill Dalton was killed again; this time by a posse of U. S. deputy marshals Cox, Heck Thomas, Bill Tightmann [sic] and fourteen others. On 8 June 1894 Bill really was killed by a posse led by deputy marshal Selden T. Lindsey. This time his wife and two brothers identified his body and his wife shipped him to California for burial. But our Bill was one tough hombre, and in 1896 he was captured in New York City (14 September THE DAILY ARDMORITE) and commited suicide in Wyoming (Harry V. Johnson, MY HOME ON THE RANGE).

There are a variety of stories about how Bill acted as a lookout or spy for his brothers during their train robbing days. How much, or even if, Bill was involved with his brothers activities may never be known for sure. He could not have been involved in the first two robberies because he was in jail in California at the time they took place. However, it is clear that Chris Madsen was the source for most of these stories. Chris claimed he went to California in October 1891 to help track down Grat Dalton. When he arrived Chris informed the officials there that Bill was back in Oklahoma because he had seen and talked to Bill in Kingfisher while enroute to California. There is no evidence that Madsen was ever in California tracking the Daltons, and Bill Dalton's trial for the Alila robbery took place in mid-October 1891. Madsen married in 1889 and then lived near El Reno, before that he was serving in the U. S. Army. Bill had been living in California since 1884 so it is very difficult to decipher just when and where Madsen was supposed to have met Bill Dalton. Chris also invented the tale that Bill was watched by detectives so wore a "loud" suit of clothes every evening when he took his wife for a buggy ride. Then Bill reportedly switched clothes with a friend and while the friend took his wife for the evening buggy ride, Bill escaped back to Oklahoma.

Chris also claimed that on the night of the Red Rock train robbery he, Judge Burford, and U. S. Attorney Horace Speed all spent a good bit of the evening talking with Bill in a Kingfisher hotel. Bill reportedly left the group, pointedly remarking on the time, 10;00 p.m. The next morning Bill supposedly rejoined Madsen and associates and made comments to the effect that he had a good alibi for the Red Rock robbery which had taken place at around 10:00 p.m. the night before.

One startling fact about Bill Dalton was completely missing from the literature until 1990 when Harrell McCullough published SELDEN LINDSEY U. S. DEPUTY MARSHAL. Harrell is the grandson of deputy Lindsey and his book presented positive proof of the arrest of all nine men in Lindsey's posse for the murder of Bill Dalton. The arrests occurred two years after Dalton's death. Why these men were arrested is still a mystery and further research on the subject only serves to raise even more questions about Bill Dalton. There are almost no official records on Bill Dalton. If there ever were any records on Bill and his supposed criminal activities the records have either been so badly misfiled than no one in the National Archives system can locate them or these records have been systematically stripped from the archives.

This lack of records raises several questions. Was Bill Dalton actually an outlaw at all? Was Bill Dalton accused, tried, convicted, and to some degree executed by the press of the day? Or, was the man finally forced into outlaw activities because the press and the law officers hounded him until he could live no other way except beyond the law? It seems certain that no one ordered the arrest of nine U. S. deputy marshals on a murder charge, two years after Bill's death, without some very compelling reason.

The first thing encountered in following Bill Dalton's story is the "well known fact" that Bill joined the Doolin Gang after his brothers met their sad fate at Coffeyville. However, the newspapers of the day seldom report any Doolin Gang. It is the Dalton Gang, the Dalton Gang, and the Dalton Gang led by Bill Dalton. There was still a so called Dalton Gang for sometime after Bill Dalton was dead. On only one or two occasions was there mention of a Doolin Gang, or a Starr and Doolin Gang. There is almost no official record of any of the activities of the Dalton-Doolin bunch until after Bill Dalton was dead. There are only newspapers, reminiscences of aging lawmen with very elastic memories, and the "western historians" to provide the data for Bill Dalton's story.

Two authors have written extensively about "The Doolin Gang". Bailey C. Hanes wrote BILL DOOLIN OUTLAW O.T. a totally undocumented history of Doolin and his gang. Glenn Shirley covered the same subject most thoroughly in his WEST OF HELL'S FRINGE and GUNFIGHT AT INGALLS and to a lesser degree in some of his other books. Both of these authors clean up the Bill Dalton story considerably. They leave out a great deal of what newspapers claimed was the work of Bill's Dalton Gang. And it goes almost without saying, that Hanes and Shirley do not agree very much on what Bill Dalton was actually supposed to have done. Hanes makes Dalton an active participant in the following: The train robbery at Caney, Kansas on 14 October 1892 [he was still in Coffeyville or Independence with Emmett then], the train robbery at Cimmaron, Kansas on 10 June 1893, present at the Ingalls gunfight 1 September 1893 and guilty of killing deputy marshal Lafe Shadley, the robbery of the Woodward Station Agent on 13 March 1894, the Southwest City, Missouri bank robbery on 10 May 1894, and the Longview, Texas bank robbery on 23 May 1894 (this one is attributed to Bill and three other men not connected with Doolin).

Shirley has Bill joining Doolin after Emmett is sentenced for the Coffeyville raid in the spring of 1893. According to his version of history Bill Dalton was involved in the following: The Santa Fe railroad robbery at Cimmarron on 11 June 1893, the Ingalls battle on 1 September 1893 (probably not guilty of shooting Shadley), the Woodward robbery on 13 March 1894, and a shoot up with Bill Carr at Sacred Heart on 1 April 1894. After this Shirley has Dalton dodging a posse in Seminole country until he joins up with Jim Wallace and Big Asa and Jim Knight [court records spell the name Nite] for the Longview bank robbery on 23 May 1894.

On 11 July 1893 the COFFEYVILLE JOURNAL reported "Another Dalton Gang Forming in the Indian Territory". The report said the Dalton Gang had made their headquarters in the Flat Iron country in the Creek reservation, and were buying supplies and ammunition in the town of Ingalls. Further, the whole gang was supposed to have ridden into Ingalls to have their horses shod a few days earlier. Deputy marshals Hueston and Wilson of Stillwater rode into Ingalls on an investigation tour and were covered by the guns of Bill Dalton, a man called Starr and two others who ordered them out of town. Starr was reported as leader of the gang. A posse was later formed to pursue the outlaws. The 20 July EDMOND OKLAHOMA SUN carried a similiar story.

The OKLAHOMA STATE CAPITAL of 5 September 1893 reported a train hold up at Mound Valley, Kansas the day before. The messenger, William Chapman, was killed during the robbery. The CAPITAL gave the credit for this deed to Bill Dalton, Dynamite Dick and other outlaws that had been involved in the Ingalls gun battle on 1 September. They also said the same men had robbed the Santa Fe depot at Independence, Kansas the night of 1 September [same date of the Ingalls fight]. Several later reports from the MOUND VALLEY HERALD, INDEPENDENCE MORNING REPORT, and ALTOONA JOURNAL told of the capture of W. A. Curry, Charley Rubaut, and George and Charley McCune for the Mound Valley train robbery. These men were captured about three miles from Ingalls.

The infamous Ingalls gunfight occurred on 1 September between 10 and 11 o'clock a.m. according to most sources. No two accounts of the story agree and four maps of Ingalls have been located; none of the maps agree exactly either. No one person can possible know in exact detail what happened that morning. All the area newspapers carried stories and a Dr. Pickering in Ingalls kept a diary and recorded his version of the event. The Winter 1958-59 issue of CHRONICLES OF OKLAHOMA contain the portions of the diary that are referred to here. Most newspaper accounts say that thirteen deputy marshals in two covered wagons (in order to be taken for settlers getting ready to move into Cherokee Outlet which was opened by land run 16 September 1893) came into Ingalls that morning. Pickering said twenty-seven marshals in three wagons came into the town. Shirley in WEST OF HELL'S

FRINGE says thirteen deputies in the original party. Then Hixon, the leader became worried and dispatched deputy Hale at Stillwater. Hale then gathered a posse of eleven along with Payne County Sheriff F. M. Burdick and City Marshal O. W. Sollers and started for Ingalls at once.

There were probably six of the outlaws in the town. The accounts of where the outlaws were vary a great deal. Some say all were in Ransom and Murray's saloon, except Arkansas Tom who was upstairs in the OK Hotel. Other accounts say some of the other outlaws were in the hotel as well and ran into the saloon after the shooting started. A very bloody battle ensued. One deputy, Dick Speed, was killed on the spot and deputies Lafe Shadley and Tom Hueston died later of their wounds. Also killed was a young man Dell Simmons, a resident of Ingalls. Mr. Ransom and N. D. Murray who ran the saloon were both wounded as were a Mr. Walker who ran a hotel in Cushing and a fourteen-year-old son of Dr. Briggs of Ingalls.

All accounts of the Ingalls battle say Bill Dalton, or that a man reported to be Bill Dalton, was there. The 1 September STILLWATER GAZETTE said Shadley was following and firing at the outlaws as they were leaving town. Shadley reportedly unmounted one outlaw, one outlaw then turned and shot Shadley three times with his Winchester. Shadley was shot while trying to get under a fence. Bill Dalton was believed to have been wounded and Newcomb was reported shot through the hips and death was expected hourly. [Newcomb, Bitter Creek and Slaughter Kid are all the same man.]

On 2 September the GUTHRIE DAILY LEADER and the DAILY OKLAHOMA STATE CAPITAL both reported on the event. One said three robbers were mortally wounded and three captured. Then later the story said Tulsey Jack, Slaughter Kid, and Bill Dalton were the wounded men. Bill Daltons's horse was reported shot from under him twice, the second time by Shadley. Shadley thinking he had killed Dalton turned toward the gunfire coming from the Hotel and Dalton walked to within an easy shot and poured four shots into Shadley.

Note: Shadley was the man who arrested Bob and Emmett for "Introducing" in 1890. Bill Dalton might well have had a king-sized grudge against the man.

On 4 September the STATE CAPITAL reported the marshals brought in Tom Jones (Arkansas Tom), John Nix, Sherman Saunders, Mr. and Mrs. George Ransom, and four boys named Case (from two different Case families). Doolin and Dalton were reported shot and another man killed. A Doctor from Stillwater had reportedly been called out to treat the wounded outlaws and had stated that Bill Dalton would never again hold up a train.

The OKLAHOMA DAILY PRESS of 4 September reported Newcomb, a flame of Tom King (Tom really got around), had been killed. Bill Dalton was shot through the leg and had escaped on one of the wounded officer's horses. This paper went on to say, "Ever since the extermination of the Dalton boys at Coffeyville Bill Dalton has been active in organizing a gang of desperate outlaws and for some time his band has numbered over twenty-five of the worst characters in the southwest." The gang headquartered in the Cherokee Strip and bought supplies at Ingalls.

On 8 September the ALTOONA JOURNAL said Bill Dalton and two other outlaws were fatally wounded. On the same date the STAR AND KANSAN said fire from the marshals had dropped both Dalton and Newcomb, who were both picked up by their comrades and carried off badly wounded. Dalton had had two horses shot from under him and Dynamite Bill was badly wounded as well.

The next day the STATE CAPITAL reported that Hixon had crippled Dalton's horse, that Shadley had shot Dalton, and then Masterson [Jim, brother of Bat] had sent a ball or two into Dalton and sent him rolling down a ravine out of sight. Another horseman had picked him up and Doolin had carried him off. It was said, "Bill Dalton will never rob another train."

The INDEPENDENCE MORNING REPORTER of 10 September said Shadley had been shot four times by Bill Dalton, who had organized the gang to avenge the death of his brothers. On 13 September the same paper reported on Bill Dalton's whereabouts and claimed that Dalton had talked to someone who had reported the following to the COFFEYVILLE JOURNAL: Dalton went directly from Ingalls to a rendezvous of the gang north of Tulsa in the Cherokee Nation and was apparently unhurt. He was accompanied by four others, two or three of them injured. Dalton had stated to the informant, that he did not fire a shot at the officers until they had killed his horse and that he was compelled to shoot Shadley in self defense. Dalton was reported determined to carry out his original plan which included a raid into Coffeyville.

Pickering's diary says.

"On the morning of Sept. 1st there was 27 deputy marshals piloted into town in covered wagons. They caused no suspicion as there was hundreds of Boomers moving the same way. 2 wagons stoped at Light's Black Smith Shop & one drove up by my house & they all proceeded to unload in a quite manner and take positions. Doolan, Bitter Creek, Danimite Dick, Tulsa Jack & Dalton was in Ransom & Murrys Saloon. Arkansas Tom was in bed at the Hotel. Bitter Creek got his horse & was riding up to a small building where Said Conley [Newcomb's girlfriend, Sadie Comley] staid & the marshalls thinking he was known to the move fired on him. Dick Speed marshal from Perkins fired the first shot. The magazine was knocked off of his, Bitter Creek's gun & he was shot in the leg. He made his escape to the southwest. Speed was shot about this time & instantly killed, also young Simmonds mortally wounded. The fires of the Marshalls was centered on the Saloon & old man Ransom was shot in the leg. Murry in arm and side. Walker shot through the liver.

By this time the outlaws had got to the stable & saddled their horses. Doolan & Danimite went out at the back door & down a draw southwest. Dalton and Tulsa made a dash from the front door. As they came out Dalton's horse was hit on the jaw & he had a hard time getting him started, but finly succeded. He went probely 75 yards when his horse got his leg broke. He then got off of him & walked on the opisite side for a ways, then left him but came back to his sadel pockets & got his wire cutters & cut a fence, then got behind one of the other boys & rode off. A great many say he shot Shadly but I seen Shadly run from my place to Dr. Call's fence & in going through it he was first shot. He then got to Ransom's house & was debating with Mrs. Ransom, she ordering him to leave when he got his last shots. He fell there and crawled to Selph's cave."

Pickering's is the only account of this entire affair to mention Bill Dalton getting wire cutters and cutting a fence.

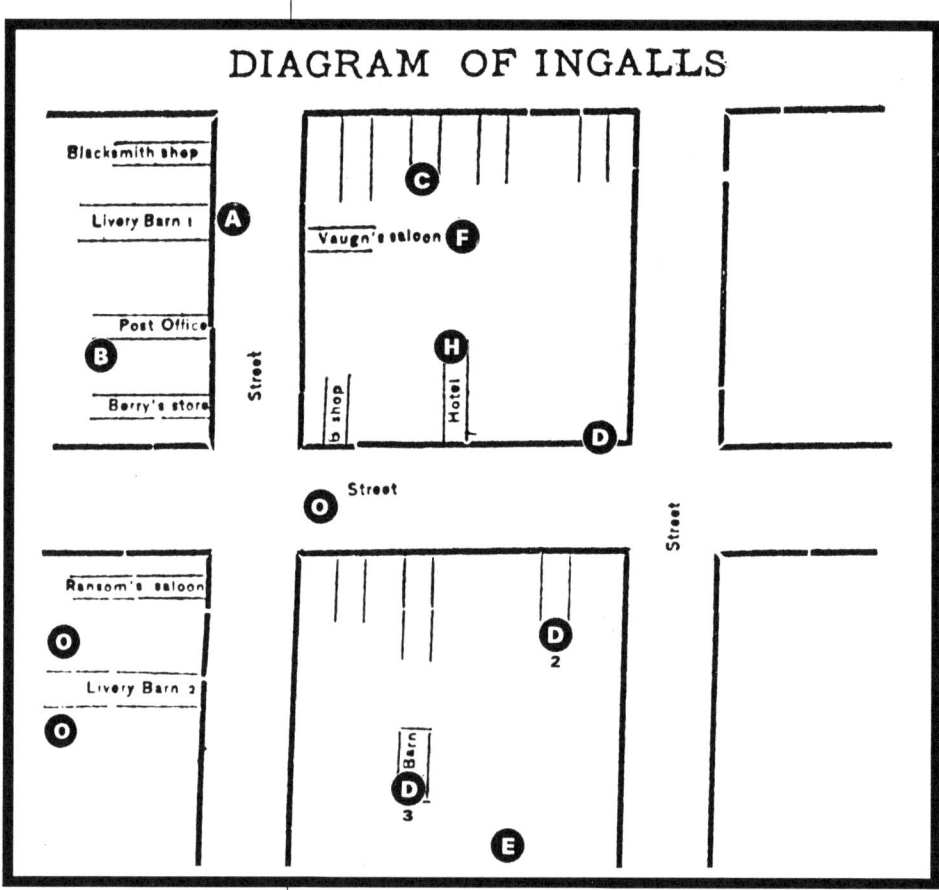

(Retyped Newspaper Article)

The marshals came in on the north street from the west. There were three vehicles arranged as follows: The Guthrie crowd drove in first in a covered wagon with mule team. The men consisted of Deputies and Possemen John Hixon, Lafe Shadley, Doc Roberts, Jim Masterson and Jim Steele, of Guthrie, and Hi Thompson, undersheriff of this county. They drove into the second street, where they turned south. Going one block south they camped on the corner of the block east of D. Shadley, Thompson and Hixon took position at D, the others remaining with the wagon. M. A. Ianson and H. Keller, of this city, next drove in, in a buggy and hitched in front of the resturant at C. Next came a covered wagon with Messrs. Tom Hueston, Dick Speed, Geo. Cox and Jim Pierce. They hitched in street just west of the north blacksmith shop, and skirmished in the rear of the various buildings, seeking for positions commanding Ransom's saloon where the outlaws were stationed. Speed, Cox and Ham Hueston went into the livery barn and took position at A. Pierce and Tom Hueston stopped behind a pile of rocks between the postoffice and Berry's [most sources give this as Perry's] store, at B. At this time one of the outlaws fired from the saloon at C. An interval of a very short time occurred when the outlaws all commenced firing at C. The marshals at B and D promptly returned their fire and a perfect fusilade was kept up for some time. Just then Marshal Speed stepped to the front door of the livery stable and was almost immediately shot. He ran back into the barn about three stalls; laid down and died instantly. Dell Simmons was at Vaughn's saloon and going to the back door, was killed at F. While the shooting was at its highest the outlaws ran from the saloon to livery barn No. 2, where they saddled their horses and rushed out. Two of them, supposed to be Dalton and Bitter Creek rode southeast to E. Thompson and Hixon ran from D to D2 firing at the outlaws. One jumped the fence and ran across a little draw south of town among some timber. The other had his horse disabled and he was thrown to the ground. Rising to his hands and knees he fired several times more, then turning made his way on hands and knees, evidently wounded, to where his comrade was waiting. Just before this one, thought to be Dalton, got away, Shadley ran from D to D3, where, as he was crawling under the fence south of the barn he was shot several times. The remainder of the outlaws rode from the rear of the barn down a little ravine west of town and circling around joined Dalton and Bitter Creek. Picking them up, they rode off south five men on three horses.

After the firing had ceased Thompson and Hixon saw smoke west of the house they were behind (D2), and at once made up their minds that there was a man in the hotel at H. Hixon kept the hotel front covered and Thompson made a wide detour around to get a rear position, which he accomplished by getting between the restaurant C and the building east. Negotiations were opened with the landlady, Mrs. Pierce, for the surrender of the man in the hotel, which was finally accomplished, he giving up to Thompson who brought him to Stillwater. The theory now is that this man, "Arkansas Tom," killed Speed and Simmons, and mortally wounded Hueston and Shadley. Both front and back windows broken and a hole through the west slope of the roof tell how he accomplished his purpose. He was taken to Guthrie Sunday, and it is well for him that he was, as a lynching would undoubtedly have occurred here Sunday night.

The letters O show where dead horses were found. Ransom, Murry and Walker were wounded in Ransom's saloon, and Dr. Brigg's little boy in the street just west of D2."
STILLWATER GAZETTE 1 Sept. 1893.

There is more to the Ingalls story but that will be covered a bit later. We now return to further reports on Bill Dalton, his whereabouts, and his actions.

The Pinkerton files contain an article from the CHICAGO TRIBUNE of 15 September 1893. Headline is, "Dalton Is Fleeing". Bill Dalton and his gang of train and bank robbers were reported to have held up a train near Kendallville, Indiana. They were believed to be hidden in the hills north of Spencer, Indiana. Pinkerton detectives from Chicago were hot on the trail.

On 29 September the STATE CAPITAL reported the notorious Bill Dalton and gang were at Wybark, I.T and had been in the vicinity of the M. K. & T. railroad for two weeks. Officers were watchful. The next day the COFFEYVILLE JOURNAL reported Dalton and two of his men were at Wagoner and the hold up of a train had been expected the night before. Three Fingered Jack, a noted desperado had just died from gunshot wounds received in a gambling den in Perry. His real name was John Patterson, and he had been mixed up in the Dalton fight at Ingalls recently.

On 10 October the CAPITAL reported the Dalton Gang in Ingalls threatening citizens. The gang were said to be sending threatening letters to citizens for taking sides with the marshals. One of the gang supposedly got an Indian drunk at Ingalls a few days earlier and stole several head of horses from him. A Mr. Berry was reported in Guthrie urging Marshal Nix to get a posse together and go after the gang.

On 24 October the GUTHRIE DAILY LEADER had a headline, "The Dalton Gang on a Lark." The gang had appeared at Cushing and all attended an oyster supper given by the ladies of the church. They reportedly conducted themselves like society gentlemen.

On 23 December the COFFEYVILLE JOURNAL (with tongue firmly in cheek) reported a dispatch from Lafayette, Indiana that the people in this part of the country were "in perfect ignorance of the tragedy". The Indiana story reported that one Eugene Bradley was the sole survivor of an deadly ambush of the Dalton Gang. A party of marshals had been hunting the Daltons. The Daltons had ambushed the party and left thirteen marshals dead to decay on the prairie.

In January there was a new series of articles. The COFFEYVILLE JOURNAL of 13, 15, and 24 January and the CHICKASAW CHIEFTAIN of 18 January 1894 all carried stories about the latest on the Dalton Gang. Supposedly friends of the gang had approached Marshal Nix in an attempt to make peace with the government. Bill Dalton, Bill Doolin, George Newcomb, Dynamite Bill, and the Slaughter Kid [Newcomb and Slaughter Kid are the same man] were all said to be willing to surrender, plead guilty (to what, not specified) and serve two years in prison. Nix was reported to be in favor of this in order to get the Dalton Gang off his hands. Attorney General Olney did not go for the deal. He intimated it would be like the government surrendering to the outlaws. The JOURNAL called Nix "the little booby who rattles around in the office of the U. S. Marshal for Oklahoma." Nix is then reported trying to raise a purse of $3000 for the capture of each of the gang.

On 24 January the JOURNAL reported that Nix was offering a reward of $2000 for each member of the gang dead or alive and that the Marshal was backed by the U. S. Government. The JOURNAL also reported that the Dalton Gang was hovering around the area and was organizing for another raid on the town. Supposedly this raid was to be one grand effort of revenge and robbery and orders were to kill first and rob after. There was a call for Coffeyville men to arm and drill and take steps at once to prepare to defend the city. Extra police were put on duty on both day and night shifts and four companies of twenty-five men each were formed, armed, and instructed. Dalton and a party of thirteen were reported on California Creek breathing dire threats. The next day the bandits supposedly moved east and the area was hit by a sudden cold spell and a blizzard. Then came another warning not to relax. The Dalton gang was expected to strike the M. K. & T. and then Coffeyville.

On 26 January the JOURNAL said the Daltons should be captured, their whereabouts was public knowledge and there were enough state, territorial, and federal officers to surround the Daltons three deep. The Daltons were then reported on the KATY line between Vinita and Pryor Creek. That night the gang was reported eighteen miles south of the town and the next day all business in Coffeyville came to a halt. Watchmen were placed on top of the mill with spy glasses, pickets were placed on the roads, and armed guards were posted on the banks. At least 200 Winchesters were reported ready for use. Then the JOURNAL followed this news with a tirade against the U. S. authorities for not protecting the town. Two or three companies of troops should be stationed along the border of the state because the deputy marshals could not be trusted to do the job. Large numbers of the deputies were no better than the Daltons, etc., etc. In the same issue of the paper the Daltons were reported in all directions, but especially sixty-five miles northeast where they supposedly robbed the bank at Pawnee. This deed was attributed to Bill Dalton, Bill Doolin, and one Sam Lewis.

On 29 January the JOURNAL reported the Daltons had robbed a settler, Robert Gilland, and left him tied up in his cabin on the Cherokee Strip. The Dalton Gang was again said to be threatening the town of Coffeyville.

The next report came from the Ardmore STATE HERALD on 22 March 1894. This time Bill Dalton and Bill Doolin had robbed the agent at the Woodward, Oklahoma train depot, then joined six other gang members a little way out of town. Supposedly twenty cavalrymen along with old Indian Scout, Amos Chapman, were out after them this time. On 5 April the HERALD reported that Bill Dalton had been shot. A party of officers had tried to arrest four of the Dalton gang near the Sacred Heart Mission in the Pottawatomie Nation. There had been a desperate fight and deputy Wm. Carr was dangerously wounded and Bill Dalton and George Thorn were reported so badly shot they will die.

On 8 April the DAILY OKLAHOMAN gave "The First Authentic Account of the Shooting of Carr" by Carr's brother-in-law, George Hill. Carr had been warned the Dalton gang was making their headquarters in the Violet Springs vicinity. The gang were coming to kill Carr because he had a warrant for the arrest of certain members of the gang. The Gang had given out the story they feared Carr more than any other deputy in the territory. Dalton and the Slaughter Kid had purchased provisions from Carr (he ran a store) and had no arms showing. They then asked for whiskey and

Carr had pulled a gun on them. A fight followed in a room 20' x 24' that contained, in addition to the two outlaws, Carr, Mrs. Carr and baby, and three other adult males. It was said the Daltons were becoming desperate due to the rewards offered for them.

On 11 April the COFFEYVILLE JOURNAL expressed its opinion that it was the Dalton Gang that had attempted to rob the Rock Island Express at Round Pond. One robber named Pitts was killed and one named Morgan was captured. A cousin of the Daltons was reported in Enid lately, and a posse was again scouring the country for the Daltons.

MET THEIR DOOM THE NOTORIOUS DALTON GANG RUN DOWN BILL DALTON KILLED was a headline in the 20 April COFFEYVILLE JOURNAL. Forty miles east of Perry, deputies had killed Bill Dalton, Bill Doolin, and one other thought to be Bitter Creek. Three marshals, a woman, and a little girl were also reported killed and the battle was still in progress.

On 25 April the CHEROKEE ADVOCATE proclaimed, DIED WITH THEIR BOOTS ON, DALTON-DOOLIN GANG WIPED OUT BY U.S. MARSHALS. The battle to the death had taken place with six members of the gang, headed by Bill Dalton. The posse of eight had unerring aim and iron nerves. The band of outlaws had over fifty murders to their credit. The fight was led by Heck Thomas and the evening before Sheriff Scruggs and a posse of twelve had left for the scene, as had a posse from Guthrie and another from Chandler. The gang was exterminated!

On 10 May the STATE HERALD reported Bill Dalton in St. Joseph, Missouri. He had been spotted on the train between Kansas City and Omaha by Frank Prather, attorney of Cherryvale, Kansas, who recognized Dalton. Dalton got off when the train stopped in St. Joe and melted into the crowd. On 24 May the HERALD reported the Dalton gang in El Reno. A posse had attacked at Yukon and gang members Ferris, Nelson, and Snyder had been wounded.

On the same day the HERALD also printed a story from the WASHINGTON POST. Deputy Marshal W. S. Feltz, brother-in-law of Marshal Nix was back in the east and had proclaimed "We will finally get the Daltons.". It was said that Bill Dalton came east frequently and had been in Washington time and again. When in the east he is a "dead swell" and when in the west a "dead tough". Dalton was reported as the toughest of the gang, and next was George Newcomb, "Slaughter Kid from Bitter Creek".

The HERALD also carried the following item.

(Retyped Newspaper Article)
THE GREAT DALTON FAMILY

The outside papers are poking lots of fun at the Indian Territory and Oklahoma U. S. marshals because of the frequency of the killing of members of the Dalton gang. It is true that half the reports of the killing or capturing of Daltons are fakes, yet a good many Daltons have been captured, a good many have been killed, and the officers have had battles with a good many others. Daltons in this country now signifies a class rather than a family. Outlaws who hold up trains, rob stores and make incursion in bands, generally in open day, are styled Daltons. They get accessions to their ranks from the states. Every escaped murderer, who has a price upon his head makes for the Indian Territory. If he reaches the haven he follows the avocation of an outlaw and becomes a Dalton, until a bullet from a marshal's gun lays him in the dust. The sparseness of the settlements of the Osage and Creek countries give ample opportunity for the declusion of such bands while not engaged in raids. Oklahoma City Journal.
STATE HERALD (Ardmore) 31 May 1894

Next came the Longview, Texas bank robbery on 23 May 1894, supposedly at exactly 3 p.m. One fact of interest must be pointed out here. Although, most of the literature about this robbery claims that two Nite brothers, named Asa (or Bill) and Jim, were involved in this robbery, not one contemporary account of the robbery ever suggested or mentioned the name Nite (or Knight or any other spelling of the name). More about the Nite brothers will follow later in the story.

The FORT WORTH GAZETTE carried a running account of the robbery and its aftermath from 24 May on until several days after Bill Dalton's death. The first GAZETTE account reported that one robber, George Bennett [later accounts say Jim Bennett] was killed; also killed was George Buckingham. Believed mortally wounded were J. W. McQueen and City Marshal Matt Muckleroy, and seriously wounded T. C. Summers and

C. S. Leonard. Two of the gang approached the cashier and president and asked for the money. The cashier grappled with one robber and his hand was mashed in the hammer of the pistol. Two robbers kept watch in the back alley between the court house and bank and kept up rapid fire at anyone who came close. Their aim was bad as they shot twenty to thirty times at deputies Howard and Stevens to no effect. One robber was throught to be Bennett's brother George who had married a Miss Renfro in the area. Another robber was fully recognized as Jim Jones, a man who worked at a sawmill in the area, leaving only one robber unknown. The dead robber wore a hat with a label from L. B. Roberson, Ardmore I. T. A posse was quickly organized and believed to be only 15 minutes behind the robbers. A reward of $500 was offered [by the bank?] and citizens had supplemented this with another $200 and the governor was asked to do the same.

On 25 May the GAZETTE believed all robbers were known. The robbers had taken $2600 of which $450 was unsigned Longview bank notes. The dead robber had married recently but had stolen her fathers horse, left, and never returned. The dead man had a good diagram of the bank in his pocket. A crowd gathered and cut the dead man's hair and beard off and tore and cut his clothes and boots to peices. A rope was placed around his neck, then he was dragged through the public square and hung from a telegraph pole. The Mayor ordered the body taken down. Jim and Will Jones were the two men who entered the bank and got the money. Jim Jones was wounded in the face and hip and could hardly travel. Jim Jones was said to have married a girl in Beckville last fall and was said to be going to Mexico. The other robber was identified as a man who had recently presented himself to a horse dealer in the area as a physician and stock owner from an adjoining county. The horse dealer became suspicious and wrote the sheriff in the next county and received a negative

Bill Dalton in death. The body was supposedly photographed at Elk before he was taken on to Ardmore. The quality of the photo is so poor it is difficult to tell if he had a mustache and goatee or not. Latta Collection: Courtesy of Christopher D. Brewer.

answer. The dealer reclaimed his horse from the man in question.

By 26 May reports were coming in from all over the country. Lawmen from many different towns were out looking for the robbers and various reports of men answering the description came from here and there. Four men had arrived in Longview in a hack leading two horses—the description matched. Jim Jones was the leader and he was also wanted for murder in Western Texas. A sheep herder with five head of horses matched the description of one robber, etc., etc. The reward was now said to be $3000.

On 27 May capture was said probable. Forty men were out guarding the Red River crossings, then the robbers had reportedly crossed the river above Albion and were making for the Oklahoma country to join the Dalton Gang. [This is the first time the name Dalton is mentioned in connection with the Longview robbery.]

On 28 May there is a detailed report of Jim Jones. He is a veteran robber and is known to be the peer of Jesse James. He is a native of Missouri too, like Jesse.

On 29 May the robber who represented himself as a physician is now positively identified as one Oscar Speight and he was the wounded man. He was reported as shot in the face by Tom McLain and shot in the side by Bob McLain. Jim Jones is said to be the same size as Jesse James but he is even more daring and dangerous. Between robberies he elopes with young ladies and is believed to have killed several of them. The Jones gang has been responsible for much of the robbing attributed to the Daltons.

On 30 and 31 May fresh posses are in pursuit. The robbers are near Kasoma I. T. and believed headed for New Mexico. The rewards now stand at $16,000.

On 5 June the report from deputies at Ardmore says that Bill Dalton and five or six of his men have been seen near Young's Crossing. The Daltons were buying whiskey and clothing and people in the area are afraid the Daltons were going to raid the town. The Longview robbers have left one set of horses behind and have stolen others; they are making for Comanche Country.

On June 8 Bill Dalton was killed and it was reported that he had led the Longview Bank robbers. This news does not, however, stop stories about lawmen chasing the Longview robbers. THE DAILY ARDMORITE of 15 June reports the robbers located in their retreat in the Arbuckle mountains. A posse was out after them and had not yet returned. On 17 June the ARDMOREITE reported deputy Tom Covington had killed John Ward, one of the Dalton Gang and one of the Longview band of robbers [this was the band in the Arbuckle mountains]. On 19 July the STATE HERALD (Ardmore) reported three outlaws killed and two of them had been implicated in the Longview robbery. A posse of deputies headed by McKee and Booker had ambushed the robbers traveling in a phaeton, a buggy, and a two-horse wagon. The deputies hid in undergrowth inside a fence and when the robbers drove into the ambuscade they were ordered to hold up their hands. The two men in the phaeton were riddled with bullets, Dave Lee, in the buggy surrendered, while John Keegan, in the wagon with his family, jumped out and ran. Keegan was killed by a shotgun blast from deputies. The dead men were all said to be wanted for various other crimes. The other two dead men were identified as Frank Chaney and George Nester. Nester was said to be one of the Longview robbers. Lee, who surrendered was not charged with any crime, but was being held until his record could be checked. It was reported that this now ended the Longview robbery chapter and that the famous gang who followed Bill Dalton had been exterminated! However, the report continued that there was still a part of this gang who followed Bill Doolin and all of them were still alive and go by the name of Dalton although there is not a Dalton in this gang. [The Gang is dead. Long live the Gang!]

The FORT WORTH GAZETTE on 9 June reported BILL DALTON DEAD and said he was one of the Longview Bank robbers. The paper said Dalton was "a victim to the unerring aim of C. Loss Hart, a deputy marshal attached to the force of Capt. Stowe of this city [this in a special dispatch from Ardmore, I. T.]. A .44 Winchester hole at the pants band on the right side of the spinal column, near the hip, shows where the little messenger of justice had rid the country of the worst outlaw who ever stole a horse or shot a man in the Southwest."

Other newspapers all over the country carried similiar stories for days to come. All reports gave deputy Loss Hart the credit for killing Dalton. The newspaper stories agreed on most of the details of the death, but there are a few variations that will be pointed out. On the previous Monday a man named Houston Wallace and a woman had gone to Duncan, I. T. and purchased a number of items with bills that were traced to the Longview robbery. On Thursday Wallace and two women went to Ardmore and were in the process of purchasing a large amount of clothing and other supplies. Wallace seemed to have a lot more cash than was normal for him, so deputy marshal Lindsey went to investigate. He found Wallace had picked up packages from the express office, and these were opened and found to contain whiskey. Wallace and the two women were then held on whiskey charges. That evening Lindsey along with deputies C. L. Hart, J. H. Letherman, C. R. Denton, J. M. Reynolds, D. E. Booker, W. B. Freeman, W. H. Glover and E. W. Roberts left Ardmore for the house of Wallace. The Wallace cabin was near Elk, about twenty-seven miles northwest of Ardmore. The next morning the posse surrounded the house. A woman, either in the house or driving in some calves, noticed the men and gave a warning to Dalton. Here reports vary a bit, but most said Dalton went outside and looked around and went back in the house for a short time. Then Dalton, with a six-shooter in his hand, jumped out a window and ran toward the posse. Loss Hart was said to be within 30 to 40 yards of the cabin, and he called for Dalton to surrender or to halt, some reports say he did this three times. Dalton tried to aim his gun and shoot at Hart. Then Hart shot Dalton with a .44 Winchester. Dalton fell, and by the time the officers got to him he was dead. One or two reports say Hart shot Dalton in the left side, but all others say that Dalton was shot in the right side, next to the spine, in either the pants band or right below the lowest rib. The bullet was said to have ranged up and lodged near the surface of the left nipple. One reporter viewed the body in the funeral home in Ardmore and gave this report that appeared in the 9 June ST. LOUIS DAILY GLOBE DEMOCRAT. "The body of the noted bandit was viewed by your correspondent at the undertaker's establishment this evening, where it is being embalmed for shipment to San Francisco, Cal., for interment. The dead robber was a fine type of physical manhood, being about 5 feet 8-1/2 inches tall and would weigh about 185 pounds. He wore a dark mustache and light goatee or beard, with dark wavy hair and unusually small hands and feet. The bullet which caused his death is of 44-caliber, and entered the body to the right of the spinal column, near the hip, just under the last rib, and ranged upward, imbedding itself over the left nipple. Not a scar or mark is visible on the body."

Several newspaper accounts gave this description of Dalton. "Dalton was a man about five feet and nine inches tall, weighed abou 170 pounds and had black curly hair; clean shaven; large head and neck and well built. He was dressed in a woolen shirt, yellow suspenders, black pants and top boots."

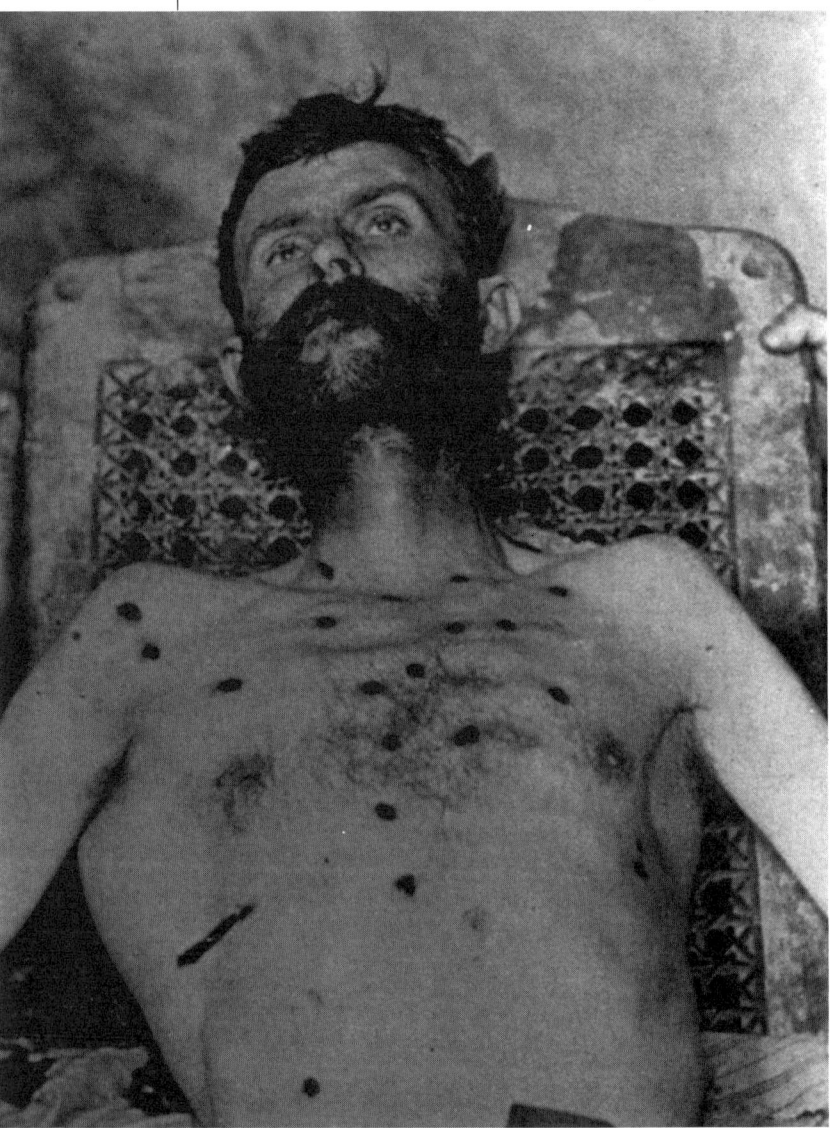

Bill Doolin after he was killed in August 1894. He was killed by deputy marshal Heck Thomas. Weapon used was a shotgun. Author's collection.

Several papers now identify the bandit killed in Longview as Jim Wallace, brother of Houston Wallace, and state that the two remaining bandits are Tom Littleton and Charles White; alias Jim Jones. Mrs. Birdie Pruitt, alias Jones, arrested with Houston Wallace was said to have married Jim Jones in Panola Co., Texas last October.

Some of the reports say Mrs. Dalton was in the house and saw her husband killed, and others say she was one of the women in Ardmore with Wallace. There is nothing that indicates which version is correct.

Sheriff Howard, Frank Fisher and J. C. Lacey came from Longview to view the body and provide identification that Dalton was one of the men who robbed the bank in that city. The DALLAS MORNING NEWS of 11 June reported as follows: "It was a moment of suspense when the sheet which covered the rigid features was raised, and the Texas officials peered long and earnestly at the distorted and swollen features. The News correspondent was surprised to find that the goatee and mustache of the dead outlaw, which when he last saw it was black, had changed its color to a dark auburn or sandy color. It was explained to him that Bill doubtless was a fastidious man and used hair dye, which when coming in contact with the undertaker's fluid as used for embalming had restored his goatee and mustache to their natural auburn color.

Mr. Fisher asked to see Bill's teeth, stating that at Longview when he smiled after his success in looting the bank they showed up very white. The lips were forced apart, as were the eyes. His hands and every feature were examined closely. The blood from the bullet wound had gone to the head, and it being such extremely hot weather the embalming was not as perfect as it otherwise would have been, as it was twelve to fifteen hours after the killing before the body could be delivered to the undertaker. Hence the features were somewhat swollen and colored. The bloodstained shirt, the hat, coat, vest, pants—in fact every article of clothing worn by the dead bandit was closely examined by the Texas officers.

'These are not the pants,' said Fisher, as Sheriff Howard held up to the gaze a pair of black checked worsted pants. 'The pants the big fellow wore when with us were blue.' he said. But the moment Fisher's eyes feasted on the boots this established the fact of his being one of the Longview bank robbers beyond all doubt. 'That's him; he's the big one that was with them. These are the identical boots. I know them by the peculiar patches in front.' remarked Fisher, and The News correspondent noticed two large diamond shaped patches on each boot, which were partly torn loose when the same were removed by the marshals from the once famous William's feet.

'I would know those boots anywhere', continued Fisher; 'they are peculiar in their make and patches.'

Sheriff Harris [Howard?] and J. C. Lacy also confirmed Fisher in that the dead bandit is one of the Longview robbers. When questioned by The News correspondent Mr. Fisher replied. 'No, I did not witness the robbery of the bank, nor can I say that the dead robber participated in the robbery, but he was with them the day before the robbery was committed. I fished with the four robbers down on the river and loaned them my boat. I saw a great deal of them that day. Bennett, who was killed in the encounter at the bank was one of the number and the dead man on the bier his companion.'"

The Wallace house was also searched and it was reported that some of the money from the Longview bank was found there. Exactly how this money was identified was never very clear. Most of the newspapers said something like, "Money found in Dalton's trunk with a coin sack such as usually used by banks".

THE DAILY ARDMOREITE reported a number of other interesting items days after Dalton's death.

(Retyped Newspaper Article)
UNTITLED ITEM (11 June)

Mrs. Dalton was arrested yesterday on a complaint issued by Commissioner Gibbons, charging her with receiving stolen money. After serving the papers Deputy Lindsay asked Marshal Williams what he should do with her. Mr. Williams told him very emphatically to turn her loose, as he did not propose to allow any such outrage perpetrated while he bore a commission.

MONEY ORDERED TURNED OVER (11 June)

Sheb Williams, United States marshal for the East Texas District is in the city on important official business. He ordered the deputies to turn over to Mrs. Dalton without delay all the money ($285) found on the person of her husband, also the pistol and letters captured.

UNTITLED ITEM (14 June)

The Longview parties left last evening for home after adjusting their share of the rewards offered for the capture of the bank robber. The bank officials identified a part of the money captured, and will take steps to recover same.

GIVEN A HEARING (14 June)

Mrs. Dalton, Miss Prudie Robinson, and Houston Wallace were put on trial yesterday before Commissioner Gibbons on the charges of receiving stolen property and introducing. After hearing a great deal of testimony from the occurrence of the Longview bank robbery to the present time. After hearing the evidence the court discharged the women on their own recognizance to answer whenever called upon to do so, and held Wallace to answer to the grand jury.

A SHAMEFUL OUTRAGE (15 June)

On the evening before Mrs. Dalton left for California she was waited upon and presented with a bill for the guards who were placed over the remains of her husband for the first three nights they were here without her request, but very greatly to her annoyance. Just why she should have been even supposed to be liable for those efficient [illegible] is the subject of much universal comment, and exacting payment of the same at her hands is considered akin to highway robbery. Wife of a dead bank and train robber as she is, she was entitled to as much consideration in such matters as pertain to money transactions as though her husband had been a banker instead of a bank robber. She paid the bill though she realized it was an outrage.

THE WEEKLY OKLAHOMA STATE CAPITOL of 23 June 1894 also contained an item of interest.

(Retyped Newspaper Article)
MR. DALTON CONTINUES DEAD

THE REMAINS HAVE LEFT ARDMORE FOR THE PACIFIC COAST

ARDMORE. I. T. June 15 [Special] Mrs. Dalton returned from the Wallace place, where her husband was killed, yesterday, bringing with her her personal effects and two children. The little girl is a cripple and goes on crutches. Mr. Clemmons, cashier of the Longview bank, is also here, and it is expected the reward offered by the bank for the capture of the robbers will be paid. Marshal Williams states the reward for Dalton is not nearly as great as has been circulated. Mr. Williams does not think it will exceed $2,500. The body will be buried in Merced county, Cal., and the remains left here on the midnight train last night. Mrs. Dalton and her children only accompanied the remains to their last resting place.

The STATE HERALD of 14 June reported that when Mrs. Dalton returned to the Wallace house she also recovered $850 from a satchel which the officers had not found during their search. She claimed it was her own money and honestly acquired and nobody seemed disposed to take it away from her.

The COFFEYVILLE JOURNAL of 12 June reported the reward was between $35,000 and $50,000 and would be paid by three states, two territories and the United States authorities to the nine officers who composed the posse when Dalton was killed.

If any reward was ever paid to anyone for the killing of Bill Dalton no record of it has been located to date. Harrell McCullough in SELDEN LINDSEY discusses this and a number of other questions that surround Bill

Dalton and his death. McCullough states that Lindsey was the man who actually killed Dalton. And indeed, several years later Lindsey did make that claim. In an interview reported in the 8 May 1932 TULSA DAILY WORLD Lindsey said, "The posse and myself rode about 30 miles that night to the Wallace ranch where I stationed my men and started the watch. I was sitting on a stump about 100 yards from the house about daylight that next morning when Dalton sent his young son out to herd up the cattle, and he, noticing one of my men, ran back to the house and told his father.

A moment later Dalton came busting out of the house in his shirt sleeves, I shot and Dalton fell dead. We found about $400 on his body. One of my deputies helped me lift Dalton's body onto a wagon and I went into the house and got the money he had taken in the Longview robbery—$4,000—which he kept in a mail pouch."

Lindsey's account does not agree with any of the 1894 newspaper accounts. All of the 1894 newspapers say Hart shot Dalton and the amount of money found on Dalton is always given as $275 or $285. The amount taken in the Longview robbery was only $2600 according to the Fort Worth newspaper.

The only indication that Lindsey might have actually done the shooting to be found in 1894 is a telegram that was quoted in several papers. This telegram was to Mayor Whitlock of Longview, "One of your robbers supposed to be Bill Dalton, was killed by my deputies, Lindsey and Booker. [Signed] Williams, U. S. Marshal, Paris, TX.

The Gregg County (TX) Historical Museum has three letters from Marshal J. S. Williams to Mr. Clemmons the Cashier of the First National Bank of Longview, Texas that mention a reward for the posse in a round about way. Clemmons letters to Williams are not in the museum so the data is very sketchy. The first letter is dated 16 June 1894 and says, "What do you think of the propriety of getting up a postal card and sending same to every national bank asking them to donate 25# [dollars?] each to boys that killed Dalton - I am in a fare way to kill or capture the other two." The letter dated 28 July 1894 says, "I have submitted your last proposition to the boys that killed Dalton, when I hear from them will notify you of their location." The third letter dated 3 January 1895 says, "Replying to yours of the 27th ult. will say I have your proposition and will submit it to the deputies participating in the killing of Bill Dalton and if agreeable to them will settle accordingly."

McCullough said his Grandfather Lindsey told him that no reward was ever paid to anyone for the death of Bill Dalton. The other startling fact reported by McCullough was the arrest of the posse for the murder of Bill Dalton in 1896. There are several newspaper accounts of this. They are as follows:

(Retyped Newspaper Article)
CHARGED WITH MURDER

THE OFFICERS WHO CHECKED BILL DALTON IN HIS CAREER OF CRIME INDICTED BY THE PARIS GRAND JURY

S. T. Lindsay, E. W. Roberts, Will Freeman, Loss Hart, D. E. Booker, J. M. Reynolds, Reagan Denton, W. H. Glover and Joe Leatherman have been or will soon be arrested on a charge of murder. It is alleged that they jointly murdered Col. William Dalton, the man who operated banks at the point of a gun and who came to his death two years ago, about twenty-five miles northwest of Ardmore while resisting arrest at the hands of the above named gentlemen. The late grand jury at Paris found indictments against them and they are now being served. Mr. Lindsay was the first to be arrested and then the warrants for the others were placed in his hands. The boys are not worried over the result, but of course the trouble and expense to them is not a pleasant anticipation. They will report in Paris tomorrow or next day.

UNTITLED ITEM

The indictment and arrest on a charge of murder by the authorities of the Paris court of the deputies who in attempting, at the risk of their own lives, the arrest of Bill Dalton and who had to slay that noted and desperate outlaw is an outrage on justice that should not go unnoticed. Of course there are none who believe they will ever be convicted and this fact alone makes the outrage more conspicuous. At best it will cost each of the gentlemen arrested money they can illy afford to spend to say nothing of the time, annoyance of being dragged and hauled around as murderers and the heavy expense to the government. The courts and

the people generally demanded the blood of Dalton and they got it, probably a little sooner than they expected; but not one moment earlier than his blood-stained record merited. The ARDMOREITE has no hesitancy in saying it is an outrage, the equal of which has not been witnessed in this country.
DAILY ARDMOREITE 22 June 1896

(Retyped Newspaper Article)
A BURNING SHAME

The indictment and arrest of the deputy marshals by the Paris authorities for the killing of Bill Dalton in the Chickasaw nation, is a burning shame. Dalton was one of the most notorious desperadoes that ever run at large, and instead of his slayers being indicted for killing him each of them should have been voted a chromo [medal?].—Gainesville Register.
DAILY ARDMOREITE 24 June 1896

(Retyped Newspaper Article)
INDICTED FOR KILLING BILL DALTON

ARDMORE, June 24—The federal grand jury now in session at Paris, Tex. has returned indictments against S. T. Lindsey, E. W. Roberts, Wm. Freeman; Loss Hart, D. E. Booker, J. M. Reynolds and other deputy marshals who killed Bill Dalton some two years ago, twenty-five miles west of this city, while attempting his capture. The papers were served this week and each of the officers appeared at Paris yesterday and gave bond in the sum of $1000 for his appearance for trial at the fall term of the court. The marshals are confident that a jury will not find them guilty.
DAILY OKLAHOMAN 26 June 1896

(Retyped Newspaper Article)
UNTITLED ITEM

The boys who wafted the gentle spirit of the late Col. William Dalton hence, have gone to Paris to stand trial for murder. We are in doubt who has the best of this, Dalton in hades or the boys in Paris, as we have only visited the latter place, but the odds seem to favor Dalton.
DAILY ARDMOREITE 28 June 1896

THEIR CASES CONTINUED

The gentlemen arrested charged with the murder of Col. William Dalton have returned from Paris. They were released on their own recognizance to appear at the next regular sitting of the United States court, at which time they expect to be ready for and accorded a trial.
DAILY ARDMOREITE 30 June 1896.

We have a dead Bill Dalton, who was reportedly running TOWARD a posse, with a .44 Winchester slug in the right side of his BACK at the waistline. The man had been, according to the newspapers, wounded numerous times in a variety of gun battles, yet there were no marks on the body except the single bullet wound. The bullet that killed the man ranged UPWARD and was imbedded above his left nipple. He was clean shaven, but had a moustache and goatee that was changed from black to auburn by embalming fluid. The man who made the identification that Dalton was one of the bank robbers was not present at the robbery, and he made the identification of only the boots not the corpse. The dead man was, at the time of his death, dressed in a woolen shirt, black pants and yellow suspenders. Yet the man who identified him was shown a hat, coat, and vest as well as a shirt and pants. The money found in the Wallace house proved Dalton was one of the robbers, yet Mrs. Dalton was allowed to retain the $285 found on the body and $850 that she found in the house after the deputies had thoroughly searched the place. A lot of things here do not not make good sense and in fact defy logic.

McCullough gives a completely different version of the killing of Dalton. He claims that Dalton first approached Lindsey's position near the cabin, Lindsey ordered Dalton to halt, Dalton then shot at Lindsey, and Lindsey then shot Dalton in the chest near the left nipple with a .38-56 Winchester carbine. Just about the time Lindsey's bullet struck, Dalton came into Hart's view and Hart then fired and struck Dalton in the back with a .44 Winchester. Hart's bullet ranged upward indicating that Dalton had fallen almost to the ground when Hart fired.

McCullough also reported on his visit with the son

of Loss Hart in 1971. Hart had reportedly told his son that he heard two shots before firing at Dalton, and had stated, "I have never said that I killed Bill Dalton."

None of the newspapers ever reported any bullet wound except the .44 in Bill Dalton's back. Clearly this all leaves many unanswered questions about the death of Bill Dalton. Emmett Dalton was certainly not a reliable reporter about many things so his claims should be considered suspect until they can be backed up with additional data. However, Emmett always claimed that Bill was shot in the back while sitting on the porch playing with one of his children. The murder charge against the nine deputies, two years later, clearly indicates that something about the killing of Bill Dalton was not kosher.

Another thing about the Bill Dalton case that does not make any sense is the absence of official records about the man. The National Archives files in Washington D.C., Fort Worth, and Kansas City have been checked and rechecked and here is all that can be found:

1. Numerous letters and telegrams that deny that Bill Dalton was ever a U. S. deputy marshal. These are the result of the Senator Vest "flap" discussed in earlier chapters.

2. Correspondence in January 1894 where Marshal Nix requests he be allowed to offer a reward of $500 each for the capture, dead or alive, of Bill Dalton, Bill Doolin, Geoge Newcomb, Tulsa Jack and Dynamite Bill. There is nothing in file that says the outlaws tried to cut a deal to surrender and serve two years, as was reported by the newspapers at this time. The reward offered is much smaller than the $2000 each the newspapers reported too.

3. There is, however, correspondence in June 1894, after Bill Dalton's death, where Bill Doolin contacted the District Court in Stillwater and said he would "give up and come in" if he would be assured of fair treatment and a reasonable (4 to 5 years) prison term. Judge Frank Dale sent this correspondence to the Attorney General and recommended approval. In his own letter Dale said, "After careful inquiry, I am in doubt as to whether any competent evidence could be obtained which would convict Mr. Doolin of any crime. We all know what those people are doing, in a general way, where they operate, and what crimes are committed by them, and yet, it would be impossible, in my judgment, to procure evidence which would convict Mr. Doolin of any serious crime."

4. Only two documents concerning the Longview bank robbery have been located in the National Archives. There is a letter from Marshal J. S. Williams to the Attorney General dated 19 July 1894.

"Dear Sir:

In the persuit of Dalton and his gang who robbed the Longview National Bank, May 23rd 1894 in which Dalton and one of his men were killed by my Deputies, we captured from Mess. Cooper & Fisher, Bills of following Nos. and Denomination:
Two Ten Dollar Bills B. and C. 409. H453916. One Ten Dollar Bill, C. 410. H453917. One Ten Dollar Bill, C. 413. H453920. all Series of 1882. and Bank No. 4077. These Bills were taken by the Bank Robbers before they were signed by the President and Cashier of the Bank, and while in possession of the Robbers were signed up by Bill Dalton. Cooper & Fisher came in possession of the money innocently, the Robbers having bought a pr. of mules from them; the Bank refuses to redeem it, Cooper & Fisher demand that I return it to them, see copy of their letter. What shall I do?

Respectfully

J. S. Williams [signed]
U. S. Marshal"

The letter from Cooper & Fisher is not in file. But there is a letter from the Treasury Department to the Attorney General that refers him to sections 5226 and 5227 Revised Statutes of the United States and to the Act of Congress approved July 28, 1892 (Vol. 27, p. 322)

Not another word concerning Bill Dalton or the Longview robbery has been found in federal records.

Not one further record on the murder charge against the nine deputies has been found either. It is not known if the deputies were ever tried. The Paris, Texas court house and several other buildings in the downtown area burned in 1916. If any records from there survive they have not been located. Also in September 1896 the jurisdiction of the Paris and the Fort Smith courts was greatly reduced. All of the Indian Territory business was taken from these two courts. Attempts have been made to locate records from the courts in the Indian Territory, but nothing on this matter has been located in any of those court records either.

Attempts were made to check Payne County, Oklahoma records. That county had jurisdiction for Ingalls and some of the other cases in which Bill Dalton was reportedly involved. The Payne County Court House burned in December 1894 and the newspapers reported that it was believed the Dalton Gang burned it in order to destroy the criminal records on Arkansas Tom. The Payne County Court House burned to the ground again in 1984.

Some records of the Ingalls affair do survive and they are of interest. The National Archives has some records. These show that William Ransom and N.D. Murray filed charges and/or sued for damages over the Ingalls fight. Murray in his letter of 19 July 1895 to the Department of Justice said, "Mr. E. D. Nix sent his deputies here [Ingalls] to shoot without giving the people warning. They shot through the saloon hitting me 4 times & crippling me for life. There was no reason for their shooting through the building as there was no outlaws near the building. The marshalls done the shooting also killed a good horse for me. They was under the influence of whiskey at the time. Now I want some advice in regard to getting damages." Supposedly Ransom and Murray lost their cases; however, no records survive the court house fires. In his book BILL DOOLIN, Hanes says the deputies laid in a good supply of "snake bite medicine" before they went to Ingalls and that the "snake bite" supplies quickly ran out.

Arkansas Tom a/k/a Tom Jones [real name Roy Daugherty] was tried for the murder of all three deputies that died as a result of the Ingalls battle. He was only found guilty of manslaughter. However, the judge sentenced him to fifty years in prison. Tom appealed the

Watron [Wharton?] I.T. Oct [??] 1892

My Dear Wife & Babes

I left Independence Saturday night and came down here yesterday (Sunday). I left Emmet getting along [nice?] and going to get well I think [Easy?]. I am going to administer on Grat & Bobs personal property amounting to about $1300. Bob had $900 in money and the people just robbed their bodies in a scandaleus manner and I will have it all to hunt up. I came down here to see [Bob Healy?] and get him to help me get my bond for administering on the estate. I have to give Bonds for double the amount $2600 and as soon as I get back up to Coffeyville I will send you the money and let you know where and when to come. Mother Eva and Ben have gone home and I am Damn glad of it. I am in a hurry so answer me at Independence Kas. and write a long letter.
Lovingly   Will

case and some records of the appeal were published in VOL. IV—JANUARY TERM, 1896 SUPREME COURT OF OKLAHOMA. The appeal was based on thirteen alleged errors, one concerning verdict and sentence. Tom thought fifty years for manslaughter was cruel and unusual punishment. Tom lost the appeal. He was, however, pardoned from prison in 1908. Several years later he was killed during a robbery.

As pointed out previously, the name Nite was never mentioned in conjunction with the Longview bank robbery up to the time of Bill Dalton's death and for some time after. The following men were all killed in June and July 1894 and were said to be Longview bank robbers: Bill Dalton, John Ware, John Keegan, and George Nester. A Frank Chaney was also killed; what he was guilty of was not specified and a Dave Lee was also taken into custody by deputies. Several other names were tossed about by the newspapers as well, but the name Nite was never mentioned.

However, in February 1897 Jim Nite was arrested and charged with the murder of George Buckingham and Charlie Learned [McQueen did not die of his wounds but remained a helpless cripple for life]. According to newspaper reports, the sheriff of Kimball [Kimble] County, Texas had been hunting other outlaws when he

Home, May 23rd 1894
Cashier, First Nat Bank
Longview
This will introduce you to Chas. Speckemeyer
who wants some money and is going to have it

This note was presented to the cashier of the Longview bank at the time of the robbery. It was supposedly written by Bill Dalton. The letter on the preceeding page is a facsimile of one of about 150 letters found in the Wallace Cabin after Bill was killed. The letter was published in the DALLAS MORNING NEWS 15 June 1896.

Both documents were reviewed by a questionable documents expert at the Connecticut State Police forensic lab. The note is of such poor quality that no comparison of the handwriting could be made.

surprised the Nite brothers in camp in the Guadaloupe Mountains. He killed Bill Nite and one other man and arrested Jim Nite. [Kimble Co. is about 400 miles east of the Guadaloupe Mountains, so one has to wonder if perhaps that sheriff was over stepping his territory just a little bit.] There are now two more dead men supposedly connected with the Longview robbery, and furthermore census records show that Jim Nite never had a brother named either Asa [Glen Shirley gives this name for Jim Nite's brother] or Bill. So who are these two dead men?

Jim Nite asked for and got a change of venue from Gregg County and his first trial was held in Smith County, in the town of Tyler. He was convicted and sentenced to life. He was immediately granted a new trial and then got another change of venue and was tried again in Rusk Co., Texas. He was again convicted and sent to the Texas State Prison, probably for life. Some of the preleminary records for the trial in Smith Co. are still in file in that county, but the trial record itself is missing. In Rusk county all the records concerning the trial are missing. All that could be found in Rusk County was the Criminal Minutes Vol. 17. These were examined from Augugt 1897 to 1902. These minutes revealed that on 22 July 1899 the judge had denied a petition in the Nite case to obtain depositions in Louisiana. The newspapers had reported that Nite had an alibi, that at the time of the Longview robbery he had been working in Teche County, Louisiana. [There is no such Co. in LA but there is a Tensas Co.] Sometime later, Nite was pardoned by Texas Governor Colquitt. The reply to a query to the Texas Department of Criminal Justice gave James Nite's date of birth as 1888 and date of pardon as 12-20-94. This data is obviously incorrect.

In January 1929 the Tulsa, Oklahoma newspapers carried several items about Jim Nite. He had reportedly attempted to hold up a drug store and he was shot five times by the proprietor of the store. Jim Nite died of his wounds.

Was Bill Dalton an outlaw? Maybe, but the evidence to prove it is extremely thin; so thin and transparent, in fact, it is hard to see it at all.

IX. Emmett and Julia

The preliminary hearing for Emmett was held in Independence, Kansas in January 1893. The 20 January COFFEYVILLE JOURNAL reported that Emmett walked from the jail and that he gave the appearance of having recovered almost entirely from his wounds, but he still walked with a perceptible limp. He was charged for murder in the killing of George Cubine and Lucius Baldwin. Emmett was bound over and held, without bail, for trial.

Bill had made a lot of boasts about how Emmett would be defended; however, it appears that Bill could not even find anybody to post bond for him to serve as administrator of Grat and Bob's estate. There was no big defense for Emmett either. Here is how the STAR & KANSAN of 10 March 1893 decribed the proceedings.

"It is not always the expected that happens. As we intimated several weeks ago might be possible, Emmett Dalton was not tried. He was brought into court on Tuesday and pleaded 'not guilty,' and his trial was set for nine o'clock the following morning. He did not manifest the same bravado as on his preliminary, but seemed a good deal cowed, and admitting that he had no funds to employ counsel, the court assigned to F. J. Fritch the duty of defending him. ...

Wednesday afternoon strong influences were brought to bear on Emmett to induce him to plead guilty. Although strenuously insisting that he killed nobody during the fight at Coffeyville, he had before expressed a willingness to plead guilty to manslaughter. This the court would not have accepted; but he was given to understand that a plea of murder in the second degree would be considered. His eldest brother, Ben, a man who has always been an honorable upright citizen, was here and urged him to make that plea. He held out for some time but finally yielded.

When the case was called on Wednesday morning the court room was thronged by a deeply interested crowd whose every eye was fastened on the mild and pleasant featured, boyish-looking young bandit who was being arraigned at the bar for the highest crime known to our laws. When he pleaded 'guilty of murder in the second degree' Judge McCue proceeded at once to pass sentence, making his remarks to the culprit very brief and imposing the greatest possible penalty, imprisonment in the penitentiary during his natural life at hard labor. Emmett's stoicism gave way beneath the unexpected weight of the penalty, and the tears commenced trickling down his cheeks while he protested that it was an unjust sentence."

Emmett always claimed he was pressured into pleading guilty and was promised a light sentence when he did so. The above article indicates that Emmett's claim about this has some validity. According to the 10 March JOURNAL he was immediately placed on a train, with a strong guard and taken to the penitentiary. On 24 March the JOURNAL reported that Emmett had been assigned to work in the carpet department of the penitentiary.

Emmett always claimed he never fired a shot at Coffeyville, and he may have been telling the truth. All of his guns were taken from him as soon as the shooting stopped and were kept by the editor of the Coffeyville newspaper and by a man in Independence until Bill took legal action to have the weapons returned. It was impossible to say for certain if his guns had been fired during the battle or not. Furthermore, Emmett carried the money bag from the First National Bank and he was shot in the right arm. He also mounted his horse and rode back to try and rescue his brother Bob. It does not seem likely that he had either a free hand or the time with which to do any shooting. Elliott's account of the gun battle never says Emmett did any shooting either.

Emmett also probably feared that he would not get a fair trial. This fear appears to have been well founded too, for the COFFEYVILLE JOURNAL of 27 January 1893 announced: "It may be fatality and it may be something else, but it does seem strange that John J. Kloehr should be drawn as a juror for the March term of District Court at which time Emmett Dalton will be tried for murder." Kloehr was the man who supposedly killed three of the four dead outlaws at Coffeyville.

Emmett appears to have been a model prisoner. The 31 March 1907 OKLAHOMA STATE CAPITAL reported that Emmett was now a prison trusty. The article went on to say that Emmett was popular with prison officials and that his conduct within the prison had won their confidence. Emmett had worked as a clerk in one of the cell houses and later as a cutter in the tailor shop. He had just been appointed as a clerk to the weighmaster and was allowed to go to the coal mine and the railroad depot in Lansing without a guard and to go into town whenever business took him there. This paper also reported that Mrs. Dalton visited her son twice a year, usually on holidays, and that she was working to get a pardon for Emmett. C. M. "Chalk" Beeson a former lawman and a member of the Kansas Legislature from Ford County was also working for a pardon for Emmett. "Beeson admits that much of his admiration for Dalton is due to his 'gameness'."

In June 1907 the COFFEYVILLE JOURNAL reported Emmett was in the hospital and suffering greatly from the wound in his arm that he received during the Coffeyville raid. The doctors said that the bone in Emmett's arm was decaying and that he should be released from prison so he could immediately go into a hospital and have the arm treated. In July Emmett

---

MARRIAGE LICENSE

STATE OF OKLAHOMA :: WASHINGTON COUNTY
IN COUNTY COURT

TO ANY PERSON AUTHORIZED TO PERFORM AND SOLEMNIZE THE MARRIAGE CEREMONY, GREETING:

You are hereby authorized to join in marriage

Mr. Emmett Dalton

of Tulsa, County of Tulsa

State of Oklahoma, aged 37 years, and

Mrs. Julia Lewis

of Bartlesville, County of Washington

State of Oklahoma, aged 36 years

And of this License you will make due return to my office within thirty days from this date.

Witness my hand and official seal, at Bartlesville, in said County this 1 day of September A. D., 19 08

J. D. Talbott Court Clerk
Clerk of County Court
By _____ Deputy

Recorded this 1 day of Sept., 19 08

J. D. Talbott Court Clerk

By _____ Deputy

CERTIFICATE OF MARRIAGE

State of Oklahoma, Washington County, ss:

I, Ralph J. Lamb
      NAME

Minister   Presbyterian Church
Official Designation   Court or Congregation

of Bartlesville in Washington County, State of Oklahoma, do hereby certify that I joined in marriage the persons named in and authorized by this License to be married, on the 1st day of September A. D., 19 08

at Bartlesville, in Washington County, State of Oklahoma, in the presence

of Elmer E. Sutton of Bartlesville, Okla.

and Mattie Lamb of Bartlesville, Okla.

I, M. A. Mikel, Court Clerk for Washington County, Okla., hereby certify that the foregoing is a true, correct and complete copy of the instrument herewith set out as it appears of record in the Court Clerk's Office of Washington County, Okla., this ___ day of _____, 19__
M. A. MIKEL, Court Clerk
By _____ Deputy

Ralph J. Lamb
Bartlesville, Okla.

Returned and recorded this 2 day of Sept., 19 08
J. D. Talbott Court Clerk
By _____ Deputy

Emmett and Julia

was placed on parole and went to Topeka for an operation on his arm. It was feared he would loose the arm if he did not get the operation. His parole was for four months. On 10 July the JOURNAL reported Emmett's operation was performed in Bethesda hospital in Topeka. He went through the ordeal well but the physicians said that another operation might be neccessary but were confident the arm would be saved.

On 15 July 1907 the JOURNAL reported that Mrs. Dalton, Emmett's mother was visiting him in the hospital. [There is never any report of Julia visiting Emmett or working for his pardon, though these stories have been spread widely.] His mother had been repeatedly working for a pardon for him. The citizens of Coffeyville were opposed to a pardon and several editorial pieces appeared against a pardon about this time. Other newspapers such as the LAWRENCE JOURNAL and the TOPEKA STATE JOURNAL were in favor of a pardon. Emmett's parole expired on 1 November and on that date he returned to the prison. On 4 November the TOPEKA JOURNAL reported that Governor Hoch had granted Emmett a full pardon. The Governor said he had reached the conclusion that Emmett had in him the elements of good citizenship. "Every officer of the institution in which he has been confined for the last fifteen years with whom I have conversed share this opinion and expressed it in the strongest possible language. ... Scores of prominent people have come to me voluntarily to speak kind words in his behalf. ... His youthfulness at the time this awful offense against society was committed must appeal to everyone familiar with the case and prompt the belief that he be given another chance."

The 9 December 1907 COFFEYVILLE JOURNAL reported that Emmett visited Scott [probably should be Scout] Younger in Tulsa on 7 December. He was amazed to see the growth and development of Tulsa since his years in prison. Emmett was at this time living in Kingfisher with his mother. The newspapers kept close tabs on Emmett for some time. In April 1908 a group of Tulsa "boosters" sponsored by the Tulsa Commercial Club made a trip through the midwest and to the east. They visited Chicago, St.

Top photo is Julia Dalton. Bottom photo is house in Bartlesville, OK where Emmett and Julia lived for a few years. Both photos courtesy Hazel Chapman.

Louis, New York, and several other cities. Emmett Dalton went on the trip and the 27 April COFFEYVILLE JOURNAL reported, "All of the Tulsa, Okla., delegation, including Emmett Dalton, had discovered yesterday that 'hustling' for their home town was no joke. All except Dalton said so. Dalton, however, when he learned that his presence here was known, sought seclusion and covered his trail as successfully as in the old days, when he was being pursued by United States deputy marshals."

Also in April two newspapers carried a similiar story about Emmett's pardon. Supposedly a letter written by Emmett in an attempt to stop the Coffeyville raid had helped pursuade Governor Hoch to approve the pardon. The 17 April 1908 OKLAHOMA CITY TIMES carried the story.

"The following letter, written by Emmet shows that he did not want to get in the Coffeyville job, but was persuaded by others because he thought in his untutored mind, that it was a coward who turned back in anything:

'____, Ind. Ter,. October 1, 1892. Dear Mother: Get somebody to see Bob at once. He has planned to rob two banks in _____ on the 5th. Am with him now, but he will not listen to me. If he pulls off this job, I will have to go with him. Grat is in it too, and I won't let them think I am a quitter, so will go with them, unless somebody talks them out of it. It's going to be close to where we used to live. If Will is in Kingfisher, send him. He knows where we are. Yours. E"

This letter was received in Kingfisher, Okla, by Mrs. Dalton, mother of the boys, from Emmet Dalton on the 3d day of October, 1892. Mrs. Dalton immediately went to Bill Dalton, who was at that time practicing law in Kingfisher, but who later turned out to be an outlaw as bad as the others, and who was killed near Ardmore a few years later, showed him the letter from Emmet and advised him to go. The place of the holdup, which turned out to be the Coffeyville affair, was not told in Emmet's letter. The dates are correct, but Bill Dalton failed to reach the boys before two of them were killed and Emmet seriously wounded.

Emmett Dalton. Courtesy of the Kansas State Historical Society.

As soon as Bill had left Kingfisher to go to the boys in the effort to dissuade them from their purpose, Mrs. Dalton went to William Grimes, then United States marshal of Oklahoma and told him of the contents of Emmet's letter. Mr. Grimes at once dispatched couriers to where he thought the Dalton boys were camped, but they could not be found.

Kansas State Prison. Tackett Collection. Courtesy of Herb Osborne.

These facts, heretofore unpublished, were brought out when Emmet made application for a pardon, and were told to the writer in person by Mr. Grimes.

...Emmett Dalton is now a reformed man. His reputation at the penitentiary was exemplary and his behavior since gaining his freedom has been such as to entitle him to the well feeling of any man. He looks and talks more like a college athlete than a man of the plains. ...Emmett Dalton is a gentleman, every inch of him. The west that he lived in is no more. He has had enough flattery since his freedom to turn the head of any ordinary man.

Recently he showed the writer a score of letters from theatrical managers from all parts of the country, from the Yukon Exposition at Seattle to the Airdome of New York, at salaries that would seem fabulous to the ordinary man, but not one has been accepted.

'I want to be a useful citizen,' he says. 'I know I did wrong. I have no complaint to make of my punishment. But I do claim the privilege to try to be an honest citizen and I shall. ..."

Emmett did become an honest and useful citizen. He wrote two books about his outlaw days and a bit later became involved in the movie business as well. He later went to California and also was involved in real estate and the construction business. He became somewhat of a spokesman for prison reform too. He wrote a pamphlet titled PRISON DELIVERY on that subject, that was published a couple of years before his death. This was reprinted in the Spring 1975 issue of OLD WEST magazine and likely in other places as well.

On 1 September 1908 Emmett married Julia Johnson Gilstrap Lewis in Bartlesville, Oklahoma. Emmett told the newspapers that he and Julia had been sweethearts in their youth. He also said this in his second book WHEN THE DALTONS RODE but made no such claim, in fact, he did not even mention Julia in the first book BEYOND THE LAW.

According to Julia's granddaughter, Julia did not

Photos this page show Emmett Dalton at various ages. Tackett Collection. Courtesy Herb Osborne.

meet Emmett until after he got out of prison. Much of what Emmett says in WHEN THE DALTONS RODE is complete fiction. There are still new stories being invented about Julia and one author, Mark Pannill, has published several real whoppers about Julia, her daughter Jennie, and Julia's second husband Earnest Lewis.

Here is a comparison between some of what Emmett and some other writers have said about Julia and what the records show.

"The Nighthawk Rider, A True Biography of Julia Johnson Dalton" an unpublished manuscript at the Bartlesville Public Library, author unknown, and newspaper stories, "Julia Johnson Dalton—Nighthawk Rider" by Ruby Cranor in the 8 May 1985 COLLINSVILLE NEWS (Oklahoma), and "Julia Dalton: Outlaw's Bride" by Madge Gilchrist Becker in an unidentified newspaper. All contain some real yarns about Julia. These claim Emmett met Julia when the Wesley [or Westley] "Tex" Johnson family was moving to the Indian Territory from the state of Texas. A group of hostile Indians attacked the Johnson wagon train but a band of brave officers of the law were nearby and drove off the Indians. The officers were led by Frank Dalton and Emmett was reportedly riding with brother Frank as posseman and helped chase away the Indians. Emmett was smitten with Julia at first sight and remained in love with her for the rest of his life. This supposedly happened in the early 1880s.

The census records show that the Daltons were still living in Bates County, Missouri and the Johnson's still in Texas in mid 1880. The Daltons moved to Indian Territory, near Vinita in 1882, and Emmett was only eleven years old at the time. Frank Dalton did not become a deputy marshal until 1884.

Emmett claimed he met Julia the spring of 1887. He was jogging along a country road and passed a church. Organ music was coming from the church of such extraordinary nature that he decided to enter the church and investigate. After all, the Daltons were a musical clan. Lewis had been a fifer in the Army during the Mexican War, Adeline played the piano and Grat, Bob, and Bill were all known to play various musical instruments. Emmett also said he serenaded Julia with a mouth-harp. Anyway, Emmett discovered the black-eyed, sixteen-year-old Julia Johnson at the organ and fell in love. Julia's granddaughter says Julia could not play any musical instrument.

Emmett goes on to tell of several visits to the Johnson home in the next few years. He described one visit in detail during the spring of 1890. He also tells how the Johnsons found out a posse was after the Daltons in 1892 after the Adair robbery. Julia supposedly waited that night until she heard Tex Johnson's snores, then dressed in brother Garrett's riding clothes and galloped off to warn Emmett about the posse. Emmett told another touching story about how he visited Julia one last time right before the Coffeyville raid. "Considerately the family adjourned with Bob to the peach-tree seat in the garden so that Julia and I might have our visit alone. ...A kitten on whose ears Julia had whimsically fastened bobbing blue pendants came purring about my legs. It clawed playfully at my rifle stock. ...We laughed until the tears rolled from our eyes. And then I rode away." It has also been reported, that a few hours after the Coffeyville fiasco, Julia Johnson was beside Emmett's bed. According to cemetery

Photo is of Julia Johnson (L) and her sister Lucy Johnson (R). Courtesy of Hazel Chapman.

records in TALKING TOMBSTONES Tex Johnson died 10 March 1891 and Martha Johnson died 25 September 1891. So Julia's parents were not even alive when Emmett was supposed to be visiting them.

Emmett's misty-eyed version of the tale can be further disputed by additional facts. The faithful long-suffering Julia that supposedly waited the fourteen and a half years for Emmett to get out of prison was a pretty busy woman in the meantime. There are a number of records in various branches of the National Archives, involving Cherokee and other Indians. Julia is well documented here. Julia first married Bob Gilstrap, a half-blood Cherokee Indian in January 1887. She was sixteen at the time of her marriage. Their daughter Jennie was born in November 1887. This marriage was a brief one as Bob Gilstrap was killed on Christmas Eve in 1889 in a shootout with a man named Frank Leno [sometimes spelled Lenno]. This occurred at the Bartle's store and according to the family, Bob had gone there to buy shoes for his daughter for Christmas. The record of Leno's trial, which opened on 26 May 1890 in the Coowescoowee district of the Cherokee Nation, does not give any information as to what the fight was about. It does show that Gilstrap tried to talk Leno out of the fight and told him he wanted no more trouble out of him. Leno insisted on a showdown and Gilstrap had to buy ammunition for his gun before the shooting began. Leno was wounded in the fight and was sentenced to nine years in prison. He apparently did not serve the entire sentence, for according to Ruby Cranor's TALKING TOMBSTONES Leno drowned on Christmas Day 1895 while swimming his horse across the Verdigris River.

Various Cherokee records show that Julia was still single in October of 1902. Sometime after that she married Earnest Lewis. She had bad luck with this husband too. Lewis was reportedly a very bad character. A number of newspaper articles show he was arrested for train robbery and broke out of jail with Tom King the notorious female outlaw who has previously been mentioned. Exactly what crimes Earnest Lewis was actually guilty of is not known for sure but he is known to have owned and operated establishments that sold liquor. Selling liquor was, of course, against the law in the Indian Territory. On Oklahoma's statehood day 16 November 1907, Earnest Lewis was killed in a shootout with two deputy marshals, Fred Keeler and George Williams. Williams was also killed in the fray. Stories abound about this gun battle but several papers reported that Lewis bragged he would kill both of the other men on the day that Oklahoma was admitted to statehood. Julia was once again a widow. She married Emmett 1 September 1908 and she had better luck this time. Julia had not waited patiently for Emmett as he would have us believe, but by all accounts the marriage was a good one.

A number of tales have circulated that Julia was married before she married Bob Gilstrap. These stories claim she was married to a Delaware Indian, named Albert Whiteturkey. A full blood Delaware, named Katie Whiteturkey Day, in an interview in 1937 (INDIAN AND PIONEER HISTORY) said Albert was her brother

Julia Dalton

This photo has been published several times and identified as Julia Johnson Dalton. It is not Julia, but is her daughter Jennie Gilstrap. Author's collection.

Death certificate of Emmett Dalton

and that he was married to Julia for eight years before Julia married Gilstrap. As Julia was only sixteen when she married Gilstrap, this story is obviously false. Other versions of the story say Julia was married to Whiteturkey only eight months. However, no record of such marriage has ever been found. In an interview with the Department of the Interior, Commission to the Five Civilized Tribes, on 18 October 1900 Julia stated that she had never been married before she married Gilstrap. The 1910 census records show her as married three times not four. Julia's daughter Jennie, told her daughters she remembered staying with Grandma Whiteturkey who was blind and who smoked a pipe. Her granddaughter believes Julia once worked for the Whiteturkey family. Julia is known to have worked taking care of elderly or sick people during her marriage to Gilstrap and during her widowhood before her marriage to Lewis.

Julia took in and kept for some time a foster child named Roy Reynolds. Roy is listed as an adopted son along with Emmett and Julia on the 1910 census. No one knows who this child really was, but there have been a lot of wild stories about him too. The boy was adopted several years later by people named Johnson, who were not related to Julia. Roy went by the name of Roy Reynolds Johnson and his wife was named Grace. This couple had at least three and possibly four children. Roy Johnson, returned to Oklahoma for a visit with some of Julia's family in the 1940s and he stated that he did not know who his birth parents were. He lived in Houston, Texas at that time. It is unlikely that he is still living.

Several wild stories are told about Julia most of which have been totally misconstrued or are entirely false. She is reported to have been abusive to her

Death certificate of Julia Dalton Johnson

daughter Jennie. There are stories that she put snakes in Jennie's bed and would put Jennie on a horse and then whip the horse. Julia's granddaughter says that Jennie liked snakes and tried to pick them up when she was a child and that Julia was at her wit's end in trying to keep the child from playing with snakes. On one occasion she reportedly did threaten to put a snake in Jennie's bed. She did not actually do this, however. The horse story is even sillier. Julia would put Jennie on an old and very tame horse that knew the way to an uncle's house, then swat the horse on the rear to get him to start moving.

Julia was also a prankster and a practical joker. She once ordered some furniture for delivery to a neighbor then stood at the window and watched the fun. One time a hired man was working for the family and Julia asked him what he liked to eat. He said to feed him anything but a chicken hawk, so Julia got someone to kill a chicken hawk and she fried it for supper. The hired man ate, then Julia told him that he had just eaten chicken hawk.

Julia did booby trap Earnest Lewis' second grave stone. The first had been vandalized and she did not like this. Her granddaughter also says it is true that Julia chased a newspaper editor down the street with a horsewhip for printing a very unfavorable story about Earnest Lewis right after he was killed.

Julia and Emmett did take the money from Jennie's Cherokee allotment and used the money to build the house in Bartlesville, where they lived for a few years. They also financed Emmett's book and an early movie with Jennie's money. Documents only recently located make this clear and the letter, in lieu of a will, by Emmett is included here.

Widow Of Famed Robber Dies In Fresno Hospital

Mrs. Julia Dalton Johnson, 73, widow of one of the famed Dalton Brothers, train robbers and desperadoes of half a century ago, died yesterday in a local hospital after an extended illness.

Mrs. Johnson, who resided at 2009 Clay Avenue, was the widow of Emmett Dalton, eleventh child in the Dalton family and author of the book, When The Daltons Rode, published in 1931. Emmett Dalton, who confessed himself an outlaw in his book, died several years ago, and his book was sold to the Universal Studios and was made into a movie.

No Valley Crimes Proved

Relatives said Emmett and his brothers, Bob and Gratten, were in the San Joaquin Valley at a time when train robberies were frequent but it never was proved in court they committed any of them.

At that time, Littleton, a brother, was working on a ranch near Clovis. William, another brother, owned a ranch near Paso Robles. Sam Oldham, a cousin, was a wheat farmer near Kingsburg and Grattan and Bob stayed with him while they were in the valley.

The family gang was broken up when they were ambushed in Coffeyville, Kan., and several were slain.

Born In Kentucky

Mrs. Johnson, a native of Kentucky, resided in Hollywood for about 10 years, and had many friends in the motion picture colony. She recently had resided here with Mr. and Mrs. Roy Johnson, 2009 Clay Avenue. Johnson is a nephew.

Surviving are her husband, John R. Johnson of Los Angeles, and a daughter, Mrs. Jennie Perrier of Tulsa, Okla. Funeral services are scheduled for 10 A. M. tomorrow in the Tinkler Mission Chapel, with cremation to follow in the Fresno Columbarium.

THE FRESNO BEE, FRIDAY, MAY 21, 1943

Obituary of Julia Dalton Johnson from Fresno, CA newspaper

The stories about Julia as the "Nighthawk Rider" who dressed in dark men's clothing and rounded up outlaws in the Territory are complete fiction. The story that she was the "Sixth Man" at Coffeyville is also nonsense. Several of the newspaper and magazine stories that have been published about Julia show a picture of a girl in a long white, lacy dress that is identified as Julia. This photo is not Julia, it is her daughter Jennie.

Julia and Emmett lived in their new house in Bartlesville for a few years then moved to California. Julia and Emmett came back to Coffeyville in 1931 for a visit. The 1 May 1931 COFFEYVILLE JOURNAL and other papers reported on the visit. The Daltons stayed with Mr. and Mrs. J. B. Tackett. Emmett and Tackett collaborated on some movies together and they corresponded for several years. Emmett had the gravestone on Grat, Bob, and Power's grave erected during his visit to Coffeyville in 1931. Up until this time Emmett was financially successful and had a very comfortable home in California. His health apparently started to fail around this time. He had a stroke and he was a diabetic. There was a story in the 1 November 1935 LOS ANGELES TIMES where Emmett was to appear in a trial in a chiropractic case. This stated that Emmett was a patient of the doctor involved for nearly a year following a stroke. This report said he had been living a quiet life, making his living largely by writing fiction, scenarios, and articles.

Emmett collaborated with western writer Charles "Chuck" M. Martin on a series of articles for a magazine. A letter from Martin to N. H. Rose dated 3 July 1937 indicates this relationship with Martin was not a smooth one. Martin said, "His mind is slipping fast, and the least we can do for the damn old outlaw is just forget his failings." Emmett had probably threatened to sue Martin over something, for Martin also said, "If he ever sues me, I'll go into court with about 150 of his letters, and chances are he will wind up behind the eight ball." There are some newspaper stories about Emmett suing Columbia Pictures Corporation too. The 2 May 1936 LOS ANGELES TIMES said Emmett lost his suit asserting story pirating. He claimed the motion picture "Beyond The Law" released by Columbia infringed on his copyrighted story and picture which dealt with the exploits of the Dalton outlaws.

Emmett also got religion during his last years. An unidentified newspaper dated 5 Oct. 1936 said Emmett, now an aging invalid, had turned to religion. He had started attending a Pentecostal church on San Fernando Boulevard. Then he started attending services at Angelus Temple, the church founded by the notorious female evangelist, Aimee Semple McPherson. Baptism records of Angelus Temple show Emmett was baptized there on 27 August 1936.

Emmett died at his home on 13 July 1937 as the result of another stroke. His body was cremated and sent back to Kingfisher for burial in the family plot. Some of the family have just recently placed a stone in the plot to mark his grave. There was a newspaper story that said Emmett's ashes were to go to Coffeyville for burial beside his brothers there. However, the article, "I Buried The Last of The Dalton Gang" in PIONEER TELE-TOPICS in December 1980 describes how the ashes were taken and buried at night. The family did not want any publicity about the burial. Funeral home records shown in an earlier chapter also show that Emmett is buried in Kingfisher.

Julia probably married again after Emmett's death. No record of the marriage has yet been located, but her obituary in the 21 May 1943 FRESNO BEE said she was survived by her husband, John R. Johnson of Los Angeles. Julia was also cremated and she was buried in the Johnson family plot in Dewey, Oklahoma. There is a very simple stone that says "Julia J. Dalton 1870-1943".

Julia's estate was not settled until August 1950. There was only $1000 worth of personal property. Her daughter Jennie was the sole heir, and the estate was settled in Tulsa County, Oklahoma. This settlement was apparently arranged in order to pass the copyrights on Emmett's books and articles on to a granddaughter and her husband, Russell W. Kurtz. Kurtz founded and was president of the Dalton Film Company and made one movie "The Dalton That Got Away". There were several articles in the TULSA TRIBUNE in October 1957 about the Dalton Film Company. Kurtz, the president, was suing KVOO-TV, Frontier City USA in Oklahoma City, The National Broadcasting Company and several sponsors, such as Colgate-Palmolive, Pillsbury, and Reader's Digest over a TV show "The Daltons Must Die". Kurtz never got anything from this suit, and he and Julia's granddaughter later divorced.

Jennie Gilstrap married twice and was widowed twice. She raised a family of two sons and two daughters. Both of her daughters are still living at this time. Jennie is spoken of with great love and respect by all who knew her.

JULIA DALTON PASSES

Julia, early sweetheart of Emmett Dalton, who dated the outlaw before the Coffeyville raid, who married another, Ernest Lewis, but faithfully sought the release of Emmett from the Kansas penitentiary, whose first husband was incidentally killed at Bartlesville when he resisted arrest by U. S. marshals in 1907, finally marrying Dalton to whom she remained true until his death at Long Beach in 1937, has, herself, now passed away. She had visited Coffeyville twice in the last few years,

Coffeyville, Kansas, LEADER, May 27, 1943.

THE COFFEYVILLE LEADER

first with her widely advertised husband and second, as his widow when Universal Pictures staged the premier here, "When the Daltons Rode," in 1940. Mrs. Dalton was credited with having the courage of her convictions. It is told that many years ago she felt that she had cause to resent the conduct of a professional man at Bartlesville, Okla. She personally administered a chastisement, using the traditional horse-whip to accomplish the task. With her death the winds of time have blown out the last spark of glamor in the Dalton family.

Obituary of Julia Dalton Johnson from Coffeyville, KS newspaper.

March 9, 1936
4439 Clarissa Ave.
Hollywood, California

Jennie Perrier
Skiatook, Oklahoma

Dear daughter Jennie:

I hope this finds you well and happy. My shoulder is getting worse.

Your mother Julia and I borrowed from your oil money when you were young to make my first picture, and also to pay Double Day to print the book When The Daltons Rode. We have never repaid you.

I am making assignment of all my rights, title, and interest including the Dalton name, to your mother Julia. This I am giving to you for the money I owe you, upon her passing, and any interest in my brother Frank Dalton's name that I used in the motion picture.

There are no other Dalton heirs, and all in perpetuum rights are yours.

Yours loving father,

Emmett Dalton

Letter from Emmett to Jennie leaving his copyrights etc. to her.

| BOOK 54 PAGE 316 | 25681 |

STATE OF OKLAHOMA,
County of Tulsa ss.   TO THE JUDGE OF THE COUNTY COURT OF SAID COUNTY:

The undersigned Jennie Gilstrap Perrier of Tulsa, Oklahoma would respectfully submit to the Court the following report of h.her acts and doing as such from 21st day of August, A. D. 19 50 to 2nd day of April, A. D. 19 51. Charges with the following, to-wit:

| DATE | | | ITEM OF RECEIPTS | AMOUNT | | TOTAL AMT. | |
Month	Day	Year		Dollars	Cents	Dollars	Cents
			Cameo pin				
			Chrystal Beeds,				
			Emmett Dalton's Bible				
			Emmett Dalton's Gun				
			Furs				
			Easy Chair				
			and all Literary works:				
			I Rode With The Daltons copyright 1935,				
			by Emmett Dalton;				
			When The Daltons Rode copyright 1930-31,				
			by Emmett Dalton;				
			Beyond The Law copyright 1919,				
			by Emmett Dalton;				
			And all property rights in and to any				
			and all stories, books, and literary works,				
			information concerning the families his-				
			tory; and all rights to copyrights and re-				
			newals thereof, and any and all property				
			and property rights incidental thereto.				

COUNTY COURT
STATE OF OKLAHOMA, TULSA COUNTY
FILED
APR 27 1951
SAMUEL W. FRY, Court, Clerk

Total value $1000.00

Total amount of moneys received or collected

List of personal property Jennie Gilstrap Perrier inherited from her mother.

X. Dubious, Doubtful, and Deceptive Daltons

There is plenty of "faction", myth, and legend mixed up in the literature of the Old West about the Dalton Gang and much of it has been accepted as history. However, there is another category of fringe folks that have popped out of the woodwork here and there making various claims. Some say they are related to the gang, others claimed they rode with the gang, and some have claimed they chased the gang. These kind of stories will never go away and true believers can be found for almost all of these tales. No story of the Dalton Gang would be complete without a sampling of these strange characters and their stories. There is also a sizable group of phony Dalton photographs in circulation, and new ones are popping up all the time. A few of these photos will also be discussed in this chapter.

Perhaps the most interesting old fraud of all times, at least in outlaw circles, was J. Frank Dalton. J. Frank was a writer, and who knows what all else he may have been. He certainly had a very vivid imagination and probably a very good memory too. He is suspected of pulling off several literary scams in Old West literature. He probably tried at one time to pass himself off as Frank Dalton, the brother killed in 1887 while serving as a U. S. deputy marshal. Burton Rascoe in his introduction to one edition of THE DALTON BROTHERS by Eye Witness says, "In 1940, a fellow claiming to be Frank Dalton of the Dalton gang wrote me from Long View, Texas. He sent me a clipping showing that he had already sold an obviously fictitious story to a New York magazine relating his adventures with Quantrel [sic] and James gangs!"

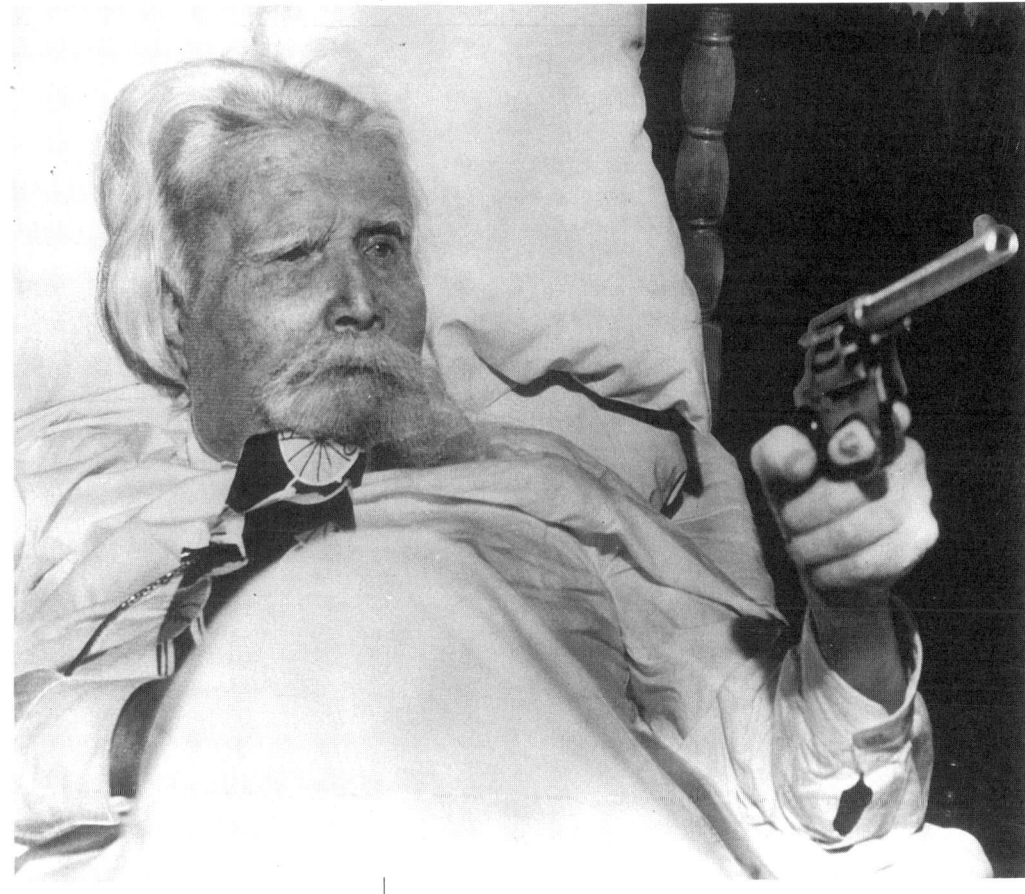

Above and following page - J. Frank Dalton a/k/a Jesse James. True identity unknown. Courtesy of Denver Public Library, Western History Department (with gun) and University of Oklahoma Library, Western History Collection.

Dalton was probably just warming up for the scam of his life, for in 1948 he convinced two newspapermen in Lawton, Oklahoma he was really Jesse James. His career really took off then. His story was plastered all over the country in newspapers and magazines. He helped promote Meramec Caverns in Missouri by claiming it was a Jesse James hide out, and started an entire new genre of outlaw literature.

Dalton said that a man named Charlie Bigelow had been killed on 3 April 1882 instead of Jesse James. This had all been prearranged to allow him [Jesse] to avoid the law and to lead a peaceful life in the future. According to Dalton, even Missouri Governor Crittenden had been in on the plot. Dalton then detailed his life since his "death" as follows: He had gone south to New Orleans and from there to South America where he served as a colonel in the Brazilan Cavalry, and later lived among a tribe of head hunters at the head of the Amazon River. In 1868 Dalton had joined the U. S. Army and had served in the Fifth Cavalry. (Never mind that Jesse was supposed to be robbing banks and trains at this time). In 1890 he was an adventurer in the Spanish American War. He went to Africa and joined the Dutch to fight against the British and later fought the Hottentots as well. He was with Pancho Villa in Mexico. In World War I he was commissioned a captain of Field Artillery in the Canadian Army, went overseas, became a pilot, transfered to the Air Force and flew for twenty-two months. Somewhere in between all of this he had gone to college. First he studied medicine and found that not to his liking and had transferred to and graduated from law school. He had also been a Texas Ranger. By the time World War II came along he was getting a little too old for active service and had only been able to aid in that conflict by selling war bonds.

A flock of folks swallowed this stuff hook, line, and sinker, or claimed they did. A flood of books and articles followed: JESSE JAMES RIDES AGAIN by Frank O. Hall and Lindsey H. Whitten, the Oklahoma newspapermen who discovered "Jesse"; I KNEW JESSE JAMES by Rudy Turilli, who along with his father-in-law, Lester Dill, used "Jesse" to promote Meramec Caverns; THE JESSE JAMES STORY by Joe Wood a former photojournalist for the ST. LOUIS GLOBE DEMOCRAT; THE TRUTH ABOUT JESSE JAMES by Phyllis Argall, (this one was published by Turilli and Dill too); JESSE JAMES WAS ONE OF HIS NAMES by Del Schroader and Jesse James III (the later was really Orvis Lee Howk and he claimed he was a grandson of "Jesse"); and JESSE JAMES AND THE LOST CAUSE also by Howk as Jesse Lee James III or "The Hawk". Dalton also convinced noted journalist and novelist Robert Ruark, and Jay S. Hoar author of a supposedly serious history book, THE SOUTH'S LAST BOYS IN GRAY that he was really Jesse James.

Those believers would have done well to investigate a bit further and to have read some of the things J.

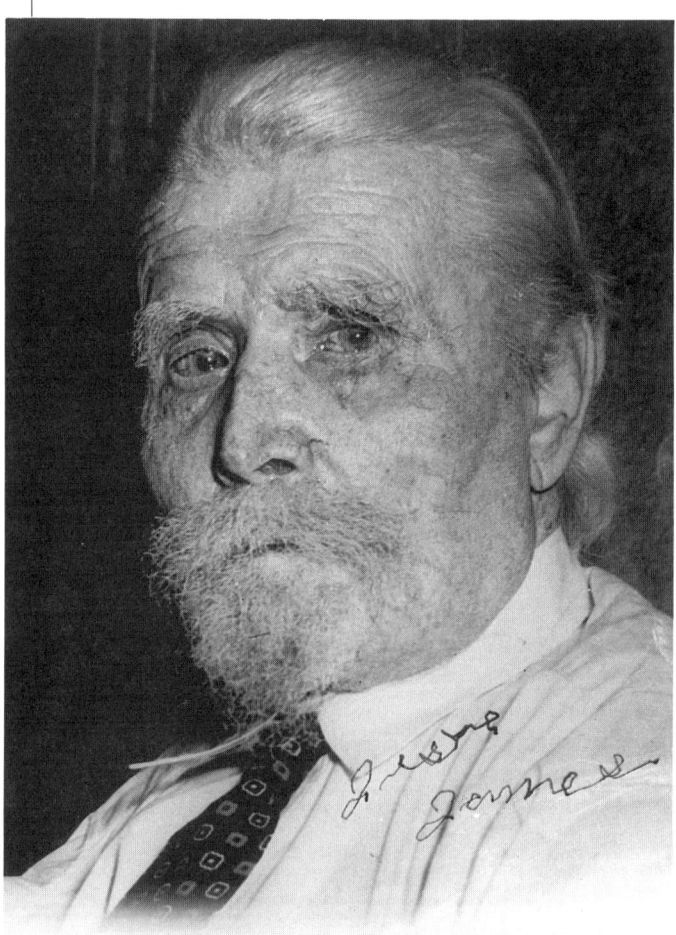

Frank Dalton himself had written. He had written a series of articles for the HENDERSON TIMES, in Henderson, Texas in the 1930s. These included stories about his days as a trail boss, a buffalo hunter, his adventures with Jesse James, the Youngers, and other Quantrell [sic] men. He also wrote about the Daltons and claimed to be a cousin to the Dalton gang. THE CRITTENDEN MEMOIRS compiled by the son of the Missouri Governor by that name also contained several of the same stories that had appeared in the HENDERSON TIMES. In the MEMOIRS, J. Frank included several letters stating emphatically that Jesse James did die when the history books said he did, and deploring the fake Jesse James' who were continually coming forward.

Who J. Frank Dalton really was is still not known. Several researchers and writers have tried to track him down, but as yet have not established his identity with any degree of certainty. Several people have thought for a long while he was really Jeremiah Franklin Dalton born near Lansing, Kansas in 1864 and son of William Clark Meredith Dalton and his wife Josephine Morris. This man was known to have married a woman named Andrea Anderson. A tip from a descendant of this William Dalton family enabled this author to track down Jeremiah Franklin Dalton. Jeremiah changed his last name to Darby and he died in Belleville, Kansas on 3 August 1947, about a year before J. Frank made his Jesse claim. The death certificate and the estate records of J. Frank Darby leave no doubt that he and Jeremiah Franklin Dalton were the same man. So the search for the true identity of J. Frank Dalton goes on.

A second deceptive Dalton is Kit Dalton who published a book, very likely written by J. Frank Dalton, titled, UNDER THE BLACK FLAG; A GUERRILLA CAPTAIN UNDER THE FEARLESS LEADER QUANTRELL AND A BORDER CAPTIAN FOR SEVENTEEN YEARS FOLLOWING THE SURRENDER OF THE CONFEDERACY, ASSOCIATED WITH THE MOST NOTED BAND OF FREEBOOTERS THE WORLD HAS EVER KNOWN. Needless to say this book is complete fiction. Kit also claimed to have been one of Quantrill's men, and a member of the James Gang, a Texas Ranger, etc., etc. Kit actually did attend a Quantrill reunion or two and he did know Frank James. Kit also claimed to be a cousin to the Dalton Gang, and this is probably about the only thing he ever said or wrote that is true. Kit's background has been traced by this author and by some other researchers. Kit was John W. Dalton, son of Caswell Dalton, and he was three years old at the time of the 1850 census. He and a first cousin, also living in Calloway County, Kentucky at the time of the 1850 census, did join the 7th Tennesse Cavalry during the Civil War. Both John W. and his cousin C. F. [Charles Fox] Dalton were reported as deserters or as AWOL in Calloway County, Kentucky from the spring of 1864 until the end of the war. What the two of them did during the rest of the war no one knows. Charles Fox died in Texas, and his widow's claim for a Civil War pension was rejected because he had deserted. Both John W. and Charles Fox are descendants of the Timothy Daltons in Virginia discussed in chapter two of this book. Thus Kit Dalton was a cousin of the Dalton gang. Kit Dalton died in Nashville, Tennessee on 3 April 1920. He was the son of Caswell and Elizabeth Hensley Dalton. Charles Fox Dalton was the son of Wyatt Dalton. Wyatt and Caswell were sons of Winston and Sarah Pullin (Seneth Pullen) Dalton of Pittsylvania County, Virginia. Winston was the son of John F. Dalton who was the grandson of Timothy Dalton Sr. of Albemarle County, Virginia.

Several references have been found to a Colonel Robert Dalton who may may well have been J. Frank in another of his roles. One undated and unidentified newspaper clipping has been found with this headline. "Dalton Scornful Calls Modern Gangster Coward". This report came from Shreveport, Louisiana and went on to say that Bob Dalton, last of the famous gang was facing charges in federal court for carrying an unregistered sawed-off shot gun. He was in the oil business and said he kept the gun to protect his payroll. He had discharged the gun accidently and was arrested and charged with intoxication. His home was said to be Meridian, Mississippi and he reportedly had a wife and a five month old child.

An article in the March 1939 PONY EXPRESS COURIER also made reference to a Colonel Bob Dalton. This article discussed the death of Emmett Dalton and his later years. This quoted Emmett as saying, "Since the day at Coffeyville, I never have committed the slightest infraction of the laws of God or man." Then the article continued, "This was true also of the later life of his brother, Bob. When the gang was the terror of the west Bob Dalton was reported to have notched his gun thirty-two times as reminders of the men he had killed. After leaving prison Bob Dalton turned respectable. He had been pardoned by President Theodore Roosevelt, Bob went to Mississippi and became a prosperous oil field developer. He was made a deputy sheriff for three Mississippi counties and received letters from a long list of national and sectional leaders attesting to his character and standing as a citizen. In later years Bob Dalton was known as 'Colonel'. He died several years ago."

On 26 September 1941 the JONESBORO (ARK.) DAILY TRIBUNE carried the following:

(Retyped Newspaper Article)
MR. AND MRS. LEE ANDERSON MEET THE LAST OF THE FAMOUS DALTONS

```
Mr. and Mrs Lee Anderson, who have just
returned from a railway organization meeting
at Chicago, today told of making the
acquaintance of Col. Robert E. Dalton of
Poplar Spring Drive, Meridian, Miss., the
```

Death certificate of Jerimiah Franklin Dalton who changed his last name to Darby.

last of the famous Daltons.

Mr. Anderson attended the Wage Increase Program meeting as international representative for the Firemen, Oilers, Helpers, Roundhouse and Railway Shop Laborers Organization. Col. Dalton gave Mr. Anderson this sketch of his unusual career:

He was born in a dugout in the Indian Territory, now Oklahoma. His grandfather died fighting with the Texans at the Alamo and he is closely related to the Daltons and Youngers who harrassed the West with their daring crimes. Col. Dalton, the youngest member of that famous outlaw gang, was arrested and spent 20 years in prison at Leavenworth before being pardoned by the late Theodore Roosevelt. He is proud of the fact that he has paid his debt to society and has "gone straight" since leaving Leavenworth.

Looking back on his past, which is distasteful to him, he recalls many colorful incidents. But regardless of the thrill of his past escapades, he feels that now is the time for "old time religion".

He took six shots in the head and three in the body but never spent a day in the hospital with any of his wounds.

He says "any man that says he can't come back decent, doesn't want to come back. I have proven that. It's a hard fight but it can be done."

He resided in Deadwood, S. D. during the days of the famous Calamity Jane, and Sidney L. Porter, who is better known to the reading public as O. Henry.

Col. Dalton is the only American citizen to serve in the Mexican cabinet, an honor bestowed upon him while he was a colonel in the army of General Obregon in 1922.

Another dubious Dalton, claimed to have been both a gang member and a lawman who chased the Daltons. He also said he was a cousin to the Daltons. He was Jack Dalton, and, in fact, it seems there were two different Jack Daltons making claims of this sort. One appears to have died around 1940 but the other was still going strong several years later. The Pinkerton files contained one article about Jack from the 21 December 1949 LOS ANGELES TIMES. This headline was, "Dalton Gang's Cousin in Court to End Contract". Jack, who said he was seventy-six and had been in motion-picture westerns was in Superior Court involved in a dispute with Promoter-Producer Robert L. Gilbert. Jack had an agreement to tell his recollections to a writer, then this material would be used for a motion picture. The contract was voided by the Superior Court Judge, because the producer had not furnished a writer to take down Dalton's recollections. Jack claimed he was a cousin of the Dalton Gang, and that he had been a deputy marshal.

On 28 September 1945 the LOS ANGELES HERALD AND EXPRESS carried a story about ex-outlaw Al Jennings and his suit for $100,000 against the Lone Ranger program and a radio network. Al was contesting a story told by Jack Dalton. Jack claimed that he was a cousin of the Dalton Gang and had been a member of Col. Nix's posse that had tracked down and captured

Frank James and Kit Dalton. Courtesy of the University of Oklahoma, Western History Collection.

Al Jenning. Jack claimed the Dalton Gang had spent the night at his ranch outside Coffeyville and that he trailed them into Coffeyville and watched the shooting. Jack was at this time living in a trailer parked in a used car lot on Broadway in Los Angeles.

A brief article also appeared in the TWENTY-FIVE YEARS AGO column of the 11 March 1948 TULSA TRIBUNE. This said, "Oklahoma Jack Dalton, 81, now in San Francisco, a relative of the Dalton boys who ranked with the James and Youngers gangs of western desperadoes, who saw Wild Bill Hickock killed at Deadwood, S. D. and was a crony of Calamity Jane, says he will carry the secrets of his turbulent career to his grave."

A lengthy article titled, "Them Daltons Ride Again" appeared in an unidentified newspaper in 1940 right after the death of a Jack Dalton who had claimed to be eighty-one years old at the time of his death. This man said he had been a member of the Dalton Gang. When Jack died a tin box was supposedly found in his dresser drawer that had papers that proved he was eighty-one and that he was a Dalton. These papers supposedly showed that he was born in a covered wagon out on the Oklahoma prairie, near Tulsa. He was born Christmas night in 1858 and his name was John J. Dalton. This article went on to rehash the history of the Dalton Gang (and to get most of it wrong). This Dalton was described as wizened, and one-eyed. It was said that he usually wore a ten-gallon hat that looked almost as old as himself. The hat had a hole up near the top of the crown that Jack said was put there by a "deppity marshal's bullet." Jack was said to be the author of a long, long ballad titled "The Coyote Howls" which recounted the deeds of the Gang. Will Rogers was supposed to have been a close friend of Jack and reportedly made a complete copy of the ballad.

Numerous other strange Daltons have been around here and there. The 11 July 1895 Ardmore (OK) STATE HERALD announced "Another Dalton Arrested" This one was in Knoxville, Tennessee and he had stolen a horse. He was also said to be wanted for committing murder fifteen years ago and had escaped that charge by stealing his father's horse and riding it to death. He was C. C. Dalton and, of course, he was a member of the famous Dalton outlaw gang which had infested the South and West a number of years go.

The March 1978 issue of REAL WEST had an article by Bill Kelly who had interviewed, "The Last of The Gun-Totin' Daltons". This one was Jim Dalton, a second cousin to the Dalton Gang and he was living in Buena Park, California. Jim informed Kelly, "Emmett, he's a second cousin of mine, and by golly we pass fer twins good, you know. Emmett was the big boy of the bunch. He had a sister that looked all around, kept the boys posted, you know, and seen how everything was; places they's wanna hit. Look out the situation. Her name was Mary. ..." Jim's daddy had been a sheriff back in Hickory County, Missouri, etc., etc.

A Henry Dalton in Farmersville, California also claimed kin to the Dalton Gang. Henry said he came to California from Texas and was a second cousin to the Gang. Henry said he never rode with the Gang but he met the brothers on some occasions, and claimed the boys used a cave in Tulare county as a hideout. He did not think the Daltons buried any treasure in the cave. He believed the treasure was buried in the east and that Emmett recovered it after getting out of the penitentiary. This story appeared in the EXETER SUN 1 December 1950. Henry died in 1965 and his obituary in the VISALIA TIMES DELTA said he was a native of Webster, Mississippi. He was buried in Visalia and he had several brothers and sisters in California and Oklahoma and children in Texas and California. His death certificate shows Henry to be the son of Jack Daulton and Elizabeth Johnson, both born in Mississippi.

There are plenty of claims around about folks that claimed to be part of the Dalton Gang, or related to them. Phony photos of Daltons are even more prevalent than dubious Daltons. A number of these have been called to the attention of the author in recent years, and there are undoubtedly several more of these around.

On 3 June 1987 the COLLINSVILLE (OK) NEWS HERALD carried a story about a collection of photos found by Wanda Brown Branham in her mother's trunk. Persons wanting to buy these photos were invited to contact Mrs. Branham. In reply to the author's query, Mrs. Branham sent a short note asking for a bid, and saying, "If you are interested please don't delay they will be sold." Photocopies of three photos were enclosed. Photos were identified as Bob Dalton and wife, children of Jesse James (3 of them) and Jesse James. It was obvious that these photos were not who Mrs. Branham claimed. The supposed photo of Bob Dalton and wife were a couple probably in their mid-thirties. Bob Dalton was killed when he was twenty-three and, of course, he never had a wife. Jesse James only had two children, not three, and the third photo was too dark to make any determination of identity.

Also in 1987 a couple named Johnson in Mulvane, Kansas sent a photo of three young men to TRUE WEST magazine's "Answer Man", Chuck Parsons. Copies also circulated to other researchers. The photo was labled Mason 24, Emmett 15 and Bob 17. Other than the fact that this is a photo of three young males, there is no resemblance to Bill, Emmett, and Bob Dalton. However, this photo and others that were supposed to be Jesse and Frank James, Zerelda Samuel, Belle Starr,

Cole Younger and other outlaws were donated to the Missouri State Historical in 1987 by this Johnson couple. All of these photos have been pronounced fakes by knowledgable researchers.

On 8 Jan. 1989 the COFFEY-VILLE JOURNAL published a photo identified as two of the infamous Dalton brothers. Several people read their paper that morning and then called the JOURNAL. Relatives of the men in the photo had immediately identified James and Earl Curry who were born in Fillmore, Missouri and who had moved to the Coffeyville area when they were young. The JOURNAL retracted with an article entitled, "Things Aren't Always What They Seem" in the 15 January issue of the paper.

In late 1988 a sizable collection of photocopies of photos were sent to the author by a man in California. The photos had been purchased in an antique shop in the gold country in California. Some of the pictures had names of Daltons written on the back. The man that now owned the photos had further assigned identities to most of the remaining pictures. All were Dalton Gang members, associates, or close relatives. These photos may well be of people named Dalton but they are not the Dalton Gang family. One photo was identified as

L to R are ? Palmer, Jack Dalton, Tex Crass, Cay Price. Photo taken at WYO (?) Picnic, May 1947, Los Angeles, CA. Courtesy of the Archives & Manuscripts Divison of the Oklahoma Historical Society.

Eugenia Moore, a fictional character from Emmett Dalton's book. One was identified as Julia and Littleton Dalton. Littleton never even met Emmett's wife Julia, so could not have been photographed with her. All of these pictures have very clear photographers names, and all were taken in studios in either Shenandoah or Clarinda, Iowa. There is no evidence whatsoever that any of the Dalton Gang family were at any time in the state of Iowa. However, writer Phillip Steele used one of these photos with an article, "The Death of Frank

Photo purchased at an auction in Ohio. Written on the back "The Dalton Gang." True identity unknown. Courtesy of Albert I. Borowitz.

This photo has been published in a couple of magazines and has been identified as Bob and Grat Dalton. None of the men look like the Daltons and from the posture of the two on the mules, neither appears to have ridden horses (or mules) before. Courtesy of the University of California, Berkeley.

Dalton" in the September 1990 issue of TWIN TERRITORIES. Steele, of course, identifies the photo as Frank Dalton.

This is a photo from the collection found in a California Gold Country antique shop. Phillip Steele has published the photo as Frank Dalton. Note the photo was taken in Clarinda, Iowa. Readers are invited to compare this photo with the two photos of Frank Dalton in Chapter III of this book. Author's collection.

Another photo that had "The Dalton Gang" written on the back of it was purchased at an auction in Ohio some years ago by Albert I. Borowitz of Cleveland, Ohio. A copy of this photo was furnished to the author by Mr. Borowitz. It is possible that these men may have been Daltons', however, they are not the Dalton Gang. Both Mr. Borowitz and the author would like to know the true identify of these men.

There will probably never be an end to Dalton tall tales, yarns, and phony photos. The Daltons will, no doubt, continue to ride on in the myths and legends of the Old West for ever and ever. It is also a pretty sure thing that a lot of new stories will surface during 1992, the centennial of the Coffeyville Raid.

This book has not been written in any attempt to replace myth and legend; those things have their place. This book has been, however, an attempt to separate the legends and myths from reality, and to take a good look at the verifiable history, warts and all, of the Dalton Gang and their family. The real history of this family has been obscured and clouded with far too many campfire tales up until this time. There are still many missing bits and pieces to the story. Any reader that has additional information, documents, etc. that would fill in any of the missing blanks in the Dalton Gang story is encouraged to contact the author and share the information. If any significant amount of new data can be located a second edition of the book will certainly be considered, and contributors will be credited, just as they have been in this book.

Nancy B. Samuelson
P. O. Box 359
Eastford, CT 06242

Sources and Author's Notes

Chapter I:

THE DALTON BROTHERS AND THEIR ASTOUNDING CAREER OF CRIME by Eye Witness.

This is without a doubt the most widely quoted source about the Daltons in existence. I have explained in my book, and presented the evidence to prove it, that Ransome Payne was the source of most of the material in this book. "Eye Witness" was first printed in a yellow paper-back cover by Laird and Lee of Chicago. The copyright was 1892 and the book was No. 6 or the Dec. 1892 issue in The Pinkerton Detective Series.

In 1954 Frederick Fell Inc. of New York brought out a reprint with an introduction by Burton Rascoe. Rascoe praises "Eye Witness" as one who sought out facts conscientiously and one who had the stuff of a true reporter. Rascoe considered Payne an incompetent fool or else a tip-off man for the Daltons. He said Payne did not merit the praise he was given by "Eye Witness". Rascoe goes on to state that the mother of the Daltons was Edith Younger, and to call the Daltons loafers, braggarts, clodhoppers, bullies, etc., etc. Rascoe says he can find nothing to substantiate that Frank Dalton was ever a deputy marshal and he does not accept that any of the Daltons were ever in California. Rascoe also presents a completely inaccurate picture of the duties of deputy marshals in the Indian Territory.

In 1977 Jingle Bob/Crown Publishers, Inc. New York, came out with a facsimile edition of "Eye Witness" with an introduction by James D. Horan. Horan says "Eye Witness" has never been identified, but thinks he was a Chicago or Kansas newspaperman. He says "Eye Witness" appears to have carefully researched the history of the Daltons, and that it is evident that a great deal of the material was obtained from Ransome Payne. He states that Payne did not exaggarate, but simply recited what he knew first hand.

CHRIS MADSEN

Madsen was one of the famed "Three Guardsmen" of the Indian and Oklahoma Territories. Chris wrote or gave in interviews several accounts of how he won the west for law and order. I have found at least six versions of Madsen's memoirs and I did not accept a thing the man said unless I could find it documented, beyond the shadow of a doubt, elsewhere. I found only one newspaper article that ever mentioned Madsen looking for the Daltons; that is included in Chapter VI: The Dalton Gang. Here are the main sources of Madsen's version of history about the Daltons:

TRIGGER MARSHAL by Homer Croy, Duell, Sloan and Pearce, New York, 1958.

A typed manuscript of Madsen's memoirs titled "Oklahoma Outlaws"
This was used extensively for:
THE DALTON GANG by Harold Preece, Hastings House, New York, 1963.

"Four Score Years A Fighter" was dictated by Madsen to Harold L. Mueller and serialized in the DAILY OKLAHOMAN from 17 November 1935 through 15 March 1936.

Letters and interviews were used extensively for:
DALTON GANG DAYS by Frank Latta, Bear State Books, Santa Cruz, CA, 1976.

"Some Recollections of Oklahoma Outlaws" is a series of letters Chris wrote to a Miss Hixson in 1939 after her request for information about Oklahoma outlaws. These letters were published under the above title in THE GOINGSNAKE MESSENGER during 1988 and 1989.

THE CLARK COUNTY CLIPPER, Ashland, Clark County, Kansas, Thursday 9 March, 1944 carried a lengthy article about Madsen after he died in January 1944. The article included letters written by Madsen in

1942 to Lon Ford, Under Sheriff of Ashland, Kansas.

Readers that have a further interest in the inconsistence of Madsen's stories are referred to the following articles by this author.

"Chris Madsen's Elastic Memory" NOLA QUARTERLY Jan.-Mar. 1992. (NOLA is National Association and Center For Outlaw and Lawman History)

"The Passing of Chris Madsen", OKLAHOMBRES, Spring 1991.

HAROLD PREECE

Preece's book THE DALTON GANG relied heavily on information obtained from Madsen and from "Eye Witness". Preece also wrote a number of magazine articles which are listed below. His material is all full of errors. There is no evidence at all for Bob Dalton's alleged love affairs with Minnie Johnson, Tom King, and Daisy Bryant. Preece also makes a lot of errors in his information about various members of the Dalton gang family. He denies that Adeline is the aunt of Cole Younger and his brothers, makes Lewis twenty years instead of ten years older than Adeline, has Lewis from Logan Co. KY instead of Montgomery Co., KY, kills off Simon at age fourteen, makes oldest son Ben into two different people, Charles and Ben, etc., etc., etc. Preece also accepts a lot of what "Eye Witness" says without question.

Preece has an entire chapter of his book devoted to "The Battle Of Twin Mounds" where he has the Daltons stealing a bunch of horses from some Missouri farmers along Beaver Creek. A posse of the farmers chase the Daltons and a William Starmer is killed and a William Thompson is wounded in the chase. Preece appears to have started this story and from here on it is repeated frequently and added to by other writers. I have searched the newspaper files of both the Oklahoma and Kansas State Historical Societies and every other place I can think of looking for data about this matter. I have found nothing. I am convinced this incident never happened.

Articles by Preece that were printed in various issues of REAL WEST are as follows:
"The Incredible Bill Dalton", January 1964.
"Bob Dalton's Bandit Bride", March 1965.
"Adeline Dalton, Outlaw Mother", September 1965.
"The Truth About Emmett Dalton", March 1966.

EMMETT DALTON

BEYOND THE LAW was first published in New York by J. S. Ogilvie in 1918. The copy I have is a reprint in REAL WEST, August 1971-April 1972. I also have a copy of this published in an unidentified magazine titled WEST OF 96 (probably ADVENTURE magazine published in England). The latter was obtained from the Eugene C. Barker Texas History Center.

WHEN THE DALTONS RODE, in collaboration with Jack Jungmeyer, New York, Doubleday, Doran & Co. Inc. 1931.

"I Rode With The Daltons" as told to Charles M. Martin, ALL WESTERN magazine May, June, and July 1935.

"Guns—Always Guns !" with Will Davis. ALL WESTERN magazine August 1939.

The only place I was able to locate copies of ALL WESTERN was in the Library of Congress. I had to make a trip there in order to obtain copies of these articles. It was not worth the effort; they only rehash Emmett's books.

"Emmett Dalton's Six Shooter" by Chuck Martin (information obviously furnished by Emmett). TRUE WEST, Jan.-Feb. 1956.

Emmett clearly wanted to put himself in the best possible light and he also wanted to give the message that crime does not pay. His various accounts of the Dalton gang do not always agree. It is obvious that all the material about Eugenia Moore and about Julia Johnson was added to WHEN THE DALTONS RODE in order to add romantic interest to the story. How much Emmett twisted and stretched the truth is difficult to tell. However, Emmett's claim that the Dalton gang got started in New Mexico by holding up a crooked gambling joint appears to be complete fiction. There is no evidence for the existance of any Eugenia Moore at all much less for her dying in New Mexico. No record of any marshal named Ben Canty can be found in New Mexico either. Emmett said Ben Canty was an old friend from Missouri, who was a marshal in or near Silver City, and that Canty introduced Bob to Eugenia Moore. I have checked the New Mexico stories with the following agencies and people and came up with a big zero:

Silver City, NM Public Library
Mother Whiteside Memorial Library, Grants, NM.
New Mexico State University, Grants Branch Community College.
Moise Memorial Library, Santa Rosa, NM.

The University of New Mexico and editor of NEW MEXICO HISTORICAL REVIEW, Santa Fe, NM.

Pat Humble and Victor A. Moitoret, residents of Silver City with a long interest in local history.

New Mexico State Records Center and Archives, Santa Fe, NM.

FRANK LATTA

I have commented throughout the book where the evidence I have found disproves or differs significantly with what Latta says in DALTON GANG DAYS. I spent an entire afternoon in December of 1988 going through Latta's papers and files also. Latta did a remarkable amount of work and made a serious attempt to get at the truth. However, why he accepted what Littleton Dalton told him, over forty years after the events, at face value and why he believed everything Chris Madsen told him are questions I cannot answer. Why he made no attempt to consult the court records of Grat and Bill's trials, and why he either did not even read the newspaper accounts of the trial or just discarded them entirely is also a puzzle.

A couple of comments concerning what Latta says about Grat and Bill's attorney, John W. Breckinridge is in order. Latta says Breckenridge was really working for the Southern Pacific Railroad and had no interest in providing a good defense for Grat. He also says Breckinridge was an alcoholic who died as the result of a bender. The evidence is not conclusive but is suggestive that Latta may be right about these two things. The probate records and "John W. Breckinridge Dead", THE MORNING CALL (San Francisco) 10 May 1892, and another obituary in an unidentified Merced newspaper indicated that Breckinridge's law partner at one time worked for the Southern Pacific. The cause of death given for Breckinridge was too many shots of morphine administered by his physician. A medical book of the period says morphine was used to treat delirium tremens.

GLENN SHIRLEY

Glenn has written more books about the Indian Territory and the outlaws and lawmen there than anyone else, to my knowledge. His work is highly respected and is frequently used as a reference by many other writers and researchers. Glen has written books, then later found out he has made errors, then written another book and corrected some of his errors; this is to be commended. However, even in Shirley's latest books I was unable to find the source documents he cited in some cases, or the documents did not say what he said they did. He simply does not cite source material for several of the things he says about the Daltons either. Some of his books contain no source material at all; then he writes another book and cites his previous book as a source. In WEST OF HELL'S FRINGE Shirley repeats the horse stealing, killing of Starmer, and wounding of Thompson story (p.47-48). He adds that Starmer's body when examined had been hit by three bullets so close together that the wounds could be covered with one hand. Then Marshal Needles read the report of Starmer's death and said "Nobody in the Territory can shoot like that except Bob Dalton." Then Shirley footnotes this and says,"'Nix (pp. 37-38) and Wellman (pp. 165-66 are incorrect in putting the Starmer killing after the Wharton train robbery. Starmer was killed May 2, 1891, and the train robbery occurred a week later. Drago (pp. 210-11) accepts the error and places the Twin Mounds fight on Skeleton Creek, nearly twenty miles west. Preece (pp. 210-11) gives a fictionalized account in which the incident occurs on 'a pair of strategically placed Ozark[?] hillocks ...a mile or two from the banks of Beaver Creek." Shirley cites no source for the incident at all, either in this book or in any other of his books.

Shirley also quotes liberally from Emmett Dalton's books and "Eye Witness". In his latest book GUNFIGHT AT INGALLS he accepts the guilt of the Daltons for the Alila, California robbery, repeats the horse stealing and killing Starmer story, claims Bill Doolin got married at Adeline Dalton's home, and makes several other statements about the Dalton family that cannot be proved. I wrote to Glenn about this book and asked what his sources were for some of these items. I received no reply.

Glenn Shirley books consulted were:

GUNFIGHT AT INGALLS, Stillwater, OK, Barbed Wire Press, 1990.

WEST OF HELL'S FRINGE, Norman, OK, University of Oklahoma Press, 1978.

GUARDIAN OF THE LAW: THE LIFE AND TIMES OF WILLIAM MATTHEW TILGHMAN, Austin TX, Eakin Press, 1988.

HECK THOMAS: FRONTIER MARSHAL, Philadelphia and New York, Chilton Co. 1962.

LAW WEST OF FORT SMITH, Lincoln, NE, University of Nebraska Press, 1957.

SIX-GUN AND SILVER STAR, Albuquerque, NM, University of New Mexico Press, 1955.

TOUGHEST OF THEM ALL, Albuquerque, NM, University of New Mexico Press, 1953.

OTHER BOOKS

Here is a list of other books consulted about the Daltons. I did not find any of them to be completely accurate. There are also magazine and newspaper articles about the Daltons too numerous to mention. Few, if any, are accurate.

Barnard, Evan G., A RIDER OF THE CHEROKEE STRIP, Boston and New York, Houghton Mifflin Co., 1936.

Breihan, Carl W., BADMEN OF THE FRONTIER DAYS, New York, Robert M. McBride Co., 1957.

Croy, Homer, HE HANGED THEM HIGH, New York, Duell, Sloan and Pearce, 1952.

Dary, David, THE LAWLESS AND LAWMEN, no other information. I have a photocopy of a chapter titled,"The Collapse of the Dalton Gang."

Dodge, Fred, ed. Carolyn Lake, UNDER COVER FOR WELLS FARGO, Boston, Houghton Mifflin Co., 1969.

Drago, Harry Sinclair, OUTLAWS ON HORSEBACK, New York, Bramhall House, 1964.

Drago, ROAD AGENTS AND TRAIN ROBBERS, New York, Mead and Co., 1973.

Drake, C. C., WHO'S WHO IN COFFEYVILLE, KANSAS AND VICINITY., Coffeyville, KS, Coffeyville Journal Press, 1943.

Eaton, Frank, PISTOL PETE, VETERAN OF THE OLD WEST, Boston, Little, Brown, 1952.

Hanes, Bailey C. BILL DOOLIN OUTLAW O.T. , Norman, OK, University of Oklahoma Press, 1968.

Harkey, Dee, MEAN AS HELL, Albuquerque, NM, University of New Mexico Press, 1948.

Hendricks, George David, THE BADMEN OF THE WEST, San Antonio, TX, The Naylor Co., 1941.

Horan, James D. and Paul Sann, PICTORIAL HISTORY OF THE WILD WEST, New York, Crown Publishers, 1954.

Hough, Emmerson, THE STORY OF THE OUTLAW, New York, The Outing Publishing Co., 1907.

Hunter, J. Marvin and Noah H. Rose, THE ALBUM OF GUN FIGHTERS, Bandera, TX, 1951.

INDIAN TERRITORY AND CARTER COUNTY PIONEERS, INCLUDING PICKENS CO. AND CHICKASAW NATIONS VOL. I. 1983. Photo in this book identified as Bill Dalton is actually W. T. Dalton who served as a member of the Constitutional Convention of Oklahoma from district #69.

James, Marquis, THEY HAD THEIR HOUR, Indianapolis, Bobbs-Merrill Co., 1934.

Johnson, Dorothy M., WESTERN BADMEN, New York, Dodd, Mead and Co., 1970.

Johnston, Harry V., MY HOME ON THE RANGE, St. Paul, MI, Webb Publishing Co. 1942.

Meeks, Beth Thomas with Bonnie Speer, HECK THOMAS, MY PAPA, Norman, OK, Levite of Apache, 1988.

Metz, Leon Claire, THE SHOOTERS, El Paso, TX, Mangan Books, 1976.

Patterson, Richard, THE TRAIN ROBBERY ERA, Boulder, CO, Pruett Publishing Co. 1991. Claims Charley Bryant had an advanced case of syphilis.

Preece, Harold, LIVING PIONEERS, Cleveland and New York, The World Publishing Co., 1952.

Raine, William MacLeod, FAMOUS SHERIFFS AND WESTERN OUTLAWS, Garden City, NY. Doubleday, Doran and Co., 1929.

Ridings, Sam P., THE CHISHOLM TRAIL, Guthrie, OK, Co-operative Publishing Co. 1936.

Shoemaker, Floyd C. ed., MISSOURI DAY BY DAY, Jefferson City, Mid State Printing Co., 1942.

Sutton, Fred E. as told to A. B. Macdonald, HANDS UP!, Indianapolis, IN, The Bobbs-Merrill Co., 1927.

Tilghman, Zoe A., MARSHAL OF THE LAST FRONTIER, Glendale, CA, The Arthur A. Clark Co., 1949.

Van Eaton, Frank L., HELL ON THE BORDER, Fort Smith, AR, Hell on the Border Publishing Co., 1953 (reprint).

Wellman, Paul I., A DYNASTY OF WESTERN OUTLAWS, Garden City, NY, Doubleday and Co., 1961.

OTHER

INDIAN PIONEER HISTORY, FOREMAN COLLECTIONS, Oklahoma Historical Society. This is a collection of interviews taken by WPA workers during the depression. None of the information found here should be accepted at face value. All should be compared with other sources in order to determine creditibility of the data.

NOVELS

Hansen, Ron, DESPERADOES, New York, Alfred A. Knopf, 1979

McCoy, Max, THE SIXTH RIDER, New York, Doubleday, 1991.

Both are very good novels, well written and enteraining. Both are based on good research but they are (and advertise to be) fiction.

CHAPTER II and III GENEALOGICAL REFERENCES

Source documents have been cited throughout the text. All of the standard tools of the genealogist have been used to compile these two chapters: census and other vital records; court records; deeds and land grants; cemetery records, wills, and estate records: military, pension, and land bounty records; etc.

Any number of other people researching Dalton, Younger, and related families have provided and exchanged data. Steve Harris and Mark Dalton mentioned in the preface to the book have been exceptionally helpful. Both of these men are also descendants of David Dalton, and thus are distant cousins to the Dalton Gang. Steve lives in Pittsylvania Co. VA in a house built by one of his Dalton ancestors. He has studied and collected genealogical data about the residents of Pittsylvania Co. and the surrounding area for most of his adult life. Mark lives in Mayodan, NC and has made several trips to Pittsylvania Co. and he and Steve together have walked creek banks, searched for survey markers, dug through the court house records, visited the cemeteries, etc., etc. in order to make the genealogical data presented in this book as accurate as humanly possible.

Any number of published books and newsletters, etc. have been consulted. County histories, historical and genealogical society publications, books of marriage records, cemetery records, family histories, etc.

The following genealogical publications primarily about Daltons have been used extensively:

THE JOURNAL OF THE DALTON GENEALOGICAL SOCIETY. The DGS was founded in England in 1970. Membership in the DGS is worldwide; the journal is published twice a year.

THE DALTON NEWSLETTER, a quarterly newsletter, published by Helen Lu of Dallas, TX from November 1974-June 1982. A lot of information on the Timothy Dalton family is located in these publications, but like all newsletters, much of it is supplied by readers. All such data should be verified whenever possible by original source documents.

DALTON DATA, Vol. I-IV, published by Mary Ann Van Zant Bell, Spokane. WA 1985. These booklets contain the bible records for some of the Lewis and Matilda Dalton family and the will of Henry Rabourn.

THE DALTON GANG AND THEIR FAMILY TIES [booklet] Nancy Ohnick ed., Mead, KS, Ohnick Enterprises, 1989.

County histories that contain Dalton gang family information are:

SILOAM SPRINGS (AR) HISTORY VOL. I, 1970. I have a photocopy of a few pages, no publication data or author is shown.

THE FIRST HUNDRED YEARS, 1872-1972, BELTON, MISSOURI, Belton Community Projects, Inc. "The Daltons of Belton" by Dorothy Lane. This contains two pages of information (given primarily by a Glenn Harrison, who got the information from his grandfather) about the Daltons when they lived near Belton, MO. pp 51-53.

Information about the earliest Daltons in America can be found in the following:

Blake, John Laurens, THE ENGLISH HOME OF MR. TIMOTHY DALTON B. A., Orange, NJ, De Vinne Press, 1898.

A number of New England genealogical publications also contain information about this Dalton family.

Other family histories:

Bobbitt, John W., THE BOBBITT FAMILY IN AMERICA, published by author, 1985, contains a fair amount of information about the Timothy Dalton family.

The Dalton Gang family:

Boecher, Lee, SHORTGRASS COUNTRY, Chisholm Trail, Montana, Pioneer Schools, 1969 is quoted extensively in the book. Boecher was a school teacher for many years in Kingfisher, OK and knew most of the Dalton family. Boecher's wife was for a time in partnership in a dressmaking business with Leona Dalton. I also interviewed Boecher's sister, Shirley Smith in Kingfisher in the spring of 1989.

The following books contain information concerning George Washington and mention his friendship and association with some of the early Virginia Daltons, mostly John Dalton of Fairfax, Co. VA:

Decatur, Stephen, Jr., PRIVATE AFFAIRS OF

GEORGE WASHINGTON, Boston, The River Side Press, 1933.

Fitzpatrick, John C. ed., THE DARIES OF GEORGE WASHINGTON 1748-1799, Boston, Houghton Mifflin Co. 1925.

Freeman, Douglass Southall, GEORGE WASHINGTON, VOL. I-III, New York, Charles Scribner's Sons, 1948.

The following contains a considerable amount of genealogy on the Samuel Dalton (of Mayo) family. Not all of the information is correct however; all should be verified elsewhere from source documents.

Horton, Lucy Henderson, FAMILY HISTORY, Franklin, TN, Press of The News, 1922.

Information about Mt. Sterling and Montgomery Co. KY and the Rabourn family came primarily from the following.

HISTORY OF LULBERGRUB CHURCH, unpublished manuscript material found in the Mt. Sterling Public Library.

THE EARLY RABURNS OF MONTGOMERY COUNTY, KENTUCKY, manuscript material and a collection of newspaper clippings from the MT. STERLING ADVOCATE. These were furnished by Lydia Jones of Mt. Sterling, KY.

Information about the Renick [Rennick] family comes from DAR records and from a Renick genealogy:

THE RENICKS OF GREENBRIER by B. F. Harlow, Jr. and Other Assistants, published privately in 1951.

Younger genealogy sources were:

Appler, A. C., foreword by Burton Rascoe, THE YOUNGER BROTHERS; THEIR LIFE AND CHARACTER, New York, Frederick Fell, Inc., 1955.

Brant, Marley, THE FAMILIES OF CHARLES LEE AND HENRY WASHINGTON YOUNGER [booklet], Burbank, CA. published by author, 1986.

Breihan, Carl W., YOUNGER BROTHERS, San Antonio, TX, The Naylor Company, 1972

Cantrell, Dallas, YOUNGERS' FATAL BLUNDER: NORTHFIELD, MINNESOTA, San Antonio, TX. The Naylor Company, 1973.

Croy, Homer, LAST OF THE GREAT OUTLAWS: THE STORY OF COLE YOUNGER, New York, Duell, Sloan and Pearce, 1956.

Younger, Cole, THE STORY OF COLE YOUNGER, Provo, UT, Triton Press, (reprint) 1988.

Brant's booklet is the most reliable. For those interested in the Youngers, Breihan has a new book, RIDE THE RAZOR'S EDGE: THE YOUNGER BROTHERS STORY that should be released by Pelican Publishing Co., Gretna, LA in April 1992. Marley Brant is also working on a full length book on the Youngers, and Bob Younger, one of the owners of Morningside Bookshop in Dayton, OH is currently compiling a genealogy of the Younger family.

Additional information has been collected from interviews, phone calls, and correspondence with the following:

Hazel Perrier Chapman, granddaughter of Julia Johnson Gilstrap Lewis Dalton. Hazel and Marjorie Johnson Lowe have also compiled a short but well documented family history titled, "Julia Ann (Johnson) Gilstrap Lewis Dalton", dated 18 December 1990. Hazel kindly furnished me a copy of this.

Glen V. McIntyre of the Chisholm Trail Museum in Kingfisher, OK. Glen's father was Leona Dalton's personal physician for many years, and Glen has had a lifelong interest in local history. He also allowed me to go through all of the files on the Daltons in the Museum.

William Dalton "Bill" Phillips, grandson of Bea Elizabeth Dalton, his mother Mrs. Annie Phillips and various other members of the Phillips family.

Lora Miller, a family historian, genealogist, and Oklahoma history researcher. She is dedicated to getting past the legends to the truth.

There are a sizable number of the descendents of Bill Dalton and Jane Bliven still living. I have repeatedly attempted to get some of this family to talk to me. Either they say they know little real information, or they say too much fiction has already been published about the Daltons and they will not talk to any writer concerning their family.

INCREDIBLE AND UNBELIEVABLE SOURCES.

Readers deserve a warning about writers that make no attempt to discover and publish the truth and who publish obvious scandalous and untrue stories about even dead outlaws and their kin. There are two writers that have been busy cranking out a sizable amount of this stuff about the Daltons in recent years. I have corresponded with both and had some telephone conversations with Mark Pannill. I am unable to determine what the motives of these two men are, but what they write is truly incredible and unbelievable and is not based on fact. Both of these men have claimed to have gotten information from people they have never met, talked to, or corresponded with. Both of these writers were taken in for a time by an elderly man who claimed at various times to be a descendant of at least two different siblings of the Dalton Gang. The elderly man shall remain nameless, because he is probably mentally ill and thus not totally responsible for his actions. Phillip Steele and Mark Pannill have no such excuse for the stuff they say and publish.

Mark Pannill has published the following booklets, all published by VinCon Publishing, Waxahachie, TX:
THE SIXTH MAN; WHO WAS SHE?, 1987.
REASONABLE DOUBT!, 1988.
ROY DALTON: THE SON EMMETT NEVER HAD, 1989.

The Roy Dalton material was also published under the same name as an article in the April-June 1991 NOLA Journal. Pannill also gave a talk on 31 January 1988 meeting of the Eastern Trails Historical Society in Vinita, OK. Pannill has imagined sexual abuse, double identity, mass murder, etc., etc. Nothing he says has any degree of credibility whatsoever.

Phillip Steele has published a small booklet IN SEARCH OF THE DALTONS. It was self published in Springdale, AR, in two editions, the first in 1985, the second in 1989. Both booklets are full of errors. Steele says the Dalton Gang family descends from a John Elijah Dalton, through the James Lewis Dalton who married Matilda Raburn (he is the great uncle not the grandfather). Dates are wrong, names change from one page to the other, individuals who have never had any contact with Steele are listed as sources, etc. Steele has also published material on Daltons in the NOLA Quarterly and he has published other booklets about the Jesse James family, Belle Starr, Ned Christie and others. All of his work is of questionable accuracy.

Chapter III. GENERAL HISTORY AND BACKGROUND SOURCES

BOOKS

Buchanan, James S. and Edward E. Dale, A HISTORY OF OKLAHOMA, New York, Row Peterson and Co., 1924.

Castel, Albert, A FRONTIER STATE AT WAR: KANSAS, 1861-1865, Ithaca, NY, Cornell University Press, 1958.

Dale, Edward Everett, and Gaston Litton, CHEROKEE CAVALIERS, Norman, OK, University of Oklahoma Press, 1939.

Davis, Kenneth C., DON'T KNOW MUCH ABOUT HISTORY, New York, Crown Publishers, Inc., 1990.

Ehle, John, TRAIL OF TEARS, New York, Doubleday, 1988.

Fellman, Michael, INSIDE WAR, New York, Oxford University Press, 1989. An excellent book, but he was taken in by Kit Dalton's UNDER THE BLACK FLAG and cites it as a reference.

Foreman, Grant, A HISTORY OF OKLAHOMA, Norman, OK, University of Oklahoma Press, 1942.

Garwood, Darrell, CROSSROADS OF AMERICA, New York, W. W. Norton and Co., 1948.

Hale, Donald R., WE RODE WITH QUANTRILL, self published, 1975.

Ingenltron, Elmo, BORDERLAND REBELLION, Branson, MO, The Ozarks Mountaineer, 1980.

Masterson, V. V., THE KATY RAILROAD AND THE LAST FRONTIER, Norman, OK, University of Oklahoma Press, 1952.

McNeal, T. A., WHEN KANSAS WAS YOUNG, New York, Macmillan Co., 1922.

McReynolds, Edwin C., MISSOURI: A HISTORY OF THE CROSSROADS STATE, Norman, OK, University of Oklahoma Press, 1954.

Monahan, Jay, CIVIL WAR ON THE WESTERN BORDER, 1854-1865, Lincoln, NE, University of Nebraska Press, 1955.

Nichols, Alice, BLEEDING KANSAS, New York, Oxford University Press, 1954.

Parish, William E., MISSOURI UNDER RADICAL RULE, Columbia, MO, University of Missouri Press, 1965.

Ridings, Sam P., THE CHISHOLM TRAIL, Guthrie OK, Co-operative Publishing Co., 1936.

Settle, William A., Jr., JESSE JAMES WAS HIS NAME, Lincoln, NE, University of Nebraska Press, 1966.

Streeter, Floyd B., PRAIRIE TRAILS AND COW TOWNS, New York, The Devin Adair Co., 1963.

Vestal, Stanley, QUEEN OF THE COW TOWNS,

New York, Harper and Brothers, 1952.

Vestal, SHORT GRASS COUNTRY, New York, Duell, Sloan and Pearce, 1941.

THE WAR OF THE REBELLION: A COMPILATION OF THE OFFICIAL RECORDS OF THE UNION AND CONFEDERATE ARMIES.

CHAPTER IV.

BOOKS

Ball, Larry D., THE UNITED STATES MARSHALS OF NEW MEXICO AND ARIZONA TERRITORIES 1846-1912, Albuquerque, University of New Mexico Press, 1987.

Burton, Art T., BLACK, RED, AND DEADLY, BLACK AND INDIAN GUNFIGHTERS OF THE INDIAN TERRITORIES, Austin, TX, Eakin Press, 1991.

Calhoun, Frederick S., THE LAWMEN, Washington D. C., Smithsonian Institution Press, 1989. Also some telephone conversations with Calhoun.

Casey, Orber, J., AND JUSTICE FOR ALL, Oklahoma City, Western Heritage Books, Inc., 1989.

Gard, Wayne, FRONTIER JUSTICE, Norman, OK, University of Oklahoma Press, 1949.

Hagan, William T., INDIAN POLICE AND JUDGES, New Haven, CT, Yale University Press, 1966.

McKennon, C. H., IRON MEN, New York, Doubleday and Co. 1967.

Prassel, Frank Richard, THE WESTERN PEACE OFFICER, Norman, OK. University of Oklahoma Press, 1972.

OTHER SOURCES

Martin, Amelia, "Unsung Heroes Deputy Marshals of the Federal Court for The Western District of Arkansas 1875-1896", FORT SMITH HISTORICAL SOCIETY JOURNAL, April 1979.

Records in the National Archives. Federal Records Group 60 in the Washington D. C. archives; records of the Fort Smith Court are in the Fort Worth branch and records of the Kansas districts are in the Kansas City branch. Researchers may be interested to know that the Fort Smith records are currently being reinventoried and reindexed. Approximately 60 pages of additional records concerning the death of Frank Dalton were just located. These records contain the testimony of all the witnesses present when Frank was killed. The telegram shown in this chapter of the book is correct, but the additional data gives the names of all of the people in Smith's camp, of people in nearby houses, etc.

CHAPTER V.

BOOKS

Block, Eugene B., GREAT TRAIN ROBBERIES OF THE WEST, New York, The Hearst Corporation, Avon Book Division, 1959.

Boessenecker, John, BADGE AND BUCKSHOT, Norman, OK, University of Oklahoma Press, 1988.

Clark, George T., LELAND STANFORD, California, Stanford University Press, 1931.

Daggett, Stuart, CHAPTERS ON THE HISTORY OF THE SOUTHERN PACIFIC, New York, Augustus M. Kelley, Publishers, 1966.

DeNevi, Don, WESTERN TRAIN ROBBERS, Millbrae, CA, Celestiar Arts, 1976. The material in this book about the Alila robbery and the Daltons is complete fiction. He also has photos of the Daltons and he identifies a photo of Ben as Emmett. Says the Daltons robbed and killed at will throughout the midwest before the California robbery. Entire book is inaccurate.

Dillon, Richard, WELLS FARGO DETECTIVE, New York, Coward-McCann Inc., 1969.

Glasscock, C. B., MAN-HUNT BANDITS AND THE SOUTHERN PACIFIC, New York, Grosset & Dunlap, 1929.

HISTORY OF CENTRAL CALIFORNIA. Photocopy of biography on Judge Gray. No publisher or date shown, but published shortly after Gray's appointment as judge.

Kirsch, Robert and William S. Murphy, WEST OF THE WEST, New York, E. P. Dutton and Co. Inc., 1967.

Lewis, Oscar, THE BIG FOUR, New York, Alfred A. Knopf, 1938.

Maxwell, Hu, suplemented by Charles W. Clough, EVANS AND SONTOG, Fresno, CA, Panaroma West Books, 1981. This is the most complete account of the Evans and Sontog saga I found. These men were also accused of robbing SP trains and were hounded until John Sontog was killed and Chris Evans captured. Evans spent years in jail for his supposed crimes. Both still declared, practically with their dying breaths, that they never robbed a train. I am inclined to believe they got the same treatment as did the Daltons and were innocent.

Smith, Wallace, GARDEN OF THE SUN 4th ed. Fresno, CA, Max Hardeson, 1960.

OTHER

Tulare County Court Records. THE PEOPLE VS. ROBERT DALTON, EMMETT DALTON, GRATTON DALTON, AND WILLIAM M. DALTON.

Sources and Author's Notes

Wells Fargo History Museum in San Francisco was contacted. They furnished photos and the reward poster shown in the book for a fee. They had no additional background information about the Daltons and the California train robberies.

Southern Pacific Railroad, the Railroad Museum in Sacramento, CA. and other various like agencies were contacted. No one could furnish any source documents of material relating to the California train robberies.

I visited the California State Library on several occasions and reviewed the micro film of all California newspapers I could find concerning the SP train robberies. I have cited many of the newspaper articles throughout this chapter of the book. Often one newspaper would carry a story, then within a day or two several other papers would carry the same story.

CHAPTER VI.

References for this chapter have all either been cited in the text of the book or have been covered by material listed for other chapters. I found no source documents in the National Archives for any of the Dalton train robberies.

CHAPTER VII.

BOOKS

Elliott, David Stewart, LAST RAID OF THE DALTONS AND BATTLE WITH THE BANDITS AT COFFEYVILLE * KANSAS * OCT-5 * 1892. Reprint of the original published by Elliott, who was editor of the COFFEYVILLE JOURNAL. This was reprinted by the Coffeyville Historical Museum, Inc. There is a one page foreward in this reprint that says that Emmett requested Colonel Elliott to take his guns after the Coffeyville raid, that Elliott was an attorney and had represented Mrs. Dalton in a divorce action, and that Emmett once wrote that he would not seek parole while Elliott was still alive because he did not want to embarrass him. All three of these statements are false, Emmett had Bill take action to recover his guns from Elliott, Mrs. Dalton was never divorced, and Emmett never wrote anything about embarrassing Elliott.

Elliott, D. S. and Ed Bartholomew, THE DALTON GANG AND THE COFFEYVILLE RAID, Fort Davis, TX, Frontier Book Co., 1968. This is another reprint of Elliott's account of the raid and Bartholomew has collected a group of newspaper items and added them to Elliott's account.

OTHER

Many other newspapers stories have been read and collected about the Coffeyville Raid. Many of them simply repeat the story that appeared in the Coffeyville JOURNAL two days after the raid. A copy of the Coffeyville newspaper was obtained from the Dalton Museum in Coffeyville, a facsimile copy of the 7 October paper is sold at the Museum.. All major city newspapers appear to have carried the story of the raid. I have copies of, or notes from articles in St. Louis, New York, Hartford, CT. and London as well as a variety of Kansas and Oklahoma newspapers.

Estate records for Grat and Bob and the trial records for Emmett's trial, such as it was, are all on file at the Kansas State Historical Society.

CHAPTER VIII.

The major source of information about Bill Dalton not covered elsewhere is:

McCullough, Harrell, SELDEN LINDSEY: U. S. DEPUTY MARSHAL, Oklahoma City, OK, Paragon Publishing, 1990.

I have also had any number of telephone conversations and exchanged a number of letters with Harrell. He and I have both searched every record location we can think of for further information on the killing of Bill Dalton and the arrest of the posse for the murder of Dalton. We have both drawn a complete blank. McCullough, makes a convincing case that Lindsey did the actual killing. Indeed, much later, Lindsey himself claimed he did the deed in an interview that I cited in this chapter. However, every newspaper at the time said Loss Hart was the one who shot Bill Dalton. Further the reporters that saw Dalton's body only describe one wound and that was the one in the back. One reporter was very emphatic, that there was not another mark on the body. McCullough says Hart shot Bill Dalton in the back with a .44 bullet and that Lindsey shot him in the chest near the left nipple with a .38-56. I don't see how it is possible for a .38-56 bullet to leave such an unobtrusive entry wound that reporters veiwing the body would confuse that wound with what they thought was the .44 bullet lodged under the skin above the left nipple.

I have also had a number of telephone conversations about Bill Dalton with Carl Breihan, who is a retired St. Louis police officer, and a western writer with a large number of books to his credit. Carl tells me that an older friend of his once had a copy of the official records concerning Bill Dalton's death. These records reportedly were obtained from the Paris, TX court house before the 1916 fire. Carl said he saw these records and that these documents lend creditablilty to Emmett's story that Bill was shot in the back while sitting down or bending over. Carl said there was no way the wound described could have been made if the man had been in an upright position. Carl's friend is now dead and no one knows what happened to these documents.

The National Archives have been searched and searched for records relating to Bill Dalton. Almost nothing has been found there. What records there are I have cited in this chapter. There are no records from the Paris, TX U.S. Marshal's office in the Archives. They are all believed to have burned. About the time the deputies should have been tried for the murder of Bill Dalton, the Paris Court lost jurisdiction over any cases in the Indian Territory. The case should have gone to the Ardmore, I.T. Court. No criminal case records for this court can be found. Many records were kept in Ardmore for years and Harrell McCullough found a basement full of dusty and molding records in Ardmore. He contacted the Fort Worth branch of the archives and these records were moved to Fort Worth. No criminal cases were among these records. What happened to the criminal cases is unknown, but there is a story that at one time someone in Ardmore decided to clean out old records, and moved boxes of them to the sidewalk, then invited town folks to come and take what they wanted. Records about Bill Dalton may still turn up in someone's attic.

I began a search for the trial records of Jim Nite in the hope that they would shed some light on Bill Dalton, the Longview robbery, and on Bill's death. To my surprise and amazement the trial records, in two counties in Texas, for Jim Nite have also "gone missing". I am convinced that someone has stripped the files about Bill Dalton's death and about the Longview bank robbery. Why this has been done I can only speculate. However, the manner of Bill Dalton's death and the fact that five or six, or perhaps more men killed by deputies were said to be the Longview robbers, raises a lot of questions about the entire affair. This is decidedly odd considering all the witnesses said there were only four robbers at Longview. The fact that Jim Nite got a change of venue, a new trial, another change of venue, and later a pardon by the Governor of Texas raises even more questions.

Then the newspapers said Nite claimed, as an alibi, that he was working in Louisiana at the time of the robbery. Yet the judge for Nite's second trial refused to authorize the taking of depositions in that state. Numerous questions remain unanswered about Bill Dalton, Jim Nite, and the Longview bank robbery.

CHAPTER IX

BOOK

Cranor, Ruby, TALKING TOMBSTONES, PIONEERS OF WASHINGTON COUNTY Bartlesville, OK, self published, 1983.

Most all of the sources relating to this chapter have been included in the notes to other chapters. However, a few comments about locating records on anything in Oklahoma and on those individuals in that area that were Indian are appropriate. Oklahoma is one of the worst places in the country to try to find genealogical records. The Indian Territory contained over thirty different tribal groups, most with their own govenment, for a long time. The entire population was a mixture of Indian, Black, White and all possible combinations of the three. There was no "White Man" legal system for marriage or divorce in much of the Territory for a long period, even after a sizable White population lived there. The area is a genealogist's nightmare in many ways. Numerous records do exist about the Indians. As Julia Johnson married a half blood Cherokee the first time, there are a variety of Indian records for her and her daughter Jennie. These have been cited throughout this chapter. There are special census records, records of testimony given to the Dawes Commission, and various other commissions, etc. These records are not in one location, but scattered in various places. Many are in the National Archives in Washington, some are in the Fort Worth Branch of the National Archives, and some are to be found in the archives of the Oklahoma Historical Society. One good reference and a starting point to locate individuals with Indian ancestry is: CHEROKEE BY BLOOD: RECORDS OF EASTERN CHEROKEE ANCESTRY IN THE U. S. COURT OF CLAIMS 1906-1910, compiled by Jerry Wright Jordan, Baltimore, MD, Heritage Books, Inc. different publication dates by Volume. This set of books is being published one volume at a time and Volume 8 is now ready for release. These books will identify names and claim numbers that will assist the researcher to locate a number of other records.

Another helpful book is, GUIDE TO THE HISTORICAL RECORDS OF OKLAHOMA, compiled and edited by Bradford Koplowitz, Bowie, MD. Heritage Books, Inc. 1990. This book gives a listing of records available in each county and town in Oklahoma.

CHAPTER X

The best and most concise thing that has been written about J. Frank Dalton is, "The Great Outlaw Hoax" by Steve Eng in the February 1986 issue of TRUE WEST. Steve, Carl Breihan, and several other researchers have been trying for years to determine the true identity of the man. I have a sizable file box full of material on J. Frank. I have letters, articles and booklets he wrote, and dozens of articles, clippings, and books about him. I also have letters Orvus Lee Howk, the man who claimed to be his grandson, wrote. None of this sheds much light on who the man really was. He moved around a lot and he may well have known some of the outlaws he wrote about. It is my guess that he really was a Dalton and may be closely related to Kit Dalton. Several of J. Frank's yarns bear a striking resemblance to other individuals in the extended Timothy Dalton family. J. Frank claimed his father was a state senator in Missouri at one time, that this family had a big plantation in the south, and that he had attended a slave sale at the plantation. There never has been a state senator named Dalton in the state of Missouri, but there was one in Mississippi. Further the Mississippi senator had a very wealthy father-in-law from Georgia, who owned a lot of slaves. J. Frank claimed he went to medical school and law school at Ann Arbor, Michigan. Another Dalton, of the extended Timothy Dalton family did graduate from medical school at Ann Arbor. J. Frank may have kept tabs on his relatives, near and far, and used some of the details of their lives as material for his own stories. Readers are warned to check any and all literature about the James Gang, after 1948, for J. Frank influence.

A FINAL WORD

In closing, readers are reminded to "count teeth" whenever reading any literature of the Old West. A lot of it is highly enteraining, interesting, and false! If the shooting sounds too fast and accurate to be true; if the outlaw had to ride 600 miles in one day to rob both of those banks; and if the lawman was in three places at once and was always brave, courageous, and bold —— be just a wee bit skeptical. By all means enjoy the myths and legends, BUT DO NOT ACCEPT THEM AS HISTORY.

Nancy B. Samuelson
Lieutenant Colonel USAF Ret.

Nancy B. Samuelson is a native of Missouri. She was born 12 November 1940 in Dent County, and is the daughter of the late Raymond and Rosa Dalton McDonough. Academic credentials include a Bachelor of Arts degree from Harris Teacher's College, St. Louis, Missouri and a Master of Business Administration degree from Syracuse University.

Nancy retired from the United States Air Force in 1984. She served for twenty years in a variety of management and command positions in the logistics career fields. She also has a considerable amount of teaching experience. She taught management and marketing courses for Park College and for five years she was an Assistant Professor of Aerospace Studies at the University of Connecticut. She is the graduate of a number of professional military schools including Armed Forces Staff College and the Air War College. Awards and decorations include the Bronze Star, Meritorious Service Medal (2 OLC) and Outstanding Supply Officer of the Year. Overseas tours of duty were in England and Thailand.

Nancy is married to Dr. Reid R. Samuelson (PhD Electrical Engineering) also a retired Air Force Lieutenant Colonel. Reid is now the Probate Judge for Eastford, Connecticut. The Samuelsons live in a 200-year-old house in rural Connecticut.

Since retirement Nancy has been busy with research, writing, and civic activities. Research and writing projects have focused on western history, genealogy, and women in the military. She is a member of a number of historical and genealogical organizations. Her articles and book reviews have appeared in the journals of THE WESTERN OUTLAW-LAWMAN HISTORY ASSOCATION (WOLA), and, THE NATIONAL ASSOCIATION FOR OUTLAW AND LAWMAN HISTORY (NOLA), OKLAHOMBRES, AIR UNIVERSITY REVIEW, ARMED FORCES AND SOCIETY, MINERVA-QUARTERLY REPORT ON WOMEN AND THE MILITARY, and in various genealogical publications. She is also the author of a booklet, THE DALTON GANG FAMILY--A GENEALOGICAL STUDY OF THE DALTON OUTLAWS AND THEIR FAMILY CONNECTIONS.

Her interest in the Dalton Gang began when she started researching her own Dalton family line. She is distantly related to the Dalton Gang; a common ancestor is Timothy Dalton who first appeared in Albermarle County, Virginia about 1732.

Order Form

Please send _____ copies of THE DALTON GANG STORY, LAWMEN TO OUTLAWS, to:

Name _____

Address _____

City _____ State _____ Zip _____

Enclose $25 for each book, plus $3 for shipping and handling to:

SHOOTING STAR PRESS

P.O. Box 359
Eastford, CT 06242